Policy Forum Series No. 39

The 2003 Federal Budget

Conflicting Tensions

Edited by
Charles M. Beach and Thomas A. Wilson

JOHN DEUTSCH INSTITUTE FOR THE STUDY OF
ECONOMIC POLICY, QUEEN'S UNIVERSITY

Published in cooperation with
McGill-Queen's University Press
Montreal & Kingston • London • Ithaca

ISBN: 0-88911-956-2 (bound) ISBN: 0-88911-958-9 (pbk.)
© John Deutsch Institute for the Study of Economic Policy
Queen's University, Kingston, Ontario K7L 3N6
Telephone: (613) 533-2294 FAX: (613) 533-6025
Printed and bound in Canada

National Library of Canada Cataloguing in Publication

The 2003 federal budget : conflicting tensions / edited by Charles
M. Beach and Thomas A. Wilson

(Policy forum series ; 39)
Proceedings of a conference held at Queen's University, Apr. 24-25,
    2003.
Includes bibliographical references.
ISBN 0-88911-956-2 (bound).--ISBN 0-88911-958-9 (pbk.)

1. Budget--Canada. 2. Fiscal policy--Canada. I. Beach, Charles
M. II. Wilson, Thomas A., 1935- III. John Deutsch Institute for the
Study of Economic Policy. IV. Series.

HJ2054.T863 2004   352.4'97103   C2004-901363-7

PREFACE AND ACKNOWLEDGEMENT

The 2003 Federal Budget: Conflicting Tensions is the tenth in the series of post-budget conferences and volumes put out by the John Deutsch Institute for the Study of Economic Policy (JDI) at Queen's University. Since its inception as a research arm of the Economics Department at Queen's, the JDI has provided periodic evaluations and appraisals of Canadian federal budgets. The JDI budget conferences since 1995 have been organized in cooperation with the Institute for Policy Analysis at the University of Toronto, and this is the fourth time that Tom Wilson has co-edited a budget conference volume.

The 2003 budget forum was held at Queen's University on April 24 and 25, 2003. A list of contributors appears at the end of this volume. The 2003 budget's distinguishing feature is that it was the final one of Jean Chrétien's tenure as prime minister and serves as a transition from Jean Chrétien to Paul Martin, his successor as prime minister and his minister of finance for the previous Chrétien budgets. Tom Courchene's introductory commentary provides an excellent overview of the papers and comments in this volume along with insights on "the Chrétien-Martin Legacy". In this preface, we therefore need only provide brief summaries of the papers and comments.

The first two papers in the volume provide background context. Jeffrey Simpson addresses the political context of the budget, focusing on the "politics of federation". Richard Harris addresses the economic context of the budget, assessing the virtues of risks of Canada's recent adherence to (at least) balanced budgets.

The next four pieces in the book look at the economic effects, and particularly a quantitative commentary, of the budget. Tom Wilson, Peter Dungan and Steve Murphy present a model-based quantitative evaluation of the budget based on simulations of the Institute for Policy Analysis' econometric model of the Canadian economy. Rick Egelton provides a quantitative appraisal of the budget's impact on financial markets and on productivity and economic growth. Pierre Fortin comments on both papers. All three pieces emphasize the importance of the interaction of fiscal policy with monetary policy under the Bank of Canada's inflation-targeting regime. With the short-term aggregate demand effects of fiscal initiatives offset by monetary policy, the analysis must focus on the allocative effects of fiscal policies. Bill Scarth, in his commentary, points out that the end of the period of deficit reduction has not been followed by a rebound in program spending (relative to GDP). He also emphasizes the importance of deficit reduction in relation to the aging Canadian population.

The 2003 budget is the first budget based on full accrual accounting principles. The next three presentations look into various accounting aspects of the budget. John Wiersema provides a detailed review of the new full accrual accounting framework. In his commentary, Mike McCracken emphasizes the need to improve budget and government accounts transparency. Alan MacNaughton draws some parallels from private-sector experience.

The next two papers in the volume are major reviews of taxation aspects of the budget. Bev Dahlby provides a comprehensive review of changes in personal taxes (the PIT and social insurance payroll taxes) and their interaction with the clawbacks of certain transfers and credits, as well as a review of changes in business taxes (the CIT and capital taxes). Jonathan Kesselman comments on Dahlby's paper, and argues for replacing the GST with a business transfer tax (BIT) or a direct consumption tax (BCT), and for providing greater incentives for savings under the PIT.

Since addressing Canada's commitments under the recent Kyoto agreement was a major feature of the budget, two studies examine the fiscal aspects of Kyoto. Both Ross McKitrick's paper and Chris Green's discussion are critical of the inadequacy of the federal government's plans for implementing the Kyoto Accords in Canada. Both authors express the view that Canada is unlikely to meet its targets set out by the government.

The last four items in the volume examine the social dimension and fiscal aspects of health care and the CHST in Canada. Armine Yalnizyan reviews the fluctuating federal support for health care, from the 1995 cuts to the CHST, to the partial restoration of CHST cash transfers since 2000. However, with the federal share of health-care spending at 20% or less, federal financial support is inadequate to finance major health-care reforms.

However, the move to create a separate CHT out of the CHST represents an improvement in transparency and accountability in this area. In his discussion of Yalnizyan's paper, Paul Boothe focuses on the fiscal sustainability of public spending on health care. He concludes that, without more radical reforms, health-care costs will continue to rise faster than revenues. Frances Woolley provides a detailed review of the various social policy provisions of recent federal budgets. Michael Mendelson explores the possible effects of the CHST on provincial spending on health, education and social services, and the prospective effects of the division of the CHST into a separate CHT and CST. He concludes that the CHT may reinforce compliance with the Canada Health Act; but without conditionality, the CST will essentially act like an unconstrained block grant (like the CHST).

As with all JDI activities and publications, the process revolves around Sharon Sullivan. She manages the conferences, coordinates the process of compiling the final versions of papers and then orchestrates the production of the final volume.

It is also a pleasure to thank Marilyn Banting for her editing skills and the Queen's School of Policy Studies' Publication Unit for valuable backup in preparing aspects of this volume.

Finally, we wish to acknowledge the marvellous cooperation we received from the contributors to this volume.

Charles M. Beach
Director, John Deutsch Institute

Thomas A. Wilson
Institute for Policy Analysis

TABLE OF CONTENTS

Preface and Acknowledgement ... iii

Introduction
The Martin/Chrétien Fiscal Legacy: Reflections from the Perspective of the 2003 Budget ... 1
Thomas J. Courchene

Session I: Budget Context

Jeffrey Simpson
The Politics of the 2003 Budget ... 29

Richard Harris
Balanced Budgets as a Canadian Fiscal Value? ... 37

Session II: The Budget and its Economic Effects: Quantitative Evaluation of the Budget

Thomas A. Wilson, Peter Dungan and Steve Murphy
The 2003 Federal Budget: A Quantitative Appraisal ... 51

Rick Egelton
Economic Impact of the 2003 Federal Budget ... 65

Pierre Fortin
The Budget: Impacts on Short-Term Aggregate Output and Long-Term Productivity Growth ... 73

William Scarth
Fiscal Policy in the Chrétien Years ... 79

Session III: Budgetary Accounting and Transparency

John Wiersema
Full Accrual Accounting ... 85

Michael C. McCracken
The Search for Budget Transparency ... 97

Alan Macnaughton
Budgetary Accounting and Transparency:
Lessons from Private-Sector Experience . . . 107

Session IV: The Tax Dimension

Bev Dahlby
The Chrétien Government's Legacy: A Tax System
for the 21ˢᵗ Century? . . . 113

Jonathan R. Kesselman
Unfinished Business: A Tax System for the 21ˢᵗ Century . . . 151

Session V: Fiscal Aspects of Kyoto

Ross McKitrick
Budget '03 and the Kyoto Process . . . 171

Christopher Green
Canada's Kyoto Commitment: Fiscal and "Real" Aspects . . . 193

Session VI: The Social Dimension and Fiscal Aspects of Health

Frances Woolley
Linking Economic and Social Policy — To Benefit
All Canadians? . . . 211

Armine Yalnizyan
The Health-Care Budget: Did it Resolve the "Crisis"? . . . 231

Michael Mendelson
The Evolution of the CHST in the 2003 Budget . . . 263

Paul Boothe
Fiscal Sustainability and the 2003 Federal "Health" Budget . . . 273

Contributors

List of Publications

INTRODUCTION

THE MARTIN/CHRÉTIEN FISCAL LEGACY: Reflections from the Perspective of the 2003 Budget

Thomas J. Courchene, Queen's University

Introduction

It was inevitable that any assessment of the 2003 federal budget would quickly give way to an assessment of the Liberal government's decade-long fiscal legacy. In his oral remarks, Simpson referred to the 2003 budget as a *fin de régime* budget. Dahlby and Kesselman in their respective papers follow along this legacy approach by assessing the issue of whether the 1994–2003 Martin/Chrétien remake of Canada's tax system is adequate to twenty-first-century needs. Yalnizyan's detailed review of health-care funding casts the 2003 budget in an even longer framework (1900–2003). Harris claims that Canada's successive seven-year series of budget surpluses has led the international community to view our penchant for budget balance as a "Canadian Fiscal Value". And where the budget had a distinctive forward impact, such as the beginning of a policy to implement Kyoto, this was again viewed as a Chrétien legacy issue. Finally, and perhaps most important in terms of the specifics of the 2003 budget, it pre-committed or front-loaded an enormous amount of future spending (health care, child benefits, elderly care, Kyoto, etc.). Indeed, Simpson aptly calls this aspect of the 2003 budget a "Honey, I shrunk the kids" budget since it reflected Chrétien's attempt to lengthen and broaden his policy legacy on the one hand and to ensure that the margin to manoeuvre for Prime Minister-in-waiting Paul Martin was as limited as possible.

Caught, thusly, between forces in Finance (and the PM's office as well) intent on preserving the fiscal legacy and the politics-of-succession fiscal gymnastics, it became very difficult for Finance Minister John Manley to claim much ownership for the 2003 budget. This is most unfortunate since John Manley was probably the only member of the Chrétien team that could have replaced Paul Martin in Finance with scarcely a dent in the Finance Department's fiscal credibility. Moreover, while Manley presided over Finance in the extremely uncertain post September 11, 2001 (9/11) period, Canada's economic performance, especially on the employment front, nonetheless outpaced that in the United States. Yet, the drama and expectations associated with the Liberal transition ensured that while political history will clearly give John Manley purchase on the 2003 budget, policy history will remain bound up with the theatrics of the personal legacies, past and future, of Chrétien and Martin.

In what follows, I also begin with a *fin de régime* approach by adding my own bit of perspective to the Chrétien Liberals' budget legacy. Then I will turn, selectively, to the various issues dealt with in both the conference and the volume, where again the perspective will, like the papers themselves, transcend the links to the 2003 budget.

More on the Fiscal Legacy

Giving Martin a Helping Hand

By way of an institutional introductory comment, this is the John Deutsch Institute's fourth budget conference and volume relating to the Chrétien era: the other JDI budget volumes relate to the 1995, 1997, and 2000 budgets respectively. To record the JDI's own fiscal legacy, the table of contents of these three previous conferences appear as the Appendix to my remarks. In this context a feat worth recording is that Thomas Wilson not only served as editor on all four budget volumes, but undertook (always with Peter Dungan, sometimes with Steve Murphy) the requisite quantitative appraisal of the respective budgets. A final opening comment is that

                                                          Thomas J. Courchene

my own expertise is such that I will not treat all sessions equally. Nonetheless, the overall collection of papers and comments is very impressive in terms of the depth and breadth of the analysis and will certainly appeal to academics, the policy community, and students of fiscal and budget matters.

The first of my perspective, or perhaps retrospective, comments is that Finance Minister Paul Martin was, initially at least, very lucky. Consider the following, all of which helped Martin tame the deficit:

- The Mulroney budgets, while never achieving budget balance themselves (although they did run operating surpluses) did soften the Canadian public for something more than incrementalism in terms of addressing the deficit.

- The Bank's shift to price stability and the Finance Department's agreement with the Bank in 1991 for an explicit target range paved the way for low and stable inflation for the entire Liberal decade (which served to lower the cost of debt-servicing).

- The fall in the dollar from its 1991 peak of 89 cents to the low 70s and later to the low 60s served to dramatically increase Canada's competitive position vis-à-vis the United States as well as Canada's tax revenues, ensuring that Martin was presiding over a strong economy.

- Even Moody's putting Canada on a "credit watch" in the first weeks of 1995 served Martin well, since he was able to lever off this to convince his fellow Liberals that fiscal restraint was the order of the day.

Later on, Martin's stellar performance arguably helped create his own good luck, as it were, but these initial bits of good fortune certainly paved the way.

Budgets and the Politics of Federalism

In his overview comments, Jeffrey Simpson directs some attention to what he calls the "politics of federalism", namely that since the federal government obtains little visibility and perhaps even less in the way of accountability for unconditional transfers to the provinces, Ottawa will push for more conditionality to be associated with future transfers. Arguably, this is what creating a separate CHT (Canada Health Transfer) and a CST (Canada Social Transfer) out of the current Canada Health and Social Transfer (CHST) is all about — to increase the "federal direction" (Simpson's term) of the transfers. In this context, I expect to see the word "additionality" become an important part of the jargon of fiscal federalism: the provinces will have to show that they are spending "additional" dollars in areas where transfers have increased. (Note that additionality may be one way around Mendelson's concern with respect to the inherent fungibility of transfer monies.) This may not work, of course; the provinces have thus far successfully ignored the conditions associated with the latest health transfer.

However, there is a much more important way for Ottawa to increase visibility and accountability, and one that is the hallmark of the Martin-Chrétien approach to fiscal federalism. This is to decrease federal transfers to the provinces while increasing federal transfers to citizens; that is, to increase *direct* transfers to citizens at the expense of *indirect* transfers through the provinces. The 1995 budget cuts to the CHST and then the later federal monies devoted to research chairs, Millennium Scholarships, and the Canada Child Tax Benefit (CCTB) and National Child Benefit (NCB) supplement are ample evidence of this trend to bypass the provinces. On a related note, it is commonplace for social activists to make the point that the Canada Assistance Plan (CAP) was a major victim of the creation of the CHST. In some ways this was certainly true, 50% welfare-sharing played an important stabilizing role for provinces hit by a negative shock, a role that has now disappeared. However, these same social advocates tend not to recognize the very substantial increases in the CCTB and NCB as more than a *quid pro quo* for the disappearance of CAP.

Budget Balance as a Canadian Value

Rick Harris' observation that, in foreign capitals, budget balance is coming to be viewed as a Canadian fiscal value is one of those insights that will immediately become part of our fiscal rhetoric. Bravo! Harris then raises the question of whether budget-balance targeting is an appropriate longer-term goal since it could well imply pro-cyclical policy; that is, raising taxes

                                                    Thomas J. Courchene

or cutting expenditures in a recession in order to stem a potential deficit. Obviously, one cannot rule out this possibility. But let me offer two possible counters to this. First, arguably Canada's most effective experience ever with stabilization policy occurred in the context of the millennium slowdown. As a result of measures in the February 2000 federal budget and the October 2000 economic statement, Canada's largest tax cut ($58 billion over five years) began to take effect on January 1, 2001, as did a cumulative $25 billion increase in the CHST. This timing coincided with the cyclical downturn and was in place for the dastardly deeds of 9/11. While this may be a one-off event and, therefore, not a meaningful answer to the Harris concern, it is arguably part of the reason why Canada has skated through this downturn more easily than have the Americans.

Perhaps the second counter is, however, that there is nothing sacrosanct about exact budget balance (i.e., a zero deficit). One can just as easily imagine balancing the budget over the cycle at a surplus of, say, $5 billion. In boom years, the actual surplus may shoot to $10 billion, and in recessions it may fall close to zero. The $10 billion swing in this example is actually less than the actual swing in Canada's surpluses (the peak was a surplus of over $17 billion in fiscal 2000/01). The point is that one can target for a given (positive) budget balance and still leave plenty of room for the operation of both discretionary and automatic stabilization policy, all the while maintaining surpluses as a Canadian fiscal value. While this is clear analytically, such a policy could run into trouble politically.

A Perspective on the Quantitative Budget Assessments

The JDI budget tradition has always been to devote a panel of the conference and volume to assessing the quantitative impacts of the budget. This has become a progressively less transparent exercise over the years. First of all, increasingly fiscal year t+1 is being influenced by budgets other than the one tabled in fiscal year t. For example, over the next fiscal year, some of the tax cuts legislated in the 2000 budget will be implemented, as will some of the pre-committed expenditures of earlier budgets (health transfers, Millennium Scholarships). Second, some of the recently legislated transfers to the provinces are in the nature of "rainy-day" funds — they can be drawn down by the provinces at any time over, say, a two or three year period. In any event, the result is that focus on the quantitative impact of year t's budget on the economy in year t+1 is becoming even less interesting. This is so because the answer to this question may be quite at variance with an equally, if not more, important question: What is the impact on the economy in year t+1 as a result of the changes in fiscal parameters from year t to year t+1? These changes in fiscal parameters from year t to year t+1 will incorporate the changes from this year's budgets as well as all relevant past budgets. The results of these quite different exercises could point in different directions, for example, one could be expansionary and the other contractionary. It is presumably the case that the fiscal authorities are fully aware of the influence that past budgets will have on the economy in the year t+1. This being the case, the budget stance for year t+1 will be designed to take these past budgets into account. Hence, my recommendation is that in any future JDI budget conferences, the quantitative budget assessment undertake forecasts of both these influences.

Beyond this, there is the reality that once monetary policy and inflation targeting are brought into the picture, expansionary (contractionary) fiscal policy will not boost (reduce) economic growth because the fiscal impact will be offset by tighter (looser) monetary conditions.

In light of all this, the important contributions of the Wilson-Dungan/ Egelton/Fortin panel is the focus on *composition* of output as a result of the interplay of the macro levers. Under the assumption that fiscal policy and output were already on track to generate inflation consistent with the Bank's target, Egelton's conclusion is instructive:

> If fiscal policy turns expansionary [as it has, T.J.C.], the Bank will increase interest rates by an amount sufficient to exactly offset the stimulus to economic growth from fiscal policy. Thus, expansionary fiscal policy will have no impact on growth but will serve to increase interest rates and push-up the value of the Canadian dollar as a result of widening interest rate differentials.

A forecast more accurate than most!

Thomas J. Courchene

Accountability and Transparency

In his paper "Full Accrual Accounting", Wiersema notes that the move to full accrual in the 2003 federal budget is viewed by some as "the biggest change in accounting for the federal government since Confederation". I commend the editors for scheduling a panel on this general issue. Complementing Wiersema's analytical paper is McCracken's valuable road map for how to improve transparency across a wide swath of policy areas and jurisdictions. And Alan Macnaughton's comment, drawn from recent earnings-management experiences in the private sector where accrual accounting is the rule, provides a timely reminder that the public sector equivalent of earnings management (e.g., deficit management) remains possible, which means that the Auditor General "has much work to do in ensuring that the introduction of full accrual accounting actually improves financial disclosure".

Indeed, the fact that fiscal year 2002/03 was selected as the year for introducing full accrual is readily explainable. Table 8.2 of *The Budget Plan: 2003* reveals that the impact of incorporating full accrual accounting adds $–0.7 billion to the surplus in 2001/02, $3.1 billion in 2002/03, $0.7 billion in 2003/04, and $0.9 billion in 2004/05. *Small wonder that fiscal year 2002/03 was chosen to inaugurate the move to full accrual accounting.* Indeed, given the pre-budget fiscal-restraint rhetoric, I was surprised that as part of the February 5, 2003 health accord, Ottawa was able to provide an additional immediate (i.e., fiscal year 2002/03) transfer of $2.5 billion to the provinces. What only Finance and the federal government knew was that their decision to shift to full accrual accounting in 2002/03 would generate an additional surplus that would comfortably finance this $2.5 billion transfer to the provinces.

One of the major accountability concerns of the Martin era at Finance related to what might be termed "deficit management", arguably the public sector equivalent to Macnaughton's earnings management in the private sector, as already noted. Heading up the list of issues here is the growing role of foundations, namely the use of third-party foundations that would receive budget monies in year t, but spent in future years. These are truly creative instruments that manage deficits by transferring funds to these foundations in budget years with large surpluses (often embarrassingly large in light of the forecast surplus). This decreases the surplus in these budget years and allows spending in later years when fiscal positions may be tight. As Weirsema notes:

> Since 1997, the government has transferred some $7.5 billion to 10 foundations ... The largest of these are the Canada Foundation for Innovation and the Millennium Scholarship Fund ... However, they haven't actually been spent for their ultimate intended purpose. [The Office of the Auditor General] found that, at March 31, 2002, only a tiny fraction of the $7.5 billion had been put to its ultimate intended use. The rest was sitting in accounts of the foundations, gaining interest. Very little had found its way to innovators and students.

Accordingly, Weirsema, and McCracken, focus on a variety of ways that these transfers to foundations can be more transparent and accountable.

At a more general level, Paul Martin's approach to budgeting certainly increased the transparency of the process — reducing the legislative period to the current fiscal year and the following two years (rather than the previous five-year projections): reliance on private-sector forecasts for variables such as gross domestic product (GDP), interest rates, inflation, etc.; adopting numerical deficit targets; and adopting explicit contingency measures to ensure "prudent" outcomes. Thanks to these measures (and to the factors alluded to earlier), almost immediately the budgetary deficit targets became credible — the financial community fully believed that Martin would achieve his deficit targets "come hell or high water" (as he earlier proclaimed). Indeed, in the event Martin exceeded his deficit targets by so much that, ironically, his projections became meaningless (except that it was certain that he would meet the deficit targets). Normally, Martin and Finance would have been skewered for consistently "low-balling revenues" so as to generate surpluses well above forecast levels. However, here is where his transparent process paid dividends: namely that the source of the problem relating to underestimating the eventual surplus did not lie in the Department of Finance. Rather, the problem lay with the fact that the private-sector forecasts consistently under-estimated key variables such as nominal and real GDP growth. In turn, this was because these private-sector estimates for Canadian GDP, etc. were driven off US forecasters' projections of comparable US variables. Thus, it was because the American forecasters consistently under-estimated the strength of the US economic boom that Canadian budget forecasts also under-estimated the eventual surpluses. While there was much concern (even from the ranks of the

                                   Thomas J. Courchene

Chrétien Liberals) about this overshooting, Martin and Finance were off the hook, as it were, because of the transparent nature of the budgetary process itself.

By way of a final comment, not all of Martin's initiatives would pass the accountability and transparency test. The obvious exemplar here is the so-called Unemployment Insurance (UI) (or EI) stabilization fund. With the economy picking up steam in the mid-1990s, Employment Insurance (EI) premiums were running roughly $6 billion ahead of EI payments to the unemployed. As part of his victory over Lloyd Axworthy and the social policy review process (see Greenspon and Wilson-Smith, 1996), Martin effectively took ownership of EI revenues. Faced with the urgency of addressing the deficit issue, he pocketed roughly $5 billion of these excess premiums and directed them toward the deficit reduction exercise. This has continued each and every year since the 1995 budget! To be sure, some pressures have developed for annual EI premium decreases, but these tended not to match the EI revenue increase from an ever-expanding employment base. Martin's rationale was that he had to build up an EI stabilization fund in order to have sufficient funds to finance the possibility of another EI deficit (payments exceeding premiums) on the scale that appeared in the early 1990s recession. But this was a *virtual* fund only. The excess EI premiums went directly into consolidated revenues. (I note in passing that at least one paper in this volume refers to the existence of the EI "fund", which is evidence of the utter non-transparency of this initiative.)

The further problem with all of this is that any excess premiums legally, were the "property" of the EI program, not of Finance. Hence, in my view, this was, and is, a misdirection of funds. What Martin ought to have done if he wanted these funds was to enact legislation to convert these excess premiums into a federal payroll tax. But for this Martin would have to assume accountability and make his actions transparent. Where was the Auditor General in all of this? Note that these issues were addressed earlier in JDI's 1997 budget volume by Dale Orr (see Appendix).

A Tax System for Century 21

Bev Dahlby's contribution, "The Chrétien Government's Legacy: A Tax System for the 21st Century?" is a veritable *tour de force* that is sure to find its way onto public finance reading lists. And the contribution is made even more valuable given that it is supplemented by Kesselman's constructive and insightful assessment. Since there is no way that I could possibly do justice to these papers in the space available, I shall focus rather arbitrarily on those features that struck me as either novel or particularly policy relevant.

Dahlby's reflections on the social insurance system are a good place to begin. As a result of the Canada/Quebec Pension Plans (CPP/QPP) premium increase from 5.85% in 1997 to 9.9% in 2003, contributions have risen from $11.7 billion in 1994 to nearly $30 billion in 2002. Two implications merit highlight. First, the maximum contribution for employees has increased from $806 in 1996 to $1,673 in 2002, the result of which Dahlby notes is to largely offset the other tax reductions (e.g., personal income tax [PIT] reductions) for low income individuals, especially single individuals. His second concern is that for the golden agers, their Guaranteed Income Supplement (GIS) is offset by 50% for any other income (including CPP/QPP payments) which, in turn, means that this doubling of premiums will not be reflected in their after-tax /after-GIS incomes when they retire. Dahlby's preference would have been to have smaller premium increases in the context of raising the retirement age by a year or two. Even the "progressive" Swedes have raised their retirement age for receipt of retirement benefits.

I would also add that at 9.9%, CPP/QPP premiums will begin to crowd out private-sector/occupational pension plans, which is another argument for supporting Dahlby's preferences for trading off some of the premium increase for an increase in the retirement age. Indeed, since much of this premium hike is designed to address the "fixed" or "sunk" costs that have arisen because the soon-to-retire baby boomers have not paid their fair share of their future pensions, the correct approach in any event is to finance this sunk cost out of *general revenues*. In an earlier context, I have addressed all of these issues under the admittedly provocative, but arguably appropriate title, "Generation X vs. Generation XS" (Courchene, 1997).

                                              Thomas J. Courchene

Among Dahlby's comments related to EI premiums is his view that true reform of EI is likely impossible because Canadians refuse to accept the principle of experience rating. I am not sure that I agree with this. I fear that experience rating would do precious little to address what ails EI. For example, experience rating in the fishing industry would clobber year-round fish farming, with attendant pressure to apply experience rating beneath the industry level, indeed eventually at the firm level with the regulatory nightmare that this would trigger. Actually, the real problem relates to the fact that short-term work attachment can lead to lengthy benefit periods. Not surprisingly, this feature is taken full advantage of by the seasonal industries: fishing, construction, forestry. It is the lack of the "insurance" feature in EI that leads to its overuse by certain industries. Were one to ensure that access to one week of benefits would require at least one week (and preferably two weeks) of work, then my guess is that most of the observed overuse by selected industries would vanish and, therefore, the rationale for experience rating would be ameliorated con-siderably.

Dahlby rightly labels the CCTB (and the associated NCB) as one of the most important tax changes of the Chrétien era since it reduces the incentive for poor families to move from welfare to work. However, the tax-back rates are such that the combined federal-provincial marginal tax rates for families with two children can exceed 60% in the $30,000 income range. Dahlby casts the dilemma as follows:

> Basically, a tax-transfer system that achieves a significant amount of re-distribution to lower income households can either impose high marginal tax rates on low income households through "targeted" benefits with high clawback rates or [impose] high marginal tax rates on high income households that finance "universal" benefits. The optimal tax rate structure depends on the responsiveness of earnings to marginal and average tax rates at different income levels.

But there may be alternative approaches here. Kesselman, for example, recommends that in-kind subsidies might be one important and appropriate part of a solution — for example, vouchers for daycare. Now that the tax system has been brought into the computer age, could one not impose a top marginal tax rate, say 40%, on a family until any and all tax-backs are achieved, at which time the family would fall into line with the regular tax system. Admittedly, 40% may not be the appropriate rate, but the idea is that one does not allow peaks to 60% for lower income levels. Rather, one extends the tax-back rates further along the income grid. Phrased differently, one establishes a maximum all-in tax-back rate that applies until the family breaks even with the system.

My final reference to Dahlby relates to capital taxes and the corporate sector, namely his concern that the efficiency gains arising because the goods and services tax (GST) does not tax intermediate inputs is being eroded by the reliance, especially at the provincial level, on capital taxes. As a result, taxes on corporations are not as low as one would presume just by looking at the corporate income tax rates. All of this appears in the context of Dahlby expressing relief that Ottawa is finally phasing out its capital taxes. He might have added that in addition to the provinces following suit, they should also convert their provincial sales tax (PST) to a GST (i.e., the six provinces who have not done so).

The reference to the GST provides a convenient bridge to Kesselman's thoughtful assessment of the Dahlby paper. From my perspective his most insightful comment is that, in the context of a Canada-US common market, the GST might become problematical.

> The open borders of a customs union would yield major benefits to the Canadian economy through lowered trading costs and increased efficiency and competitiveness. However, this prospect would be thwarted by Canada's existing high indirect consumption tax rates, which require border controls to enforce.
>
> Sales tax rates are only about half as high in most of the United States, whereas 45 states impose a retail sales tax but where there is no federal counterpart to the Canadian GST. To overcome this obstacle would require eliminating or changing the format of either the federal or provincial sales taxes in Canada. Changing the GST to a more direct form would raise the tax-paid price of goods and services produced in Canada, but the exchange rate would adjust to restore the nation's international trade competitiveness.

The reference to a "more direct form" for sales taxes would include the business transfer tax and the direct consumption tax both of which deserve more attention than they heretofore have received, especially if Canada and the United States move in the direction of a customs union.

                    Thomas J. Courchene

The 2003 budget also announced that the federal government will look into the possibility of introducing tax-prepaid savings plans (TPSPs) in Canada. These are after-tax deposits that then earn interest tax free and are non-taxable when withdrawn. In a 2001 C.D. Howe publication, Kesselman and Poschmann (2001) proposed this option for Canada and then elaborated on the advantages of these TPSPs relative to RRSPs (registered retirement savings plans). Kesselman is unduly modest about Finance's decision to devote further study to his proposal, but Dahlby appropriately sings its praises.

Health Care

Armine Yalnizyan's paper, "The Health Care Budget: Did It Resolve the 'Crisis'?" will also end up on reading lists in a variety of disciplines — economics, political science, health policy, public administration, etc. It is a nice combination of theory and practice that traces some key analytical features through the 1995 CHST cuts and then through the two federal-provincial-territorial accords (September 2000 and February 2003) that returned some of these monies to the provinces. To have all of this in one place is a valuable service to students and professionals alike.

Among the many analytical points Yalnizyan makes is that the federal cuts to CHST transfers over the last half of the 1990s did not really reduce provincial expenditures on health care since "cost containment is taking place in other areas of government expenditures", with the result that "health care is taking a bigger bite out of provincial expenditure with every passing year" (with Ontario leading the way with health-care spending now in 2001–02 at 44% of provincial spending). She goes on to argue that the first of the CHST cash infusions (September 2000), although nominally a health-care deal, was really an unconditional cash transfer, "making amends for the hard years of the 1990s". Arguably, this was also the case for the $2.5 billion cash component for fiscal year 2002/03 that was part of the February 5, 2003 health accord (since the fiscal year was almost over). Much of the remaining $30 billion or so in the 2003 agreement was intended to be more "transformative" in nature, following along the lines of Romanow and Kirby. However, I share with Yalnizyan the concern that these new monies are unlikely to buy much reform. One reason is that about 80% of the cost of the roughly $75 billion in health-care spending relates to various labour inputs. Much of the new money will simply go to maintaining the supply of qualified personnel, given that up to half of these health professionals will retire within the time frame of the accord. A second reason why these monies may not buy transformation is that the provinces remain unsatisfied with Ottawa's *share* of health-care funding. Yalnizyan notes that Ottawa's share of provincial health spending will rise to nearly 20% over the next year or two, but then fall back to 18%, whereas the appropriate federal share should be 25%. Elsewhere, I have argued that the provinces are insisting on Ottawa abiding by the "golden rule" of fiscal federalism: if you won't supply the gold, you can't make the rules. This being the case, the provinces are not likely to embark on major transformation without more certainty and sustainability to, let alone a more appropriate share for, Ottawa's financial commitment.

In terms of issues that will likely emerge over the next few years, one that Yalnizyan highlights is the Canada Health Act (CHA) principle of public administration. My preference here (Courchene, 2003) would be to support the Kirby view that the public administration principle in the CHA refers only to how the health-care insurance plans are administered, and not to who actually provides the services. In other words, there will be a single payer (government) who should be agnostic about whether health-services providers are government-owned, not-for-profit, or for-profit enterprises.

Paul Boothe, in his discussion of the Yalnizyan paper, focuses most of his comments on financial sustainability. While the feds and the provinces are fighting over the appropriate shares, the reality is that health costs are rising faster than the revenues of all governments — "it seems that Canadians and their political leaders are not yet ready to face up to the fact that "free on demand" health care can never be affordable in a world of rapid technological change and rising public expectations and that more radical reforms will be needed to preserve our equity-based, single-payer health system". Readers wishing to find out in more detail what Boothe has in mind can consult his recent paper with Carson (2003), *What Happened to Health Care Reform?*

                                             Thomas J. Courchene

The Social Dimension

Frances Woolley's "Linking Economic and Social Policy: To Benefit *All* Canadians?" addresses in some detail the specific social policy provisions contained in the 2003 budget. As such, these program descriptions do not lend themselves easily to analytical reflections. However, in terms of the economic and social policy linkages that Woolley attempts to draw, I think that they are related, and more important, linkages that have been characteristic of the Martin budgets. The first is that Finance has taken over not only the funding for social policy but, arguably, the design as well. This began, of course, with the triumph, prior to the 1995 budget, of Martin and Finance over Lloyd Axworthy and Human Resources Development Canada. Henceforth, Martin largely called the social policy shots (and even took control of the EI premiums, as noted above). Once the deficit was tamed, the linkage began to unravel a bit, especially with respect to the health funding envelope. It will be interesting to see if the 2003 budget proposal for splitting the CHST into the CHT and the CST will be accompanied by a further loosening of the grip by Finance over these areas.

The second linkage is that in a progressively advancing information era where knowledge is increasingly at the cutting edge of competitiveness, social policy (in its knowledge or human-capital development dimension) is rather indistinguishable in its impact from old style economic policy. Not only was Martin fully aware of this, but he forged the way for Ottawa and the Department of Finance to make important federal inroads into these areas that, to a large degree, fall under provincial jurisdiction: Millennium Scholarships, Canada Research Chairs, etc.

With Martin as prime minister, both of these linkages will presumably continue, but the interesting question is whether they will continue to be coordinated/orchestrated by Finance or whether the oversight will come directly from the Office of the Prime Minister.

Michael Mendelson's focus is on the implications of splitting the CHST into a separate health and social transfer (CHT and CST). His answer is two-fold. First, from a fiscal objective, since the provinces have sufficient access to revenues (which preludes the existence of a fiscal imbalance between the two levels of government), the real fiscal issue is that *between* provinces. And for this one would prefer an equalization-type program than a CHST-type. Presumably, this is especially the case, given that all the recent infusions to the CHST have been equal per capita transfers, eroding the erstwhile degree of equalization embedded in CAP and Established Programs Financing. The part of this that is not persuasive to me is the suggestion that there is no fiscal imbalance between the two levels of government. There are competitive limits to how high our tax rates can be on our mobile factors. For many of the shared taxes, Ottawa got there first, so that there is no competitive room for the provinces to raise marginal rates, even if they have constitutional powers to do so.

Mendelson's second point is that, from a programmatic vantage point, the movement toward a CHT and a CST will only make a real difference if these transfers become conditional (or perhaps "additional" as noted in the introductory paragraph). I guess I would add that conditionality is likely only if Ottawa agrees to commit itself to paying 25% of health costs in terms of a case transfer. But I have already made this point in a previous context.

Kyoto

When it comes to the environment, I am definitely a consumer of information, not a producer. Accordingly, I benefited substantially from the descriptive and analytical contributions on the Kyoto Protocol by Ross McKitrick and Christopher Green. McKitrick begins with what turns out to have been a correct presumption, namely that Kyoto would fail because the Russians would not ratify it in part because the withdrawal of the United States from the Protocol meant that the potential value of Russia's tradeable emission permits would now be worth less. This is just as well, given his conclusion with respect to both the 2002 Climate Change Plan and the environmental provisions in the 2003 budget:

> In sum, it is hard to see any evidence that actually implementing the November 2002 Climate Change Plan in the next few years was seriously in mind when this [2003] budget was written. This would not be surprising since the November 2002 plan cannot be taken seriously. It is a hodgepodge of comically bad ideas, and the lack of any specific cost estimates cannot disguise the fact that it would be ruinously expensive while at the same time accomplishing no significant public good.

                                        Thomas J. Courchene

Chris Green's assessment is even more critical — Canada's environment policy is launched along the wrong trajectory:

> If the federal government really wants to make useful investments on the climate change front, it would do better to make investments that could really make a difference, rather than use those funds in a scattershot and eventually futile attempt to achieve essentially meaningless GHC (greenhouse gases) emission targets.

By way of elaboration:

> After all, what affects climate is *not* annual emissions (a flow), but the *global* atmospheric concentration of GHGs (a stock). The relevant question is what will it take to stabilize the atmospheric concentration of GHGs at a level that avoids a "dangerous interference" with climate. Contrary to popular belief, including that of many climate policymakers, the facile view ... that a combination of energy efficiency improvements and renewable energies are capable of achieving stabilization, has been shown to be fundamentally flawed.

Toward this end, Green suggests three possible projects that could be used in Canada and elsewhere to help stabilize the stock of GHGs: carbon capture and sequestration, nuclear fusion, and nuclear-generated electrolytic hydrogen.

The Chrétien Budget Legacy and the Provinces

I want to conclude with a provincial perspective of the fiscal legacy of the Chrétien Liberals, drawing in part from my earlier assessment (2002). The starting point is two-fold. First, from the vantage point of 1995, there was no way for Ottawa to move to a zero deficit without, initially at least, shifting much of the existing federal deficit to the provinces. Second, and increasingly important, what sells electorally to Canadians are citizen-related issues: health, education, income distribution, child poverty, etc. Since these areas are largely under the jurisdiction of the provinces, Ottawa has to find ways to "invade" provincial jurisdiction. The CHST cuts announced in the 1995 budget were the key to solving both of these problems. The decrease in cash transfers from roughly $17 billion to $11 billion created enormous damage to provincial finances. To be sure, the strength of the ongoing boom allowed the provinces to accommodate these cuts on a temporary basis. (As an important aside, while Ottawa has restored some of these transfers, the reality is that the 2003 budget forecasts for 2007/08 indicate that federal cash and tax transfers will still account for a smaller level of GDP than they did in 1995. On the other hand, health expenditures have grown much faster than GDP). However, part of the way that the provinces managed to maintain (indeed increase) expenditures on health was to starve virtually every other provincial policy area. As a result, citizens became very receptive to the types of policies that have been the hallmark of the Martin budgets — policies that deal directly with citizens and bypass the provinces — Millennium Scholarships, CCTB and NCB, research chairs, homelessness. In response to mounting provincial pressures for redressing the resulting fiscal imbalance, Ottawa is finding new ways to justify maintaining its current revenue share: sharing gasoline taxes with the cities, expanding the health-care envelope, increased defence and aid spending, etc.

Hence, the provinces are facing deteriorating finances (except for Alberta) and witnessing a federal end run of their spending responsibilities, an end run that appears to have the support of the majority of Canadians. So far, this bit of fiscal brinkmanship has paid off handsomely for the federal government. One can confidently predict that the provinces will not take all this without protest. The federal-provincial fiscal tug of war will soon be again afoot. This may not be news, but it's certainly Canadian, eh?

References

Boothe, P. and M. Carson (2003), *What Happened to Health Care Reform?* C.D. Howe Institute, Commentary No. 193 (Toronto: C.D. Howe Institute).
Courchene, T.J. (1997), "Generation X vs. Generation XS: Reflections on the Way Ahead", in K. Banting and R. Boadway (eds.), *Reform of Retirement Income Policy: International and Canadian Perspectives* (Kingston: School of Policy Studies, Queen's University).
__________ (2002), *Half-Way Home: Canada's Remarkable Fiscal Turnaround and the Paul Martin Legacy, Policy Matters* 3(8) (Montreal: Institute for Research on Public Policy).

                                                    Thomas J. Courchene

__________ (2003), "Medicare as a Moral Enterprise: The Romanow and Kirby Perspectives", *Policy Matters* 4(1) (Montreal: Institute for Research on Public Policy).

Greenspon, E. and A. Wilson-Smith (1996), *Double Vision: The Inside Story of the Liberals in Power* (Toronto: Doubleday Canada Ltd.).

Kesselman, J. and F. Poschmann (2001), *A New Option for Retirement Savings: Tax-Prepaid Savings Plans*, C.D. Howe Institute Commentary No. 149 (Toronto: C.D. Howe Institute).

Appendix

The 1995 Federal Budget: Retrospect and Prospect
TABLE OF CONTENTS

Acknowledgement

Preface

Session I: The International Dimension

Leo de Bever
International Impact of the Federal Budget

Sylvia Ostry
The 1995 Federal Budget: The International Dimension

Session II: A Quantitative Assessment

Thomas A. Wilson and D. Peter Dungan
Economic and Fiscal Effects of the 1995 Federal Budget: A Quantitative Appraisal

Session III: The Expenditure Dimension

William B.P. Robson
Federal Spending in Four Dimensions

Bryne B. Purchase
Born Again Government?

Session IV: The Federal-Provincial Dimension

Robin Boadway
The Implications of the Budget for Fiscal Federalism

Thomas J. Courchene
The Federal-Provincial Dimension of the Budget: Two Cheers for the CHST

                                                   Thomas J. Courchene

Session V: The Taxation Dimension

Jack M. Mintz and Duanjie Chen
The Budget's Tax Policy: A Ship Lost at Sea

Session VI: The Social Policy Dimension

Sherri Torjman
The 1995 Federal Budget: a.k.a. The Real Social Security Review

Keith Banting
Who "R" Us?

Session VII: Assessment and Perspectives

Pierre Fortin
Six Observations on the Budget

William Scarth
The Federal Budget: Assessment and Perspectives

The 1997 Federal Budget: Retrospect and Prospect
TABLE OF CONTENTS

Acknowledgement

Preface/Executive Summary

Session I: The Martin Budgets: An Assessment

John McCallum
The Martin Budgets

William Watson
Paul Martin's First-Term Record

Andrew Sharpe
Perspectives on Federal Fiscal Policy in the 1990s and Beyond

Session II: A Quantitative Assessment

Thomas Wilson, Peter Dungan and Steve Murphy
The 1997 Federal Budget: A Quantitative Assessment

Session III: The Child Benefits Package

Ken Battle
The 1997 Budget and the Child Benefits Package

Lisa M. Powell
Revamping the Child Tax Benefit System: An Assessment

Session IV: Payroll Taxation

William B.P. Robson
Not as Bad as it Looks: An Intergenerational View of the CPP Tax Hike

Dale Orr
Employment Insurance Premiums: An Economic Policy Analysis Perspective

 Thomas J. Courchene

Session V: Jobs and NAIRU

Pierre Fortin
Canada's Job Growth Potential

Peter Pauly
Canada's Job Growth Potential: Comments

Session VI: Provincial Perspectives

Paul Boothe
Fiscal Reform in Alberta: The Dinning Budgets

Teresa Courchene and Chris Forbes
Provincial Finances: From Deficits to Debt Reduction

Session VII: Assessment and Perspectives

Leo de Bever
Fiscal Policy: Reclaiming the Ability to Choose

Rick Egelton
Fiscal Finances: Debt Burdens and Policy Choices

Harvey Lazar
The Social Policy Legacy

The 2000 Federal Budget: Retrospect and Prospect
TABLE OF CONTENTS

Acknowledgement

Introduction

Session I: The 2000 Federal Budget: Implications for Canadian Federalism

Harvey Lazar
The Social Union Framework Agreement and the Federal Budgetary Process

Thomas J. Courchene
Taxation, Fiscal Federalism and the 2000 Federal and Provincial Budgets

Session II: The Budget and its Macroeconomic Effects

Thomas A. Wilson, Peter Dungan and Steve Murphy
Macroeconomic Effects of Budget 2000

Rick Egelton
Macroeconomic Effects of the 2000 Federal Budget

Gregor Smith
Macroeconomic Forecasts and the Budget

Session III: The Taxation Dimension

William B.P. Robson
Counting Chickens and Unhatched Eggs: The Post-Budget Outlook for Canadian Taxes

Michael Smart
How Do Recent Tax Reforms Affect the Behaviour and Welfare of Families?

Robin Boadway
Tax Changes in the 2000 Federal Budget

Session IV: The Expenditure Dimension

Lars Osberg
Federal Expenditures in Canada:The Millennial Vision and its Tensions

Lise Bastarache
Federal Budget 2000: The Expenditure Dimension from a Provincial Perspective

Session V: The Social Policy Dimension

Frances Woolley
Budget 2000: A Children's Budget?

Keith Banting
Do We Know Where We Are Going?

Session VI: Assessment and Perspectives

Jim Stanford
Paul Martin's Tax Revolt

Pierre Fortin
Fiscal Stabilization and the Allocation of Fiscal Dividend:An Assessment

Session VII: Budgeting in the New Millennium

Jack M. Mintz
Some Reflections on the Budget Process and the Fiscal Issues Confronting Canada

Session One
BUDGET CONTEXT

THE POLITICS OF THE 2003 BUDGET

Jeffrey Simpson, *The Globe and Mail*

I feel like a heathen among the believers. I am a journalist among scholars and I am a political scientist, so I am doubly ill-suited for this task. But I console myself with the fact that all budgets, although they are principally economic documents, are political statements in the sense of being part of the ongoing partisan battle between the government and its political adversaries. They are also a political statement of the government of the day's preferences, values, intentions, and strategic choices. This budget was very much of that sort, but there were two other observations that made this budget quite particular. It was a unique sort of budget because it was the prime minister's last and it was in effect two budgets crammed into one. I mean this in the sense that at least some of the spending incorporated in the 2003 budget — some of the choices, if you like, that were reflected in the spending options of the 2003 budget — would likely have been included in the 2002 budget but for the terrorist attacks in the United States and the very sudden requirements that these attacks imposed on the Canadian government to spend money on such matters as security and border issues and intelligence. It is obviously not possible to know which spending items would have been included in the 2002 budget but for those terrorist attacks, but I think it is reasonable to say that at least some of the measures that were announced in the 2003 budget would have figured in the 2002 budget but for the very sudden change of priorities that swept over the federal government in the fall of 2002 as a consequence of the attacks in the United States.

You can go back and say that some of the spending items that we saw in 2003 had actually been outlined in principle, but, of course, not in detail in the Speech from the Throne of January 2001, which followed on the Liberal Party's successful re-election in the fall of 2000. That speech did outline a quite ambitious spending agenda for the duration of what the prime minister then hoped would be a full mandate for him. It included extensive references to health-care spending, child poverty, climate change, and other matters.

One should look at the 2003 budget in the context of what did not happen in 2002 because of the terrorist attacks. Also, between the Speech from the Throne of January 2001 and the September 2002 Speech from the Throne, there was another seismic political development — the then prime minister lost his grip on the Liberal Party. Therefore, he had to concede in the late summer of 2002 that he would not lead the party into the next federal election campaign. He, in effect, had to telescope into a shorter time frame what he had intended or hoped to accomplish during the rest of the mandate. He said, you may remember, in the late summer of 2002, when he announced his departure for February 2004, that he wanted to have two more budgets. But, in reality, he only had one, which was the 2003 budget. I should add, however, that, although remote, Chrétien might have tried to introduce one last budget. But this would likely have provoked a severe revolt inside the Liberal Party.

I should say that what Chrétien did in the late summer of 2002, for those of us who are observers of political theatre, is going to go down in Canadian political history as an absolute master stroke. I know that it left the Martin people literally dumbfounded because the prime minister had lost control of the rank and file of the Liberal Party and of the majority of the Liberal caucus. Therefore, he had a hand that was extremely weak. I remember having had many conversations with the Martin people in which I said to them, "Look the deal is going to be that he's going to ask you to cancel that February 2003 convention in exchange for him staying for a little longer, maybe a couple of months, until maybe June." The Martin people, figuring that they had all the high cards in their hands said, "Well we might give him until May maybe June." One or two of them said maybe September, but that will be the deal — no convention, he stays until May or June, then we take over. They were thunderstruck when he said "I'm staying till February 2004." So thunderstruck, you may remember, that they had to retire for two or three hours to consider their options because this was one they had never considered. It was a complete masterstroke and the prime minister read the party correctly and that it would prefer to let him stay until February 2004 in exchange for no blood. It gave him 18 months of additional time in office.

Prime ministers have a heavy and often a decisive hand in what goes into a budget. But I would say that, in this case more than in most, the budget was shaped by the prime minister. Remember that Chrétien's minister of finance, John Manley, was quite new. He had no constituency of his own inside the party or in the country. He could not go to the prime minister and say, "You know, I've got a large number of people who agree with me in the caucus. I've got a constituency in the country that agrees with me as opposed to you." So a variety of broadly defined political assumptions factored into shaping the budget.

First, this being Chrétien's last budget, it was going to be his legacy budget. Now, he was right when bearded about this legacy business in saying his legacy was 40 years in public life and nearly ten years as prime minister. That is all true. But all prime ministers, at least in my experience, as they come toward the end of their time in office, do think rather more about how they will be viewed by history. They try, insofar as they can, to make decisions and shape events to give a final positive interpretation to their years in office. He had already identified in that Speech from the Throne of 2001 his priorities for his last mandate while holding open the option that he might run again. Of great significance, he put Alex Himmelfarb in charge of the coordination within the government of the priorities of the government. Himmelfarb had moved over from deputy minister of Canadian Heritage to become the Clerk of the Privy Council.

Second, the budget had to be balanced, since one of the two or three enduring legacies of the Chrétien government had been the elimination of deficits. If you think back to public opinion prior to the 2000 election and even the late 1990s, all of the polling data and all of the internal political intelligence in the Liberal Party said that the party was being positively reviewed by Canadians because they had brought the era of deficit to an end. They had brought fiscal stability to the country. To plunge the last budget back into deficit would have imperilled, and probably risked completely, the undoing of some if not all of the positive political legacy of the previous years of sound fiscal management. So additional spending had to be placed in the context of a balanced budget.

Third, if you look at the way they viewed their political/economic imperatives, they were in order: first, significant new spending; second, a balanced budget; third, tax reduction; and fourth, way down the list, debt reduction. So why spending at the top? As a general observation, I would say that Liberals are more comfortable with it. It suits their sense of what government is there for. The party's own polling, public polling, and their own caucus feedback suggested that spending was more popular than additional tax cuts, and it was particularly more popular for the Liberal's core constituencies that include low-income women, immigrants, and francophones. It is true that *National Post* readers wanted the reverse priorities, but *National Post* readers do not vote Liberal. And there was inside the Liberal caucus a kind of ambivalence with the previous budgets that had brought about the fiscal balance. Yes, Liberals recognized that they were being rewarded for that, but, on the other hand, there were pent-up demands inside the party for spending in a variety of areas.

The politics of surplus are very different than the politics of deficit. It is much more difficult to say "no" with a surplus than with a deficit. All political people have a sense of themselves, and this prime minister's self-reading was of a battler for the little guy. I have watched Chrétien over many years and I would say that spending restraint is something he will do if he must, but spending is what he will do if he can.

Fourth, it was obvious that health care was going to eat up the largest amount of available and discretionary dollars.

Fifth, the spending was going to be spread out over a number of years. I would say that, of all the budgets that I have written about and read over many years, this spreading out of the spending over many future years was more pronounced. Why? It makes planning easier and therefore can be argued to be good policy. If you are going to launch a new policy initiative like climate change, for example, or if you are going to engage in funding urban infrastructure, these projects do not take just one or two years. If you are going to put a lot of money into the health-care system and you hope that the money will bring about reform, those reforms will, of course, take many years. So spreading out the spending over a certain number of years can make good planning sense.

But there was another agenda, although not everybody agrees with me on this. The spending also ate up surpluses that Paul Martin might have hoped would be available for him as prime minister. In that sense, it was rather a "honey I shrunk the kids" budget. I cannot remember another budget that pre-committed so much spending over such long-term contracts. For example, $34.8 billion for health care over five years; $3 billion for infra- structure over ten years; $172 million for Aboriginal languages over 11; $114 million for official languages over five years; $2 billion for climate change over five; $320 million for affordable housing over five; $935 million for child care and early learning over five; $800 million for the military per year; $965 million for the National Child Benefit over three years; and $600 million for water and waste water treatment for Aboriginal reserves. Plus an agreement to continue with commitments for 8% annual increases in the foreign aid budget with no time limit, a continuation of the long-term tax reduction plan, a continuation of the previously announced six-year plan for $5.2 billion for agriculture. And so on. In other words, an awful lot of three, five, six, ten, eleven-year spending commitments. This was a budget not just for this fiscal year and for the next, but for fiscal years extending well into the future. You could argue that this really is not what the prime minister's final budget should be about. You could argue that, under other circumstances and with different personalities, an out- going prime minister might have said he would only make commitments to the end of his time in office or for a brief period of time thereafter in order to maximize the flexibility for his party and his successor.

But knowing Chrétien and knowing his animus toward Martin, the thinking ran exactly the opposite; namely, how can I use up as much of the future fiscal room as possible. And if this pre-committed spending causes any fiscal headaches down the road, I will be gone and Martin will have to deal with them all. Believe me, that is exactly how the Martinites interpreted what went on. But they were completely helpless to stop it. They were not going to foment a caucus rebellion and furthermore, the kind of social- spending commitment in this budget was very popular with the Liberal caucus, including with a number of people who were strongly committed to Martin. There was not going to be a caucus rebellion in the Liberal Party, even among the Martinites, for improving the National Child Tax Credit.

Martin had already committed himself to a greater federal role for cities. Do you think there was going to be a caucus revolt over spending more money on health care? I do not think so. This was an absolutely correct reading by Chrétien. So, my interpretation is that Chrétien, as I said, pulled off one of the great political masterstrokes of our time in surviving 2002 and then introducing a budget in 2003 that at least had the ancillary intention, if not the primary one, of making the margin for manoeuvre of his successor as limited as possible.

The caucus was overwhelmingly in favour of Martin, but the caucus lacks the internal party constitutional authority to replace the leader. All the caucus can do is stew and, on occasion, raise sort-of revolts over tertiary issues such as how to elect committee chairs. The fact that Liberal members of Parliament were generally satisfied with the spending priorities in this budget illustrates again that the politics of a surplus is more difficult than that of a deficit, because it is very hard to say "no" when the government looks to be running a surplus. Once a consensus emerges as it did in 1994–95 in the party and in the country that a deficit has to be tackled, it is possible for a minister of finance to say "no" to a lot of people. Caucus members at least have the cover of saying "no" to aggrieved constituents because they are saying it to all kinds of groups. Everybody's ox is being gored. In a surplus situation that kind of defence no longer applies, so that competition inevitably emerges, as it did with great intensity before the last budget, to see which interest or which region will be favoured by the budget.

The public reaction to the budget was curious, although perhaps entirely in keeping with the political problem of having a surplus. This reaction took the government by surprise. Despite spreading so much money around, nobody seemed happy. Interest groups grumbled. Provincial premiers complained bitterly that health-care spending was insufficient and was too tied. Business groups huffed about too much spending and no further tax reductions. But, after two or three days of that kind of reaction, all became quiet and, apart from this conference, nothing has been heard about the budget since.

This is not the place for an extended discussion of health-care policies. Suffice it to say that for several years before this budget, it became clear that health-care concerns were public priority number one and there was no

                                                                    Jeffrey Simpson

chance that this government was going to deviate from the principles of the Canada Health Act. The only questions, therefore, were how much additional money would be spent and for what purposes. There had been the $24 billion hurry-up promise made in the first week of the 2000 election, but even then, there was the sense that the Liberals knew that that was not going to be enough. Of course, it was not enough because the early monies spent out of that allocation were largely eaten up by the health-care workers. The first infusions of money did not lead to any discernible improvements that any Canadian could feel in the delivery of health care. Public anxiety remained high and provincial premiers continued to complain.

The Romanow Commission on Health Care was established to look into what to do about health care. It was quite significant that the prime minister knew Roy Romanow, knew his general views about health care, and knew that he was not going to call into question the principles of the Canada Health Act. Romanow's job was essentially to produce a dollar figure on the health-care bill and to affix certain conditions to how that additional money would be spent. Indeed, the terms of reference for the commission made it perfectly clear that that is what his job was. He was never going to recommend anything that called medicare into question. Nor was a centralist such as Chrétien going to write the premiers a large cheque and be done with it. He is of the school that the federal government never receives credit from the provinces in terms of publicity and attention, so he was not going to turn over great amounts of money to them without significant federal direction and that, of course, was the essence of the argument between the two levels of government. You can call this partisan politics if you like, but it is more accurately described as the politics of federalism.

Whether all of this money on health care will actually deliver an improved health-care system is a question that will be answered long after Chrétien is gone from the political scene. But it is one that is absolutely central to the next major political debate we will have in the country.

BALANCED BUDGETS AS A CANADIAN FISCAL VALUE?

Richard Harris, Simon Fraser University

It seems like a very long time has passed since John Deutsch Institute conferences dealing with the budget were somber events with a highly pessimistic overtone on the state of Canadian public finances. We can now gratefully push those memories to the back of our minds — but not too far. In those "bad old" days the typical conference presentation began with a weary description of the failure of governments to run balanced budgets over the cycle and speculation on the ultimate consequences of the ever rising public debt. It all seems so surreal now. Today, as we discuss the budget of February 2003, we have nothing but good news — six consecutive balanced or surplus budgets in the context of remarkably strong economic growth and phenomenal job creation.

However, as practitioners of the dismal science, it is useful to remind ourselves that there are both cyclical and structural aspects associated with the current favourable fiscal situation, and both of these are subject to change. In almost all other Organisation for Economic Co-operation and Development (OECD) countries, current fiscal policy discussions are dealing with emerging deficits for a variety of reasons. The Canadian case is therefore quite unusual viewed against the global situation. Secondly, the Canadian public, media and politicians all now display a remarkable preference for surplus budgets. This has now translated according to some pundits as a new "Canadian value". This is indeed a remarkable shift in public and private attitudes. Many fiscally conservative economists will argue, with some justification, that this has been a major public policy success on the part of the mainstream economics profession. Yet it is clear that this enthusiasm has not been exported abroad. Many other governments, including the United States, are now running large deficits. Which leads one to wonder if the Canadian situation is likely to persist? In my comments I first briefly review the recent budget in light of recent developments, and then go on to discuss the pressures and risks to a fiscal framework built around the concept of forever balanced budgets. My basic argument is that the current Canadian preference for budget surpluses is likely to change in the face of cyclical and structural developments over the medium term.

The 2003 Budget

This year's budget document is highly self-congratulatory (see Canada. Department of Finance, 2003). After reading it, one is given the impression that the current federal government is almost entirely responsible for the favourable fiscal developments. In many ways this seems natural given that, compared to almost any other country — in particular the European economies, the United States and Japan — Canada stands out as a model for fiscal prudence.

It is also clear that the cyclical performance of the Canadian economy has been exceptional. Average economic growth in Canada in the first three-quarters of 2002 was 4.4%, the strongest among the G7 countries. Strong domestic demand balanced weakening external demand as other economies recovered from the recession which began with the stock market crash in spring 2000. Job growth has been very good. As emphasized in the budget, during 2002 the economy created 560,000 jobs, more than 60% of which were full-time. And in the game of Canada-US comparisons, we look even better in 2002 as the US economy lost 229,000 jobs. The employment rate in Canada is now about the same as the US rate for the first time in 20 years. On the fiscal side, the federal debt as a percent of gross domestic product (GDP) has gone from a peak of 67.5% in 1995/96 to 44.5% in 2002/03. Department of Finance are predicting a budget surplus of approximately 0.7% of GDP for the current year. To what do we owe these favourable developments? The following quote is the explanation given by the Government of Canada:

The solid performance of the Canadian economy at a time of global weakness reflects Canada's sound economic policies. Five consecutive budgetary surpluses, a sharp drop in public debt and large tax cuts supported confidence and domestic demand. This sound fiscal policy, together with low inflation, allowed the Bank of Canada to reduce short-term interest rates to their lowest level in more than 40 years, boosting consumer spending and confidence.

The government is therefore claiming credit for the lower interest rates, due to both a confidence channel running from sound fiscal policy and to a low inflation rate produced by the Bank of Canada. From a textbook perspective one wonders to what extent the low interest-rate environment in Canada has been "made at home". A skeptic might argue this can be almost entirely ascribed to external developments. After all, Japan has the lowest interest rates in the world, but one of the worst fiscal records. However, we can ask whether relative interest rates and growth performance can be squared with this or other possible explanations. In the textbooks, shifts in aggregate demand with a stable NAIRU (non-accelerating inflation rate of unemployment) usually produce increases in interest rates when output grows. Recall the United States has had the classic textbook case of reductions in interest rates accompanied by sub-par output growth. What other theoretical explanations might we give? Here are two possible textbook answers.

- The economy was hit with very favourable productivity shocks lowering the NAIRU, which in turn leads to accommodative monetary policy with little inflation. With this explanation, fiscal policy is basically a sideshow with the improvement in overall fiscal stance a by-product of low real interest rates and high growth all driven by the exogenous productivity shock.

- Give all the credit to monetary policy. In the Mundell- Flemming model with falling real interest rates abroad together accompanied by a very accommodative domestic monetary policy you get lower interest rates and a depreciating real exchange rate. The low dollar and low interest rates take up the slack. Under this explanation you give a lot of credit to the foreign exchange markets for producing what most view as an overly cheap Canadian dollar.

It is possible to give some explanations based on changes in fiscal policy. There is a literature that relates contractionary fiscal policy to lower real interest rates and output expansion — what is sometimes referred to as the German Fiscal Policy theory.[1] There is now a large number of papers on this but the international evidence is mixed. In the German fiscal policy theory, which is not too far from what the 2003 budget appears to claim, the stimulative effect of a fiscal contraction comes through an expectations or credibility channel. Reduced expectations of future fiscal crises lower expected future taxes and government spending; this increases investment, reduces the risk discount on government bonds, increases business confidence and interest rates then fall more in response to fiscal tightening, than would be explained by a simple fiscally induced shift in the IS curve. Perhaps this story may be relevant for Canada, in which case it is the poster-boy for the German fiscal policy theory, but we clearly need more research before going with this explanation.

The performance of the US economy post-stock market crash in 2002 has played an important role in the Canadian fiscal recovery. US demand after the tech bubble burst did fall, but the composition effects have been decidedly in Canada's favour. The Federal Reserve aggressively cut rates which led to strong growth in US demand for autos and housing. This fortunately just happens to be what the Canadian economy exports to the United States. Moreover, 9/11 seems to have had a more dramatic impact on US domestic consumer confidence than was the case in Canada. All in all, I would argue that favourable cyclical developments in Canada post-2000 have had a lot to do with good luck and accommodative monetary policy here and in the United States. Fiscal policy at best played a minor but at least supportive role.

None of this matters except that, as in the case of duffers explaining their golf scores, governments always attribute success to their own decisions and attribute failure to external factors or bad luck. It is important that in judging the emergence of the "northern tiger" we sort out what was policy induced. If Canada had been hit with it's own terrorist attack or demand shock equivalent , and the US Fed had not cut rates so aggressively, would we have been as satisfied with the policy rules that currently guide Canadian macro management?

---

[1]The classic reference is Giavazzi and Pagano (1991).

                                                        Richard Harris

The Case for Countercyclical Fiscal Policy

The current stated preference on the part of the public and politicians for balanced budgets runs against both a long history of counter-cyclical fiscal activism in Canada, and also what is generally going on elsewhere in the world economy. The current discussion in Canada of fiscal policy is remarkably different than is the case in either the United States, which has seen the reemergence of Reagan-style military Keynesianism, Britain (a more muted form of modified Keynesianism), Japan — a case of fiscal desperation with monetization looming, or in Europe where the straightjacket of the Growth and Stability pact is running up against the reality of fast emerging structural deficits in Germany and France. This is a remarkable change since the mid-1990s in all these countries. One could conclude that in matters of fiscal fashion, growth-oriented fiscal activism appears to be alive and well. Looking at the United States this conclusion seems clearly warranted. Alan Auerbach stated that "the strong support for this most recent stimulus package reminds us that policy makers may go where economists fear to tread. No politician wishes to be cast in the title role of 'It's the Economy, Stupid' " (Auerbach, 2002).

Canada's position on the wisdom of pursuit of counter-cyclical fiscal policy may be rationally rooted in the evidence. The evidence, however, is mixed. Auerbach (2002) reviews the literature and draws a number of conclusions on the US experience:

1. The cyclical response of the economy (referring to the United States) to fiscal policy has been weakened by greater openness to trade.
2. Counter-cyclical responsiveness of US tax and spending appears to have increased over the last two decades, driven either by use of discretionary policy, or by changes in the structure of the automatic stabilizers.
3. Romer and Romer (1994) argue that fiscal policy worked in the right direction, but was far less powerful than monetary policy.
4. Blanchard and Perotti (1999) present evidence that shows that unexpected tax cuts do increase consumption, thus discretionary fiscal policy could work in practice.

What does one take from this? From the US perspective, it appears that counter-cyclical policy continues to be treated seriously as a policy tool.

One issue is that the US case may not be relevant for Canada. First, Canada is more open to trade. The presumed stabilization benefits of counter-cyclical fiscal policy may simply be too small to worry about. Second, Canada has a different fiscal history than the United States. The latter is important because the fiscal history of an economy may condition the response of that economy to fiscal stimulus or contraction at any point in time. For example, an economy that has been persistently in surplus and growing, but suddenly finds growth slowing, may respond more positively to fiscal stimulus than an economy that has had a history of weak growth and budget deficits (such as Japan). Expectations and response to initiatives by macro authorities are conditioned by credibility of those authorities. This is really more in line with the German theory of fiscal credibility. It may well be at this point that any indication the fiscal authorities are abandoning balanced budgets will create a crisis in credibility, which in turn would destabilize the economy. Whatever counter-cyclical fiscal policy gains delivered in terms of Keynesian employment benefits or New Classical tax-smoothing, these would be more than offset by increases in interest rates and loss in confidence. As in the case of all "cost of credibility" arguments, it is difficult if not impossible to quantify this effect before the event. It is clearly an argument George Bush does not worry about.

Balanced Budgets as a Long-Term Rule: A Canadian Value?

When the Canadian fiscal crisis occurred in the first half of the 1990s, getting to balanced budgets was the fiscal equivalent of the Holy Grail. Yet to be honest, relatively few economists at the time, if pushed, would necessarily have argued that balanced budget fiscal rules were an optimal policy in the usual welfare maximizing normative sense. It subsequently evolved that way, in my view, largely as a response to the politics of debt and deficits. If the public supports balanced budgets, this is vastly superior to an alternative in which deficit finance is viewed as costless, and more-over constrains politicians in a socially useful way. One could even go so far as to say that there might in 2003 be substantial public support in Canada for enshrining balanced budgets within the constitution as the Europeans seem to have done with the Growth and Stability Pact.

                                                           Richard Harris

Looking at other industrial democracies, though, I am somewhat skeptical that this is a Canadian value which will endure beyond the current business cycle. I think there are both structural and potential cyclical reasons the whole framework for fiscal policy will be revisited. It is worth thinking about these issues now if only to prepare ourselves for the public debate, and hopefully to prevent a return to a US-like situation in which the government behaves as if a permanent structural deficit is not a problem.

Eventually a large recession will occur in Canada, a deficit will result and there will be calls for fiscal stimulus from business, labour, and provincial governments. This is inevitable. Not *if*, but only *when*. Paul Martin, as the prime minister, may be able to duck the issue if he is lucky enough with the current economic cycle, but it is anybody's guess at this point (April 2003). With the contingency reserve there is some minor room for a negative shock but a large recession on the scale, for example, of 1989–91 will simply overrun the current budget plan. Why should we worry about this issue? My claim is that there are two major risks that are being built into the current fiscal framework which will ultimately come back to haunt us.

First Risk

First there is the risk that public expectations are being created that cannot be delivered on in the obvious case of a significant negative shock to the national economy on either the supply or demand side. Politicians and officials are not sufficiently attentive to the fact that the public holds the government responsible for the performance of the economy, and at the same time holds them accountable to their rhetoric — that is, balanced budget rhetoric in this case. When the next recession hits, therefore, the government may well quickly do an about face and engage in what appears to be reckless fiscal policy; this in turn may induce a sudden loss in the fiscal credibility of the federal government at the point when it is most critical. Perhaps officials need to do a better job of educating the Canadian public as to what the intermediate target of fiscal policy is, and the expected response of the deficit is to a negative shock, rather than dwelling on the current cyclical success. The cyclical success of the Canadian economy has postponed the fact that long-term fiscal targets have not really been set, nor is there a framework in which these are embedded within a realistic view of the business cycle.

Second Risk

The opposite scenario is a government that puts fiscal credibility ahead of all other objectives. Canadians are well acquainted with a pro-cyclical fiscal response by government. It is what many provinces do routinely. This raises the question "Do you really want the federal government to raise taxes and cut spending in the face of a recession for the purposes of sustaining fiscal credibility?" Both the New Classical optimal tax-smoothing argument and standard Keynesian argument say "no". Realistically, one can expect a political response to this type of development. A government that pursues this course in the face of major recession is unlikely to be re-elected. In the end it is a lose-lose situation. As in the case of the first risk, the public and the government would be better served by articulated fiscal values which dealt with the reality of recessions.

The Long-Term Structural Context

Budgets and fiscal rules also operate within a longer-term structural context, of course. Most of the time economies are in expansion and any fiscal framework should account for this. There have been lots of proposals for fiscal rules ranging from targeting debt-to-GDP ratios, to budgets balanced over a typical cycle, to target levels of real government expenditure per capita — to name only a few. If the current expansion continues and the budget stays in balance, then the debt-to-GDP ratio will continue to decline. As debt declines the percentage of revenues devoted to interest payments on the debt decline and this allows for increases in program spending or tax cuts — whichever is preferred. At least over the medium term we have room to think about the longer-term objectives of fiscal policy. There are three factors I think are quite likely to play an important role in future debates on long-term fiscal targets. In each case they create problems for sustaining balanced budget objectives, but the reasons are quite different.

Productivity Growth

The US acceleration in labour productivity growth in the 2.5 to 3% range seems to be thus far quite durable. Canada remains well below that although, as noted, we are doing much better on the job-creation front than the United States. If Canadian labour productivity growth does accelerate toward the US level, then the debt-to-GDP ratio will fall faster than in the current projections. On the other hand, if the United States continues to grow at its current pace, there is the unfortunate reality that the gap in living standards between Canada and the United States will grow, despite Canada's superior fiscal performance. If this situation persists, there will be a growing debate on a trade-off between reducing the debt as opposed to more direct fiscal initiatives targeted at increasing growth; for example, tax cuts, increased human capital, and innovation spending. It is not at all inconceivable that we will see the government rationalize deficit spending within an overall framework focused on raising growth rates.

The US Budget Deficit

The United States faces a long-term fiscal imbalance, given the trajectory based on its current fiscal policies. The main sources of the imbalances are large, unfunded, transfer programs, an aging population, and a continuing rise in health-care spending per capita and new defence spending. Based on the most recent Congressional Budget Office (CBO) projections, Auerbach *et al.* (2002) estimate that the current imbalance, which the primary surplus would need to increase to deliver a stable debt-to-GDP ratio expression, is between 4 and 8% of GDP. This seems almost unbelievable; it is larger than any conventionally measured primary deficit during the postwar period. It is certain that the growing US deficit cannot remain unchecked so something will undoubtedly have to change. But overall the emergence of this deficit in our largest trading partner together with (a) good economic performance in the United States and (b) little political resistance by either the Republicans or Democrats may lead in Canada to significant shifts in political opinion on the merits of balanced budgets. This will be particularly true if there is little evidence these deficits are leading to increased interest rates or increased inflation. In general, I think the whole political distaste for budget deficits may begin to erode on both the left and the right if the current trends in the United States continue. I should add that I do not view this as a good thing. The other possible endgame is a major recession in the US coincident with large-scale fiscal retrenchment. Such an episode will give credence to the "I told you so" crowd, but the reality is that it will just turn a US structural problem into a major cyclical problem for Canada.

The Aging Population

The "aging problem" is now on the policy horizon. This has a number of consequences, including increased demands for spending on health care and declining labour force growth. The Canadian population growth is predicted to decline steadily, from an annual average rate of just over 1% in the 1990s to an average of 0.5% per year over 2016 to 2025. There is now a growing body of literature which deals with the fiscal issues that emanate from this trend. The timetable on which this will feed into the Canadian fiscal policy debate will undoubtedly hinge on such factors as the pace at which employment growth slows, the nature of specific policy responses to deal with aging, and the experience of countries whose demographics are much worse than Canada's: for example, Italy and Japan. One essential point, however, is that fiscal policy, through its impacts on stocks of debt, redistributes income across time and across generations. In the medium term one can imagine that there will be demands for increased public saving in anticipation of future public spending on the baby boomers in the latter years of their life. Such demands will be based on two arguments. One is the fairness in the tax-expenditure system, and the limited ability of a smaller cohort of younger workers to carry the implied fiscal burden necessary to deliver public services to the older cohort beginning about the middle of the next decade. It is certain that there will also be claims that governments can deliver these services in the future without increased taxes or debt, but those arguments I believe will be dispensed with in short order. Two, there is clearly future risk to the current boomer generation as they come to realize their capacity to extract future health and pension benefits from a government facing a rapidly slowing labour force growth will be severely constrained. For either of these reasons the fiscal choices in the very long run (when the boomers have all aged) are (a) higher taxes, (b) increased deficits and debt, or (c) running down accumulated public assets. Choice (c) will only be an option if there is a significant period over the next decade in which either the public debt

                                    Richard Harris

is run down (to levels well below normal) or there is actually net public asset creation. Running down the debt will require significant structural budget surpluses over a sustained period of time leading to a public debt contraction equivalent of a boomer Heritage Fund.

Should this rationale find political support it will create a major issue for the conduct of fiscal policy in that the size of the structural surplus and the pace at which debt-reduction occurs will come to the front of the debate on fiscal policy. It is clear we are still a long way from that point now.

References

Auerbach, A.J. (2002), "Is There a Role for Discretionary Fiscal Policy?" NBER Working Paper No. 9306 (Cambridge, MA: National Bureau of Economic Research).

Auerbach, A.J., W.G. Gale, P.R. Orszag and S.R. Potter (2002), "The Budget Outlook and Options for Reform", in H.J. Aaron, J. Lindsey and P. Nivola (eds.), *Agenda for the Nation* (Washington, DC: The Brookings Institution Press).

Blanchard, O. and R. Perotti (1999), "An Empirical Characterization of the Dynamic Effects of Changes in Government Spending and Taxes on Output", NBER Working Paper No. 7269 (Cambridge, MA: National Bureau of Economic Research).

Canada. Department of Finance (2003), *The Budget Plan 2003* (Ottawa: Department of Finance).

Giavazzi, F. and M. Pagano (1991), "Can Severe Fiscal Contractions Be Expansionary? Tales of Two Small European Countries", *NBER Macroeconomics Annual*.

Romer, C.D. and D. Romer (1994), "What Ends Recessions?" in S. Fischer and J. Rotemberg (eds.), *NBER Macroeconomics Annual*, 13–57.

Session Two
THE BUDGET AND ITS ECONOMIC EFFECTS: Quantitative Evaluation of the Budget

THE 2003 FEDERAL BUDGET:
A Quantitative Appraisal

Thomas A. Wilson, Peter Dungan and Steve Murphy, University of Toronto

Finance Minister John Manley's first budget uses up virtually all of the available fiscal room through program-spending increases. With the federal government once again "back-loading" a number of spending initiatives, the budget surplus for 2002–03 is reduced to the $3 billion contingency reserve. This represents the minimum commitment to debt reduction, and signals a shift in priorities toward additional spending.

There were several important tax reductions announced in the budget. While these tax changes will improve the efficiency of the tax system, their combined impact on the budget balance within the planning period is quite small. Leaving aside the enhancements to the Child Tax Credit, which is really a transfer payment program, tax reductions in 2002/03 are only $0.5 billion. In 2003/04, the phasing in of additional tax reductions generates a $1.2 billion net reduction in taxes. Over the three-year period, program-spending increases (including increases in the Child Tax Credit) account for 90% of the total fiscal stimulus.

Over the two-year forward planning period, these budget initiatives eliminate the available "surplus for planning purposes". As a result, the fiscal plan allows for a $4 billion surplus in 2003/04 and a $5 billion surplus in 2004/05, reflecting the $3 billion contingency reserve and appropriate allowances for "economic prudence". Canada remains the only G7 country to plan for budget surpluses.

Tax Measures

The budget included several tax reductions which should improve the Canadian tax system. The capital tax for large corporations is to be phased out over five years. The elimination of this tax will reduce the net tax burden on capital formation, and should provide a modest stimulus to investment over the medium term.

Other corporate tax measures include a planned increase in the small business deduction, and a planned reduction in the corporate income tax rate for large resource companies (coupled with the replacement of the 2.5% resource allowance by deductions for royalties and mining taxes and a new tax credit for exploration expenses). These measures will be phased in over four and five years respectively.

As for personal income taxes, the budget provides a long overdue increase in registered retirement savings plans/registered pension plans (RRSP/RPP) limits. These limits will be increased to $18,000 over the next three years (with corresponding adjustments to pension accounts under defined benefit RPPs).

The budget also includes a 12¢ reduction in the basic Employment Insurance (EI) employee contribution rate, effective January 1, 2004. As indicated in previous Policy and Economic Analysis Program (PEAP) analyses, this measure will have a favourable, albeit modest, supply price effect.

As noted above, increases in the Child Tax Benefit should be viewed as an increase in transfer payments, rather than as a tax reduction. Increases in the National Child Benefit supplement and a new Child Disability Benefit will cost $240 million in 2003/04 and $350 million in 2004/05.

Program Spending Initiatives

Not surprisingly, increased spending for health care was the most important spending initiative, accounting for almost half of the new spending initiatives over the three-year period of the budget plan. Of the total increase in

 Thomas A. Wilson, Peter Dungan and Steve Murphy

health-care spending of $8.2 billion, over one-half ($4.7 billion) is back-loaded to the 2002/03 fiscal year. Most of this spending, of course, will involve increased transfers to the provinces.

The budget provides $1.8 billion over three years for research, education, and innovation. These investments in human capital and research and development should enhance Canada's longer-term growth potential. Roughly one-third of this spending is back-loaded to fiscal 2002/03.

Increased spending on defence, security, and international assistance will total $3.75 billion over the three-year period. Environmental and related spending initiatives account for about $1.8 billion over the next two fiscal years.

Overall, total spending initiatives amount to $15.4 billion over the three-year period, of which $6.4 billion is charged to fiscal 2002/03. If the Child Tax Benefit is included under spending, the three-year total is increased to $16 billion.

Economic Effects of the Budget Measures

Relative to a status quo fiscal projection, the budget clearly provides a net fiscal stimulus over the next two years. However, the timing of this stimulus on the economy is difficult to determine since:

- As noted, a significant amount of spending is back-loaded to fiscal 2002/03.
- Some of the spending on health care and research is through third-party trusts or foundations.
- Some of the increased provisional health-care funds to the provinces are drawn upon at the discretion of the provinces.

Further complicating an analysis of fiscal policy at this time is the fact that some of the funds provided through third party foundations in previous budgets remains to be spent.

Based on information provided in the budget, it appears likely that, on a National Accounts basis, the bulk of increased federal spending will occur in fiscal 2003/04. We estimate that $10.6 billion of federal spending and $0.5 billion of tax reductions should occur in this fiscal year. In 2004/05, incremental federal spending will be about $5.3 billion, whereas the magnitude of the tax reductions would increase to $1.2 billion.

Our estimates of the total fiscal impacts are presented in Table 1 and Figures 1 to 3. It is clear that the main thrust of the budget is on the spending side. Over the next three years, the total fiscal impact is $26.6 billion, of which $23.4 represents increased spending. Almost two-thirds of the additional federal spending involves transfers to the provinces (sometimes via third party trusts).

Although the total federal fiscal impact of $11.1 billion in fiscal 2003/04 drops to $6.5 billion in fiscal 2004/05, the lagged reaction of the provinces will likely smooth out the fiscal impacts. As shown in Table 1, we assume that the provinces will not spend all of the additional federal transfers in the current year, but their spending increases will be greater than federal transfer increases over the next two fiscal years.

Table 1: Federal Budget: Fiscal Impacts ($ billion)

	2003/04	2004/05	2005/06	Three-Year Total
Federal spending initiatives	10.6	5.3	7.5	23.4
(Of which transfers to provinces)	7.6	2.6	4.7	14.9
Federal tax reduction	0.5	1.2	1.5	3.2
Total	**11.1**	**6.5**	**9.0**	**26.6**
Provincial spending	4.3	4.4	6.1	14.8
Joint fiscal impacts	7.8	8.3	10.5	26.6

                    Thomas A. Wilson, Peter Dungan and Steve Murphy

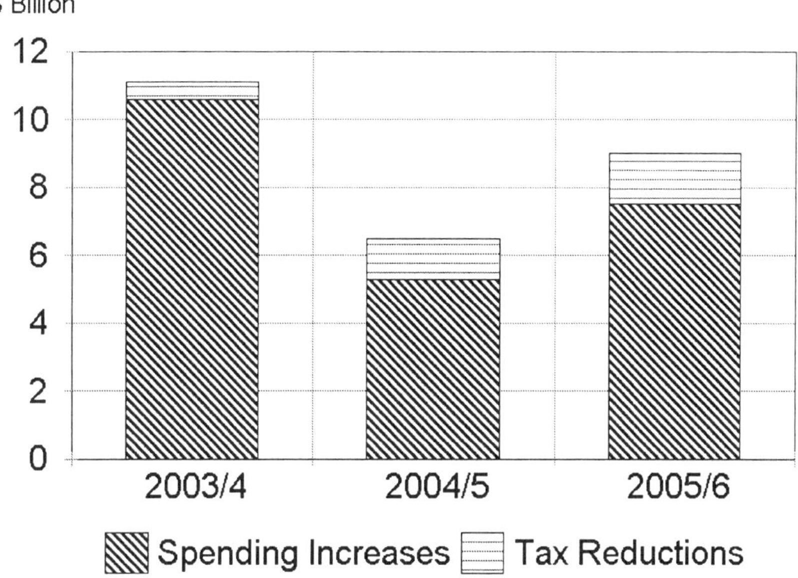

Figure 1: February 2003 Federal Budget: Federal Fiscal Impacts

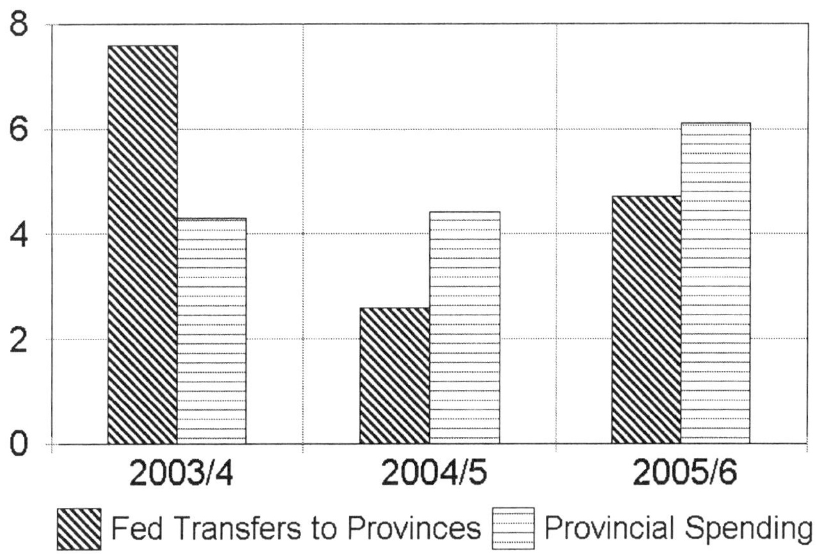

Figure 2: February 2003 Federal Budget: Provincial Fiscal Impacts

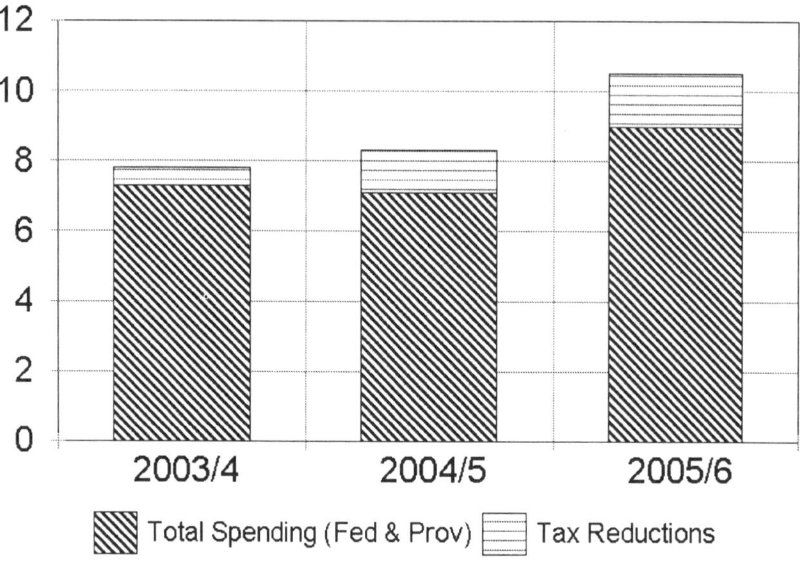

As a result of this delayed provincial spending, the total fiscal impacts on the economy should be $7.8 billion this year, increasing to $8.3 billion in fiscal 2004/05 and to $10.5 billion in fiscal 2005/06.

With a net fiscal stimulus of $7.8 billion this year, the Bank of Canada will be more likely to increase short-term interest rates sooner and by larger amounts, in order to contain inflationary demand pressures. The fact that all measures of inflation are currently near or above the top of the 1 to 3% inflation target zone means that there is little leeway for the central bank to maintain its current accommodative monetary policy stance.

Modelling the 2003 Federal Budget

We have implemented the 2003 federal budget in the FOCUS model of the Canadian economy. All expenditure initiatives are implemented by changing exogenous spending variables within the model. The assumed provin-

 Thomas A. Wilson, Peter Dungan and Steve Murphy

cial spending responses are also implemented via appropriate changes to exogenous variables.

Most of the tax reductions are incorporated by changing add factors to relevant revenue equations, except for the small EI rate cut, and the phasing out of the corporate capital tax. The latter was modelled as being equivalent to an investment tax credit, but with corporate tax revenues added — factored to reflect the intramarginal revenue effects of capital tax reductions. In modelling reductions of this tax, we have assumed that firms will take into account future rate cuts when making their investments in 2004 and 2005.

Interaction with Monetary Policy

In the current monetary policy environment of inflation targeting, one must allow for a monetary policy response to any fiscal initiatives. The results of our model simulations presented in Tables 2 through 4 and Figures 4 to 6, show the net economic effects under three alternative monetary policy responses. In the first simulation, there is no monetary policy response. While unrealistic, this simulation provides a picture of the potential economic effects of the budget.

The second and third simulations show the economic and fiscal effects of the budget when it is accompanied by a reactive monetary policy. In the second simulation, monetary policy acts to neutralize the exchange-rate effects of the budget; in the third it acts to offset the price-level effect by engineering an appreciation of the Canadian dollar.

We would view the simulation with price-level targets as the more realistic case under current economic conditions.

As the first simulation indicates, the 2003 budget is an expansionary budget. Without a monetary policy reaction, real GDP would be increased by 0.9%, 1.2%, and 1.3% over the next three years. The consumer price index (CPI) would be 0.5% higher next year, and 1.1% higher in 2005/06. In the current economic situation, with inflation at or above the upper bound of the Bank of Canada's target range, a fiscal stimulus of this magnitude should trigger a monetary policy response.

Table 2: Macroeconomic Effects of the Budget Measures: Monetary Policy Targets Money Supply
(impacts are percentage changes)

Real Output and Components	*2003(F)*	*2004(F)*	*2005(F)*
Real gross domestic product	0.85	1.18	1.32
Consumption	0.37	0.90	1.18
Government current & capital spending	2.46	2.16	2.76
Residential construction	1.06	1.99	1.51
Non-residential construction	0.39	0.88	0.84
Machinery and equipment	0.67	1.48	1.63
Exports	0.13	0.36	0.55
Imports	0.26	0.73	1.23

Table 3: Macroeconomic Effects of the Budget Measures: Monetary Policy Targets Exchange Rate
(impacts are percentage changes)

Real Output and Components	*2003(F)*	*2004(F)*	*2005(F)*
Real gross domestic product	0.63	0.62	0.53
Consumption	0.32	0.69	0.76
Government current & capital spending	2.46	2.14	2.70
Residential construction	0.72	1.04	0.37
Non-residential construction	−0.15	−0.28	−0.53
Machinery and equipment	−0.35	−0.73	−1.00
Exports	0.00	−0.04	−0.14
Imports	0.25	0.62	0.92

Table 4: Macroeconomic Effects of the Budget Measures: Monetary Policy Targets CPI

(impacts are percentage changes)

Real Output and Components	*2003(F)*	*2004(F)*	*2005(F)*
Real gross domestic product	0.01	−0.12	0.14
Consumption	0.20	0.26	0.35
Government current & capital spending	2.45	2.10	2.62
Residential construction	−0.31	0.30	0.23
Non-residential construction	−1.87	−0.79	−1.14
Machinery and equipment	−2.91	−4.06	−1.00
Exports	−0.38	−0.61	−0.80
Imports	0.31	0.27	0.50

Figure 4: February 2003 Federal Budget: Real GDP Impacts

Percent

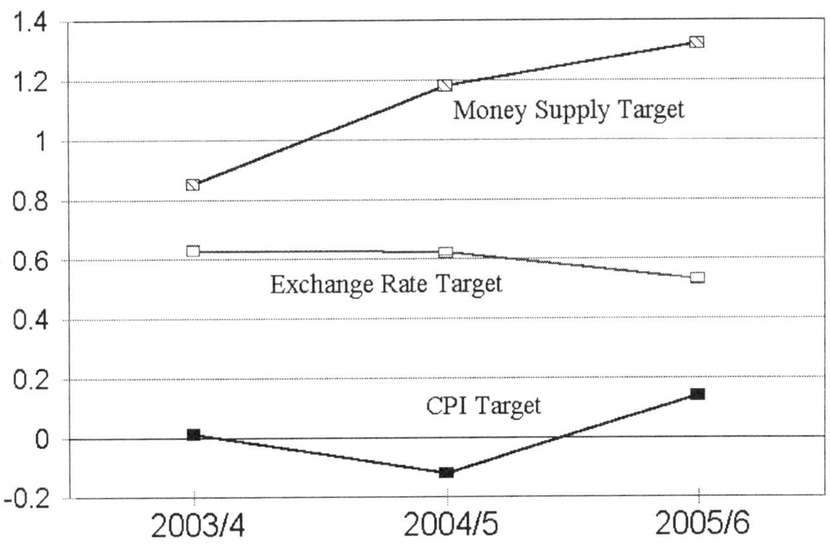

Figure 5: February 2003 Federal Budget: CPI Impacts

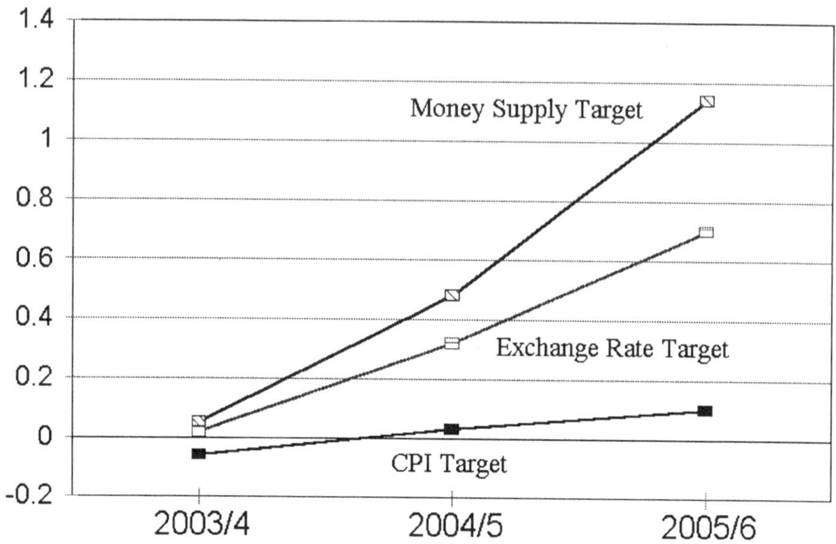

Figure 6: February 2003 Federal Budget: Unemployment Rate Impacts

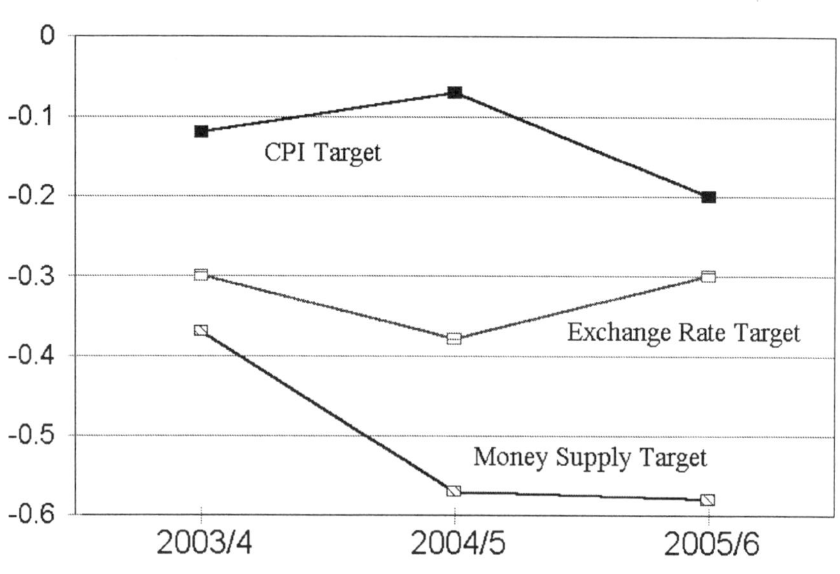

   Thomas A. Wilson, Peter Dungan and Steve Murphy

The second simulation presents the "intermediate" case where the Bank of Canada offsets the impacts of the expansionary fiscal policy upon the external value of the Canadian dollar. As shown in Table 3 and Figures 4 and 5, exchange-rate targeting would cut the aggregate effects of the fiscal stimulus almost in half. Real GDP would be up by 0.6% to 0.5% over the next three years, with the CPI impacts reduced to 0.3% and 0.7% in 2004/05 and 2005/06 respectively.

When we move to the more realistic case of CPI targeting, the monetary policy reaction eliminates the aggregate demand stimulus provided by the budget.[1] With the Canadian dollar appreciating by almost 1%, the price level and real output effects of the budget are roughly offset by the tightening of monetary policy.

When monetary policy offsets the real aggregate demand effects of fiscal policy, the effects of the budget in the composition of demand are clear. Budget 2003 shifts the composition of demand toward government spending (up 2.6% by fiscal 2005/06) and away from business investment and net exports. Consumption and residential construction increase very modestly.

Fiscal Effects

The model simulations also show the total fiscal effects (including indirect effects) of the budget under alternative monetary policy responses (see Table 4 and Figures 7, 8, and 9).

Because of tax recaptures, the total fiscal impacts of the budget are substantially smaller than the impact effects when there is no monetary policy reaction. Under exchange-rate targeting, tax recaptures are more limited. The federal budget balance would be reduced by $4.4 billion this

---

[1]Of course, the Bank of Canada's actions will also depend on other factors which affect the economic outlook. If the outlook were to worsen because of weaker growth in the United States, for example, the Bank may choose not to offset the budget's aggregate demand stimulus; in effect substituting fiscal expansion for the monetary expansion which otherwise would have been necessary to achieve the Bank's inflation target.

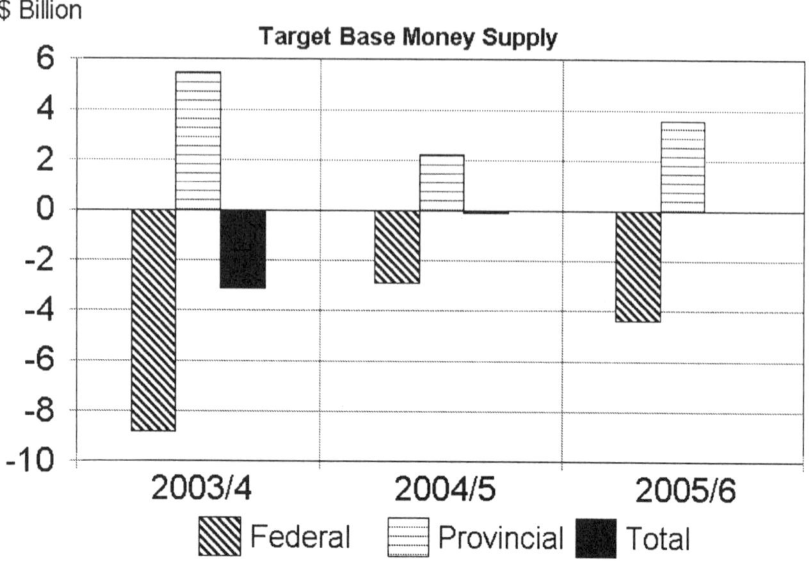

Figure 7: February 2003 Federal Budget: Budget Balance Impacts

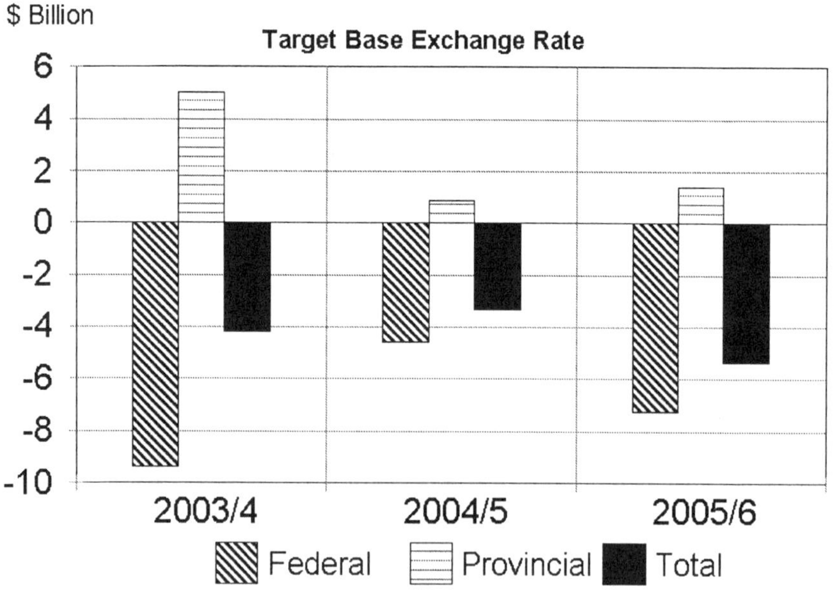

Figure 8: February 2003 Federal Budget: Budget Balance Impacts

    Thomas A. Wilson, Peter Dungan and Steve Murphy

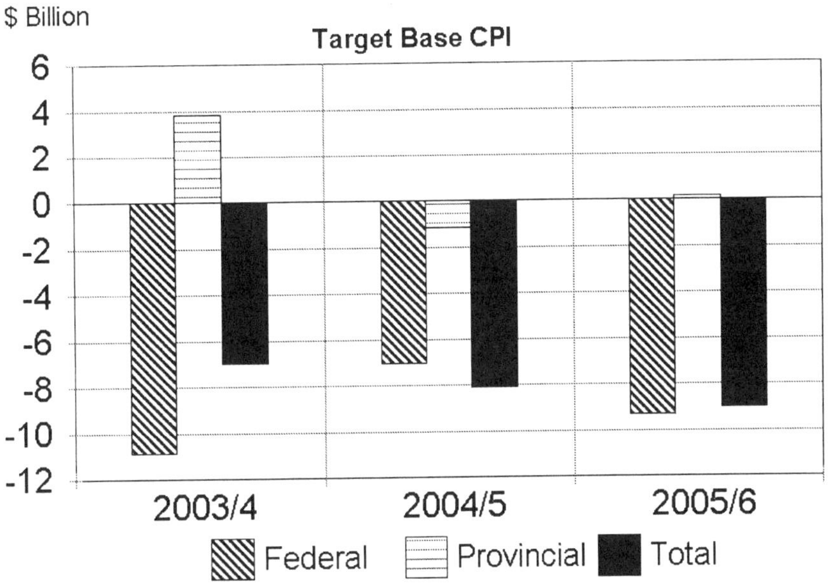

year, and by \$4.6 and \$7.3 billion in fiscal years 2004/05 and 2005/06 respectively. When monetary policy acts to offset the aggregate effects of the budget, not surprisingly, the model results are quite close to the original fiscal impact effects.

Summary

The 2003 budget is an expansionary budget, with most of the fiscal stimulus provided by increased spending. Since a significant portion of the rise in federal spending involves transfers to the provinces, increased provincial spending on goods and services will result. Because of the impact of the budget on prices, however, a more restrictive monetary policy will be required to maintain inflation within the 1–3% target range.

Although the tax measures may have modest supply-side effects, and some of the spending measures will contribute to longer-term growth, these effects will be negligible over the current year and very modest in 2004. Given the central bank's focus on an 18–24 month forecast period, we anticipate a significant tightening of monetary policy over the coming months. This combination of fiscal and monetary policy will raise the value of the Canadian dollar,[2] and shift the composition of demand from net exports and investment to government spending and consumption.

---

[2] A September postscript on these developments may be useful. Over the six months following the budget, the Canadian dollar appreciated by 8.8% relative to the US dollar, and by 8.5% on a trade-weighted (G6) basis. Partly as a result of this sharp appreciation, the Canadian economic outlook weakened. Consequently, on July 15, 2003 the Bank of Canada reversed the 25-basis point increase in the Bank rate which it had previously implemented on April 15.

   Thomas A. Wilson, Peter Dungan and Steve Murphy

ECONOMIC IMPACT OF THE 2003 FEDERAL BUDGET

Rick Egelton, BMO Financial Group

Finance Minister John Manley, following closely in the footsteps of his predecessor Paul Martin, brought forward a balanced budget with cautious economic and revenue assumptions, a $3.0 billion contingency reserve, and an "economic prudence" reserve, which grows over time. The results of this approach, as shown in Figure 1, have been impressive. The figure shows the budget fiscal target for the fiscal year in which the budget was unveiled, the actual fiscal outcome, and the value of initiatives implemented in the budget that were allocated to that fiscal year.

With the help of a buoyant economy during the second half of the 1990s, this cautious approach to fiscal planning has allowed the federal government to meet or significantly exceed its fiscal targets in each and every year since 1995. From a deficit of just under $40 billion in 1994/95, Canada has run budgetary surpluses every year since 1997/98. Canada is the only G7 country that will not run a deficit in 2002/03.

Less impressive, however, has been the year-end spending binges by the federal government over the last several years. As the year-end approached and it became clear that the government would better its fiscal target, the fiscal room to manoeuvre would be used to front-end load significant amounts of new spending into the current fiscal year. As Figure 1 illustrates, this has occurred in each of the last seven federal budgets. This approach to fiscal planning is biased toward spending since tax cuts, unlike spending, must typically be ongoing and cannot effectively be implemented in a one-time fashion.

Figure 1: Federal Government Surplus/Deficits in Billions of Dollars

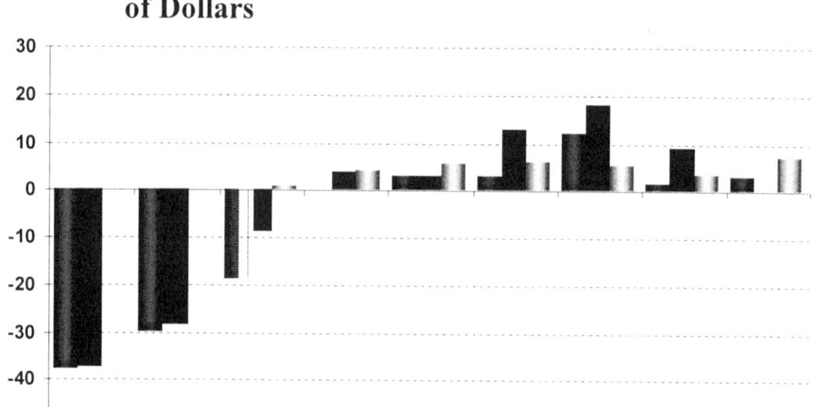

Source: Department of Finance.

The purpose of this paper is to assess the impact of the 2003 federal budget on Canada's near- and medium-term economic outlook. The 2003 budget cannot be viewed in isolation and the impact of previous budgets must also be taken into consideration. I have divided the analysis into three areas:

- the impact on debt levels and financial markets;
- the impact on near-term economic growth; and
- the impact on productivity and long-term potential growth.

Debt Levels and Financial Markets

The combination of budgetary surpluses since 1997/98 and fairly strong economic growth has resulted in a dramatic improvement in the federal government net indebtedness, both in an absolute sense and relative to other industrialized countries. As Figure 2 shows, federal debt as a share of gross domestic product (GDP) has fallen from a peak of 67.5% in 1995/96 to around 45.0% in 2002/03.

                                                      Rick Egelton

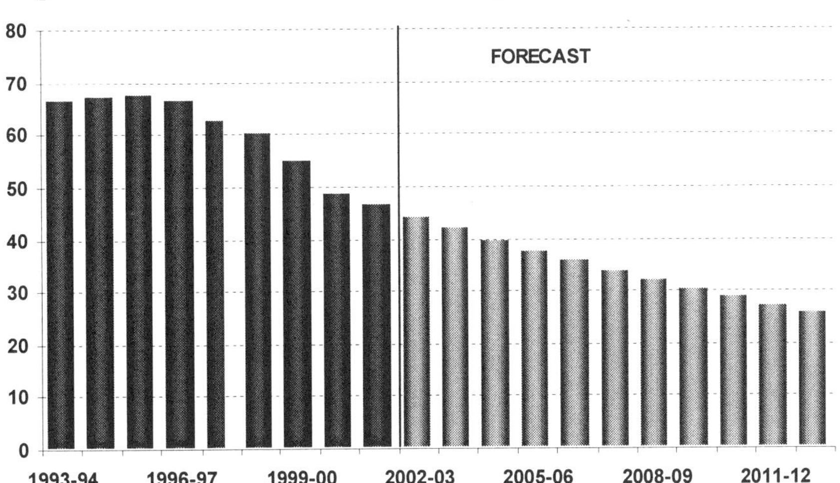

Source: BMO Financial Group and Department of Finance.

Internationally (Figure 3), Canada has moved from having the second highest debt burden in the G7 to what will likely be the second lowest in 2004.

Theoretically, one would expect that lower debt burdens would lead to lower real long-term interest rates, reflecting a reduction in government borrowing relative to the size of the economy. Second, it would seem reasonable to conclude that Canada would be less vulnerable to external shocks, in which a "flight-to-quality" response in capital markets invariably causes funds to flow out of high-debt countries — thereby pushing up domestic interest rates — and into safe haven markets like the United States. While it is beyond the scope of this paper to examine these assertions in detail, the low long-term interest rates over the past several years, particularly vis-à-vis the United States, and the less volatile interest-rate environment in Canada would appear to lend some measure of support to the aforementioned propositions.

There are two areas where we have seen a concrete reaction to Canada's improved fiscal position. First, the improved government debt climate has led to the restoration of Canada's AAA credit rating, slightly lowering the cost of borrowing, not only for the federal government but also for other entities whose

Source: OECD.

credit rating cannot exceed that of the sovereign. Second, the lower debt burden, together with the reduction in interest rates, has significantly reduced debt-service payments as a share of total federal government revenues. This has left the federal government with more room for other initiatives like tax cuts, debt reduction or program spending.

The Impact on Near-Term Economic Growth

Figure 4 shows the change in the federal government's primary cyclically adjusted balance since 1995. Periods in which the balance is rising represent contractionary fiscal policy, whereas years in which the primary cyclically adjusted balance is negative conform to expansionary fiscal policy. After the extremely contractionary fiscal policy in the 1995/97 period, fiscal policy in Canada has generally been expansionary. This expansionary posture is expected to continue through 2004 with the implementation of measures contained in the recent budgets.

                                              Rick Egelton

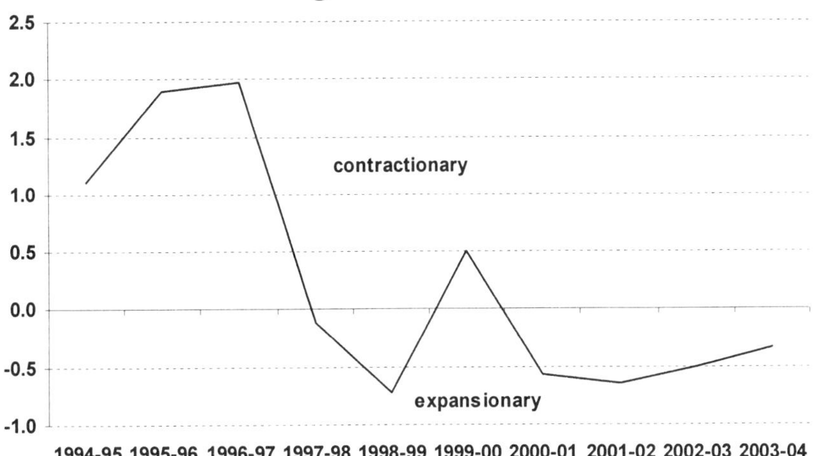

Figure 4: Change in the Primary Cyclically Adjusted Balance as a Percentage of GDP

Source: Department of Finance.

The impact of the stance of fiscal policy on economic growth, however, cannot be viewed in isolation of the stance of monetary policy. The goal of monetary policy in Canada is to keep inflation at 2%. To achieve its goal, the Bank of Canada will manipulate short-term interest rates so that economic growth and the output gap follow a path that will generate the desired inflation target.

In such an environment, expansionary fiscal policy will not boost economic growth because the fiscal stimulus will simply be offset by tighter monetary conditions. Consider the situation in which fiscal policy is neutral and the Bank of Canada believes that growth and the output gap are on a path to generate the inflation target of 2%. If fiscal policy turns expansionary, the Bank will increase interest rates by an amount sufficient to exactly offset the stimulus to economic growth from fiscal policy.

Thus, expansionary fiscal policy will have no impact on growth, but will serve to increase interest rates and push-up the value of the Canadian dollar as a result of widening interest-rate differentials. The composition of growth will also shift toward more government and consumer spending — to the extent that tax cuts are part of the expansionary fiscal policy — and away from interest and exchange rate sensitive categories of demand like residential and business investment, and international trade. In short, therefore, it is likely that the expansionary fiscal stance will have more of an impact on the composition of growth in 2003 and 2004 than on boosting the overall rate of economic expansion.

Productivity and Long-Term Potential Growth

In order to assess the impact of the 2003 federal budget on productivity and long-term potential growth, the 2003 federal budget initiatives were broken down into four categories:

1. non-productivity enhancing;
2. productivity enhancing;
3. long-term productivity enhancing; and
4. unconditional transfers to the provinces.

By productivity enhancing, I mean measures that will contribute to either trend factor productivity growth, labour productivity growth or will increase hours worked. This does not mean that measures that do not enhance productivity are not worthwhile. A foreign aid program in sub-Saharan Africa will not contribute to Canada's productivity growth but may nonetheless be extremely worthwhile from a humanitarian perspective. Similarly, a health-care program designed to enhance the quality of life of terminally ill people may be an excellent use of taxpayers' money, but it will have little impact on productivity growth.

I have classified the following expenditures as non-productivity enhancing: (i) defence and security; (ii) international development assistance; (iii) health; and (iv) cultural.

I acknowledge that certain defence expenditures may have an impact on productivity via the development and transfer of new technology to the private sector, and that measures that successfully increase the health of the population can also have a positive impact on labour participation and productivity. However, on balance, it is far from clear that the increased resources devoted

                                    Rick Egelton

to these areas in the 2003 budget will have a meaningful impact on productivity growth.

The various small tax measures, together with the capital tax reduction and the Employment Insurance premium rate cut, were classified as productivity enhancing. The research and innovation expenditures and the skills and learning initiatives were classified as long-term productivity enhancing due to the likely long time lag from expenditure to actual productivity improvements.

The impact on productivity of the increased transfers to the provinces is unclear since we do not know exactly what the provinces will do with the increased resources.

In sum, as illustrated in Figure 5, more than two-thirds of the budget measures in terms of dollar expenditures will have little impact on productivity growth. Therefore, the impact on growth via productivity from the 2003 budget is quite limited.

Figure 5: Share of Budgetary Initiative

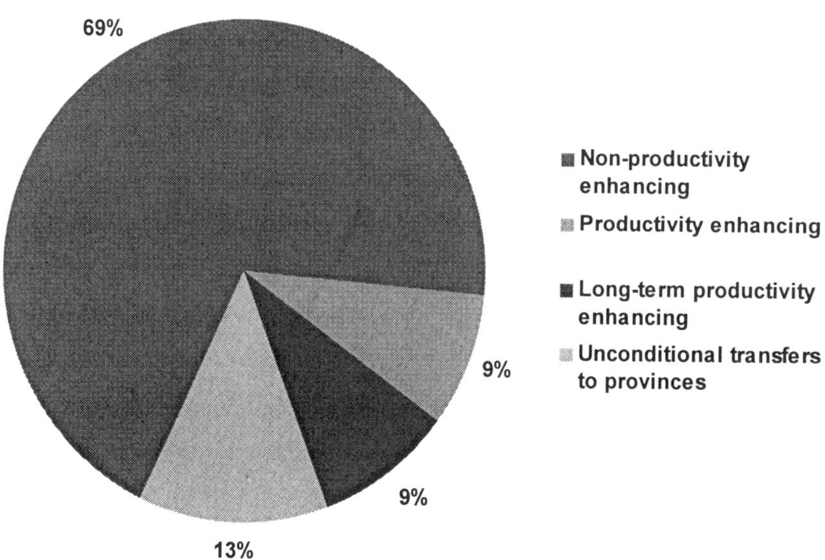

THE BUDGET: Impacts on Short-Term Aggregate Output and Long-Term Productivity Growth

Pierre Fortin, Université du Québec à Montréal

The two papers presented in this session are by the University of Toronto team (Tom Wilson, Peter Dungan and Steve Murphy), and by the BMO Financial Group (Rick Egelton). They address the economic consequences of the 2003 federal budget for short-term stabilization and long-term growth. In good division of labour, University of Toronto focuses more on short-term stabilization, and BMO more on long-term growth.

No Effect on Aggregate Output

As a basis for their analysis of short-term macroeconomic effects, Wilson, Dungan and Murphy first estimate that the fiscal initiatives will cumulate to a significant $26.6 billion over the three fiscal years 2003/04, 2004/05 and 2005/06. These initiatives have three key characteristics: (i) almost 90% are accounted for by spending increases; (ii) almost two-thirds of federal spending increases involve transfers to the provinces; and (iii) while 40% of the cumulative federal stimulus is back-loaded in 2003/04, the lagged spending reaction of the provinces will smooth out the timing of the fiscal stimulus more equally over the three years.

The University of Toronto team examines the short-term macroeconomic effects with the help of three simulation exercises done with the FOCUS macroeconometric model of the Canadian economy. These three runs of the model calculate the alternative effects of the same given rightward shift of the IS curve along three LM curves with increasing slopes in aggregate output/ interest rate space.

The first LM curve is the standard positively sloped LM curve constructed with a fixed money supply (M1) and described in intermediate macroeconomics textbooks such as Abel, Bernanke and Smith (2003, ch. 9), Blanchard, Johnson and Melino (2003, ch. 5), or Mankiw and Scarth (2001, ch. 10). When Wilson, Dungan and Murphy implement the fiscal stimulus in the model, the rightward shift of the IS curve along this LM curve raises aggregate output (real gross domestic product) by 1.3%, and the real interest rate by 0.2 percentage point, after three years. (The LM curve actually shifts to the left a bit on account of the increase in the price level.) There is a useful pedagogical benefit from this exercise: it makes it possible to estimate the value of the federal spending multiplier — since most of the stimulus arises from the spending side — generated by the standard IS/LM short-run macro-model. I calculate that this multiplier is equal to about 1.3 in the first year, and 1.5 in the third year after the stimulus. Teachers of intermediate macroeconomics should take note.

However, as the three authors recognize, this first simulation is totally unrealistic as a description of the real world. With an unchanged money supply relative to the base case, the consumer price index increases by 1.1% and the inflation rate by 0.7 percentage point. The Bank of Canada will definitely not allow this to happen. It will instead reduce the money supply relative to the base case in order to offset the inflationary consequences of expansionary fiscal policy. Since inflation is an increasing function of output via the supply side of the economy — the Phillips curve, in other words — preventing inflation from rising amounts in essence to eliminating any increase in output. The central bank will react by reducing the money supply so that *the effective LM curve will be vertical at the initial (and final) level of output.* In this realistic setting, which describes the third simulation by the University of Toronto team, the fiscal stimulus pushes the IS curve to the right along the vertical LM curve. The outcome is unchanged aggregate output (and inflation) and higher interest rates than in the first simulation.

Wilson, Dungan and Murphy also report an "intermediate" simulation in which the Bank of Canada adjusts the short-term interest rate so as to keep the Canadian-US exchange rate unchanged from the base case. Since in the FOCUS model a fiscal stimulus with given money supply leads to an exchange rate depreciation, this alternative simulation requires that the money supply be decreased to prevent depreciation. There follow positive multiplier effects on real GDP that are smaller than in the first simulation with fixed money supply. But this simulation is not particularly relevant to the actual policy context. *Pas rapport.*

I conclude, first, that the fiscal expansion will have zero impact on aggregate output, and that it will increase interest rates a bit over the medium run; and second, that we do not need complicated simulation exercises to arrive at this conclusion. A little logical thinking would have been enough, based on the idea that the Bank of Canada, and nobody else, is in the driver's seat to target output and inflation. But I am thankful for the estimate of the spending multiplier that can be extracted from the first simulation with a fixed money supply. I will use it in class.

The third simulation by the University of Toronto team may lead to zero impact on aggregate output, but it is not without effect on resource allocation. As the authors note, higher interest rates and the appreciated Canadian dollar in this exercise shift the composition of aggregate demand away from net exports and business investment and toward government spending. The most important question here is whether this compositional shift is good or bad for long-term growth.

A Productivity Enhancing Budget?

The consequences of the federal budget for long-term growth is the main focus of Rick Egelton's paper. The impacts of the budget on growth flow through two channels: debt accumulation and compositional changes. Egelton reminds us that the federal debt reached a maximum of 68% of GDP in 1995/96, and will have dropped to 42% of GDP at the end of the current fiscal year. BMO Financial Group projects a further decline toward 25% of GDP in 2012/13. After emphasizing all the good things that the declining federal debt burden brings to the Canadian economy — higher private investment, lower external debt, more budget stability, more room available for new budget initiatives, less dependency on lenders, etc. — Egelton points out that the 2003 federal budget will likely slow down the rate of decline of the federal debt-to-GDP ratio a bit. But this is a small change he does not seem to be too concerned about. It is hard to disagree with him.

Egelton is more critical of the compositional shift induced by the budget — away from net exports and business investment and toward government spending — that Wilson, Dungan and Murphy notice too. He splits the tax and spending measures into four categories. The first puts together "non-productivity enhancing measures" such as defence and security, international development assistance, health, culture, and the environment. They make up 69% of all measures. The second and third categories include short- and long-term "productivity-enhancing measures" such as the Employment Insurance premium rate cut, the capital and other tax cuts, and spending on research, innovation, skills, and learning. These sum up to 22% of all measures. The fourth category is made of "unconditional transfers to provinces". These amount to 9% of all measures. On this basis, Egelton concludes that productivity is not an important concern of the budget.

In this kind of assessment, one should be cautious not to take a too-narrow view of productivity, though. I can see at least five reasons that Egelton underestimates the magnitude of favourable impacts of the federal budget on productivity. First, the largest item in his "non-productivity-enhancing category" is health. I understand that the National Accounts classify health expenditures as consumption, not investment. But I think, as many others, that the National Accounts are wrong. Spending on health is replacement investment in human capital. A sick or dead population is not going to be very productive.

Second, Egelton does not consider spending on the environment as productivity enhancing. I suggest we wait and see what our productivity becomes when our ability to function and survive in this world is threatened by too much UV radiation, too much congestion, too much air and water pollution, and rising planetary temperatures.

Third, Egelton may be right to classify some spending on culture as non-productivity enhancing. But surely some of it is investment in identity-building and social capital, which according to much recent research is not unconnected to the efficient functioning of economic organizations.

                                                      Pierre Fortin

Fourth, part of international development assistance winds up helping productivity to grow in poorer countries. Should we really discount this as an opportunity lost by Canada to enhance its own productivity?

Fifth, Egelton excludes unconditional transfers to provinces from the productivity-enhancing category. But those grants finance what provinces do. To a large extent, they spend them on health, education, and public infrastructures, all of which have significant productivity-sustaining components.

All things considered, it is arguable that a dominant portion of tax and spending measures announced in this budget will have favourable impacts on productivity. (Full disclosure: I am *not* a card-carrying member of the Liberal Party of Canada.) There is, however, an opportunity cost. The measures will have to be paid for by a reduction in net exports and private investment that both the University of Toronto and BMO underline. Whether the *net* impact on the economy will be growth promoting or not would require a detailed quantitative assessment that none of the authors really addresses.

References

Abel, A.B., B.S. Bernanke and G.W. Smith (2003), *Macroeconomics*, 3d ed. Canadian (Toronto: Addison Wesley).

Blanchard, O., D. Johnson and A. Melino (2003), *Macroeconomics*, 2d ed. Canadian (Toronto: Prentice Hall).

Mankiw, N.G. and W. Scarth (2001), *Macroeconomics*, 2d ed. Canadian (New York: Worth Publishers).

FISCAL POLICY IN THE CHRÉTIEN YEARS

William Scarth, McMaster University

I will summarize very briefly a few background issues. Since the 2003 budget is expected to be Chrétien's last, there has been much talk of legacies. I begin by noting that there is less evidence of some of the oft-noted legacies in the Chrétien-era budgets than many commentators have suggested, and this remains true of the 2003 budget.

Here are the broad facts. Shortly after the Liberals took office, they embarked on a battle to "slay the deficit". I refer to this first period (until the end of fiscal 1998/99 when this objective was achieved) as Period One. The announced intention was to rely primarily on expenditure cuts, not tax increases, to eliminate the deficit. In absolute dollar terms, the data indicate that the government did not achieve its intended emphasis on spending cuts. During this period, federal program spending fell by just \$8.5 billion, while taxes rose by \$27 billion. Nevertheless, when expenditures and revenue are expressed as percentages of each year's gross domestic product (GDP), the data do support the government's stated policy after all. Because our GDP grew, the program-spending ratio fell dramatically, by 4.4 percentage points, during Period One, while the tax-to-GDP ratio increased by only 1.1 percentage points. I conclude that, for consistency, we should evaluate the more recent history, Period Two (fiscal 1999/00 to 2002/03), in terms of GDP proportions as well.

With the deficit eliminated by the start of Period Two, the government's plan was to enjoy the "fiscal dividend" in the following proportions: half was to take the form of program spending increases, and the other half was to be split between tax cuts and debt reduction (running budget surpluses). There has been a significant fiscal dividend; during Period Two, federal debt-interest payments have fallen by 1.3 percentage points of GDP. But again, reference to absolute dollars is not helpful if we are looking for data that indicate a government that is delivering on its promises. During Period Two, program spending increased by $27 billion, but taxes also increased (by $23 billion). This is the sort of evidence that supports the notion that Chrétien is comfortable with a return to a bigger tax-and-spend government. But in terms of GDP percentages, a different interpretation is warranted. During Period Two, the ratio of program spending to GDP fell by another one-fifth of one percentage point (and it is projected to fall even a little further), and the federal tax-to-GDP ratio fell by 1.7 percentage points (and it too is projected to keep falling a little further). This is not evidence of a big switch back from smaller to bigger government.

It is customary to evaluate budgets according to efficiency, equity, and stabilization objectives. As conference participants have noted, there has been some progress on efficiency grounds (for example, some levelling of the international tax playing field). Nevertheless, we still have a long way to go regarding very high marginal tax rates for some low-income individuals, and we could do more to harness the force of private incentives in the provision of some public services. There have been improvements on the equity front as well, but since incidence studies show that most of the government's redistribution is done on the expenditure, not the tax, side of the budget, I have some concern about the effectiveness of our redistribution efforts as time proceeds.

Stabilization policy refers to the government acting as a shock absorber. In a short time frame (the duration of a typical business cycle), the new commitment to avoiding even temporary deficits "come hell or high water" has caused some to fear that one of the legacies of the Chrétien years is a loss in macroeconomic built-in stability. But, as Jean-Paul Lam (at the Bank of Canada) and I have reported, this concern can easily be exaggerated. As long as our central bank is committed to limiting *both* inflation that is "too high" *and* inflation that is "too low", real-output volatility does not appear to be seriously affected by shifting away from the Keynesian approach to budget deficits, and to a renewed focus on avoiding deficits.

                                                    William Scarth

In a longer time frame (the duration of each generation's working life), the government's stabilization role involves spreading the effects of bad shocks across generations. This strategy was applied quite successfully as the national debt was run up during the depression of the 1930s and World War II, and then the debt-to-GDP ratio was pulled back down to about 20% by the early 1970s. This strategy was applied much less successfully between the early 1970s and the early 1990s, as the debt ratio increased by 50 percentage points without there being an obvious negative influence on living standards that needed to be shared with future generations. Since the early 1990s, fiscal policy has been focused on reversing this build-up in debt before the next (more justified) need for a shock absorber arrives.

Some commentators have expressed concern that the government's debt-reduction effort is not proceeding fast enough, since they see the aging of the baby-boom generation as that next big "hit" to average living standards in Canada. I am more optimistic regarding this concern. I agree that the aging of the population is a significant challenge. However, as Harriet Jackson and I reported at a conference similar to this one a few years ago, getting the federal debt ratio down to 20% by 2010 may be sufficient to raise living standards by approximately the same amount as the aging population will lower living standards.

Is it credible to assume that the government will achieve a debt ratio of 20% by 2010? I think so, but I have one concern. There is an increased propensity for many participants in fiscal policy debates to assume that program spending can be projected to grow at a rate equal to the sum of the population growth rate and the inflation rate (on the grounds that constant real per-capita spending is adequate). But this planning assumption puts insufficient emphasis on Baumol's "cost disease of the service sector" point. Civil servants (such as health-care workers and teachers) will want to share in the productivity gains that are enjoyed by their counterparts in other sectors. It is not credible to make projections on the assumption that public-sector workers will accept an ongoing deterioration in their relative income position. I hope that this point is appreciated (by scaling public spending to the sum of the population growth rate, the inflation rate, and the productivity growth rate) as budgets are set in the future. Only if this is done, is it likely that progress on debt reduction will be sufficient to permit the government to act as a shock absorber in the face of baby-boom aging.

Session Three
BUDGETARY ACCOUNTING AND TRANSPARENCY

FULL ACCRUAL ACCOUNTING

John Wiersema, Office of the Auditor General of Canada

The theme of this session is budgetary accounting and transparency. I have been asked to talk about the announcement in the 2003 budget of the government's plan to adopt full accrual accounting. I will also discuss its continued use of year-end transfers to foundations.

I can already see the heads starting to nod. But I assure you, for those of us who work in the Office of the Auditor General, these issues are absolutely riveting! Accountants are not boring people. We just get excited about boring things. I am sure you too will find these issues interesting, once you see their implications for transparency in government.

Introduction

Before I begin, let me provide you with a brief overview of what we do. In short, the role of the Auditor General is to audit government operations. Led by the Auditor General of Canada, Sheila Fraser, we provide information that helps Parliament hold government accountable for the stewardship of public funds.

Overall, we audit some 70 federal government departments and agencies, 40 Crown corporations, 10 departmental corporations and 60 other entities and special audits. We also audit the governments of the three territories,

15 territorial agencies, and several United Nations agencies, including UNESCO (Canada. Office of the Auditor General, 2001, p. 6). To do all that, we have nearly 600 staff members. And we need all those people. After all, as the saying goes, it takes three accountants to deal with a $1.00 mistake in an expense report: one to find the mistake and two to discuss the significance of it. Actually, that is not true. The Auditor General employs more than just accountants. We have engineers, lawyers, management specialists, sociologists, and even economists. Thus, you could say it really takes one accountant to find the mistake and two economists to explain what it all means.

Of course, not everyone wants to hear about our work. A former president of the Treasury Board was once overheard to say about one of Fraser's predecessors: "Why give him more money to hire more people to find more mistakes?" Therein lies the most common misconception about our audits. The Office of the Auditor General does not go looking for mistakes. We are not on the hunt for boondoggles. Our goal is simply to make government more efficient, effective, economical, and more environmentally sustainable.

The Impact of the Auditor General's Reports

People often ask if these reports are worth the effort. Does government listen? Does it implement our recommendations? Many people think that, after the media hoopla, a report gets stored on some forgotten pathway of cyberspace. If you do manage to track it down and click on the link, it will just say "Document Not Found". The opposite is true. When we speak, people generally listen. And then they take action. Among the recommendations we have made over the past five years, departments have already completed nearly a quarter of suggested changes. And satisfactory progress is being made on half (Canada. Office of the Auditor General, 2002a, p. 3).

The Change to Full Accrual Accounting

That brings me to the current topic. It has taken a long time, but the federal government has announced that it will implement full accrual accounting, something we have been encouraging for many years.

Let me give you some background. Accrual accounting recognizes transactions and other events when they occur, rather than when cash or its equivalent is received or paid. Up until now, the government has been reporting on a modified accrual basis. That is to say, it has been recording tax revenue and capital expenditures largely on a cash basis, even though it has been recording many expenses on an accrual basis. This model does not require the government to record and disclose some significant costs, assets, and liabilities. In other words, we have not been seeing the full picture.

The government first announced its intentions to adopt full accrual accounting in 1995 (Canada. Department of Finance, 1995, p. 38). But it has taken until the 2002/03 financial year before this good intention will actually result in an audited set of accounts on a full accrual basis of accounting (Canada. Department of Finance, 2003, p. 177 and Annex 6, p. 277).

It does not sound like an earth-shattering decision. But, in fact, changing the accounting practices for a huge organization like the federal government is an enormous undertaking. Some have called this the biggest change in accounting for the federal government since Confederation.

Impact of Changes on Non-Financial Assets, Tax Revenues and Liabilities, Etc.

So what are the implications of full accrual accounting? It means the government's summary financial statements will include, for the first time, tangible capital assets, inventories, environmental liabilities, taxes receivable, prepaid expenses, employee future benefits other than pensions, and revised methods of accounting for Aboriginal claims (ibid., p. 197). As a result of these changes, the government will recognize tens of billions of dollars of assets and liabilities that were not previously valued and recorded. For example, according to Annex 6 (ibid., Annex 6, p. 277) to the government's 2003 budget, the move to accrual accounting will add $71 billion to the government's recorded total liabilities as at March 31, 2002, $44 billion in financial assets and $55 billion in non-financial assets. To a lesser extent, the changes will also affect the annual surplus or deficit.

Accrual accounting will also help eliminate the distortion of reported financial results caused by altering the timing of cash receipts or disbursements. For example, in the December 2001 budget, the government announced a six-month deferral of small business income tax installments for the last quarter of 2001/02. The government estimated the take-up of this initiative at some $600 million. While the $600 million clearly relates to economic activity in 2001/02, it would be reported as revenue in 2002/03 under a modified cash basis of accounting (Canada. Receiver General Canada, 2001/02, p. I.36). In other words, the government's finances are coming more clearly into focus. We are starting to see the whole picture.

I want to stress, however, that this change in government accounting practices will in no way alter the government's underlying fiscal situation. In other words, there is no new cash for spending. Full accrual accounting merely changes the timing of recognition of certain revenues and expenses to better capture the government's financial situation.

However, if one assumes that projected annual surpluses are available for spending decisions and the measurement of these surpluses changes as a result of accrual accounting, arguably, the process for making spending decisions might be affected.

Benefits of Full Accrual Accounting

Full accrual accounting has several benefits, both for the government and for taxpayers (Canada. Office of the Auditor General, 2002b, ch. 5; Canada. Department of Finance, 2003, p. 284). It provides a more complete measure of the overall size of the government. It will allow the government to present its financial results on a more appropriate and widely recognized basis of accounting. It will allow these financial results to more adequately reflect the economic realities of the period in question. And finally, and perhaps most importantly, it will help government better manage its resources in three important ways:

- First, since full accrual accounting will recognize physical assets, it will encourage managers to develop better policies for managing those assets and to make better decisions about whether to buy, lease or sell buildings and equipment.

- Second, it will show more accurately the cost of owning and operating capital equipment, giving a better picture of what it costs to provide some programs and services.

- Third, it will provide a more complete recording of the government's liabilities, which will encourage departments to better manage those liabilities.

PSAB Standards

I want to talk briefly about an initiative related to the adoption of full accrual accounting. About the same time that the government decided to go ahead with the new accounting system, new standards for government reporting were released by the Public Sector Accounting Board (PSAB) of the Canadian Institute of Chartered Accountants.[1]

These standards stress that government has to go beyond reporting on the annual deficit or surplus. The board argues that it takes more than one number to encompass the complexities of a government's financial condition. It calls for five indicators to come into play: net debt (financial assets less liabilities), the accumulated surplus or deficit, annual surplus or

---

[1]Landmark government reporting model issued; senior governments will provide a more complete picture of their finances, *PSAB Bulletin* (Issue 17, January 2003) and *Media Release/Communiqué* (February 10, 2003), retrieved April 23, 2003, at <www.cica.ca>.

deficit, change in net debt in the year and cash flow in the year. Governments need to include these numbers and explain them in their financial statements. This will help taxpayers understand what is really going on.

Impact on Management Practices

These new standards will not be adopted overnight. It takes the right people with the right skills to champion the cause of effective financial management. In that regard, I can point to two key players.

First, at the departmental level, managers have a special responsibility. They need to improve financial management and control and to help foster a change in their department's culture. Changes are more likely to take hold if everyone can be made aware of the benefits (Canada. Office of the Auditor General, 2002b, ch. 5, para. 5.60).

Second, there is the Treasury Board Secretariat, which is the federal government's management board. It can play a much stronger leadership role. Our audits have found that, while the Treasury Board Secretariat is committed to change, it needs to provide much clearer guidance and direction (ibid., para. 5.65). The Secretariat must also monitor the progress of departments and agencies in implementing these initiatives and provide periodic feedback both individually and collectively (ibid.).

Impact on Budgeting/Appropriations Still Under Study

Our audits show that departments are struggling to adjust between accrual-based accounting for reporting purposes and modified cash-based accounting for budgeting and appropriations (ibid., para. 5.39). Nowhere is the leadership of Treasury Board more needed than on this issue. Government managers are waiting for the government to commit to accrual-based budgeting and appropriations. We have pushed for this to happen. The House of Commons Standing Committee on Public Accounts continues to back our recommendation. But, to date, Treasury Board's response has been slow (ibid., Exhibit 5.39). It has held preliminary consultations with

John Wiersema

departments. In August 2001, it hired a manager to complete a study and make a recommendation by the fall of 2002. Other than that, there has been little progress (ibid., para. 5.41). A recommendation has not yet been put forth. In our view, it is critical to resolve this issue.

Year-End Transfers to Foundations

I would like to wrap up with some thoughts about year-end transfers to foundations — an issue closely related to full accrual accounting. Over the last few years, the government has made increasing use of foundations to achieve specific goals. These foundations were entrusted with the responsibility for billions of dollars of taxpayers' money.

Since 1997, the government has transferred some $7.5 billion to ten foundations. A listing of these foundations and the amounts transferred to them is attached as an Appendix (which is a reproduction of Table 4 from the Auditor General's Observations on the 2002 Public Accounts). The largest of these are the Canada Foundation for Innovation and the Millennium Scholarship Fund. The idea was to encourage innovation and to help students with postsecondary education costs. There are several issues that concern us about these transfers (Canada. Receiver General Canada, 2001/02, p. I.34).

First, the government entered the $7.5 billion as an expense into its accounts. However, they have not actually been spent for their ultimate intended purpose. Our audit found that, at March 31, 2002, only a tiny fraction of the $7.5 billion had been put to its ultimate intended use. The rest was sitting in the accounts of the foundations, gaining interest. Very little had found its way to innovators and students (ibid.).

In our view, the government's accounts would better reflect economic reality if the expenses were recorded in the year when the foundations either make grant payments to recipients or use the money according to their agreements with the government. This would be consistent with the way these transfers are handled in the National Accounts by Statistics Canada (ibid., p. I.37).

The second issue has to do with the accountability and governance arrangements for these foundations. In the 2003 budget, the government announced a number of improvements to these arrangements. However, important issues remain (Canada. Office of the Auditor General, 2002c, ch. 1, paras. 1.2–1.5):

- None of the foundations submit corporate plans for tabling in Parliament. And some do not provide annual reports that describe their accomplishments in a credible way. Reporting to Parliament is not adequate for proper scrutiny.

- The government has set up these foundations in an ad hoc manner. Parliament has not had the chance to fully consider how it authorizes and oversees this kind of public spending.

- Weak oversight of foundations means that ministers are not able to answer properly about their results to Parliament, and ultimately, to all Canadians.

- Finally, Parliament only receives financial statements audited by the private sector for the foundations. In our view, broad scope value for money audits conducted by Parliament's auditor, the Auditor General of Canada, are also necessary to provide for proper accountability to Parliament for the use of taxpayer's money.

The government needs to change its accounting policies as they relate to the foundations. Doing so would go hand-in-hand with the announced change to full accrual accounting. It also needs to further strengthen the accountability and governance of the foundations.

Conclusion

I have given you a very brief tour of the implications of full accrual accounting, and why it is important. I think the government's decision to adopt this system is one example of how the work of the Office of the Auditor General makes a difference. We play an important role to make sure that taxpayers get value for their money. But it goes deeper than that.

                                                                     John Wiersema

Improving public-sector performance helps build stronger public institutions and a healthier democratic society.

Transparency is a hallmark of democracy — one that is envied by citizens
of many countries around the world. Full accrual accounting helps bring it
about. And through its regular reports, the Office of the Auditor General
also encourages transparency.

Change may take longer than we would like. But change does happen. The
Office of the Auditor General is proud to play a role in bringing it about.

Appendix
Major Federal Foundations

Foundation[1]	Government Expenditures Recorded in Fiscal Year Ended March 31 ($ millions)							Foundation's Cash and Investments[2]
	1997	1998	1999	2000	2001	2002	Total	March 31, 2002
Canada Foundation for Innovation	801		200	900	1,250		3,151	2,964
Canadian Health Services Research Foundation	13	13	13	73	13		125	124
Canada Millennium Scholarship Foundation		2,500					2,500	2,346
Aboriginal Healing Foundation		350					350	278
Genome Canada				160	140		300	276
Green Municipal Investment Fund[3]				100		100	200	211
Other foundations under $100 million[4]				72	52	10	134	133
Canada Health Infoway Inc.					500		500	516
Foundation for Sustainable Development Technology					100		100	101
Pierre Elliott Trudeau Foundation[3]						125	125	125
Total	814	2,863	213	1,305	2,055	235	7,485	7,074

Notes: [1] The foundations included in the table have each received over $10 million in total funding from the government since 1997 specifically for spending in a future year more than a year ahead; this has been announced publicly in a budget or in some other way.
[2] These balances are at the date of the latest annual report where March 31, 2002 financial statements are not yet available. It is estimated that $1 billion of interest and other returns on investment were earned on the $7.5 billion transferred, $1.3 billion has been paid to ultimate recipients or used for the ultimate purposes, and $0.1 billion has been paid in administration costs, leaving the balance of $7.1 billion at March 31, 2002.
[3] These are endowments, that is, only the earnings on the endowment are disbursed.
[4] These are: Foundation for Climate and Atmospheric Sciences; Clayoquot Biosphere Trust Society; Forum of Federations; Pacific Salmon Endowment Fund Society; Canadian Institute for Research on Linguistic Minorities – University of Moncton; and Frontier College Learning Foundation (Endowment fund).

John Wiersema

References

Canada. Department of Finance (1995), *The Budget Plan* (Ottawa: Department of
    Finance).
__________ (2003), *The Budget Plan* (Ottawa: Department of Finance).
Canada. Office of the Auditor General (2001), *Performance Report*, period ending
    March 31, 2001 (Ottawa: Office of the Auditor General).
__________ (2002a), *Performance Report (Estimates)*, period ending March 31,
    2002 (Ottawa: Office of the Auditor General).
__________ (2002b), *Report of the Auditor General of Canada*, December
    (Ottawa: Supply and Services Canada).
__________ (2002c), *Report of the Auditor General of Canada*, April (Ottawa:
    Supply and Services Canada).
Canada. Receiver General Canada (2001/02), *Public Accounts of Canada*, Supple-
    mentary Information Observations of the Auditor General (Ottawa: Supply and
    Services Canada).

Web Site and Other References

In the interest of keeping this document brief and focused on its most essential
content, many items that could be of interest to you are accessible through our web
site or other web links.

Office of the Auditor General of Canada

Reports of the Auditor General	http://www.oag-bvg.gc.ca/domino/ other.nsf/html/99repm_e.html
Performance Report	http://www.oag-bvg.gc.ca/domino/ other.nsf/html/99menu5e.html
Report on Plans and Priorities	http://www.oag-bvg.gc.ca/domino/ other.nsf/html/99menu5e.html

Other

Information about the new Government Reporting Model	www.cica.ca/PublicSector
Public Accounts of Canada, Summary Report and Financial Statements, 2002	http://www.fin.gc.ca

THE SEARCH FOR BUDGET TRANSPARENCY

Michael C. McCracken, Informetrica Limited

Background

Governments in developed countries are under continual pressure to be more open or "transparent" with respect to their activities. This reflects a desire to be assured that the operations of governments can withstand scrutiny and partly a hope that such transparency will prevent the most egregious forms of malfeasance.

> The bottom line is that, in my view, the federal government's current financial statements and annual reports do not give policymakers and the American people an adequate picture of our government's overall performance and true financial condition. (David Walker, Comptroller General of the US, 2003, p. 3)

In Canada, the Auditor General has been pointing out the weaknesses in federal reporting since the early 1980s. In 1995, Finance Canada agreed to adopt accrual accounting, and finally implemented it in 2002/03. However, the achievement of full transparency remains elusive.

The notion of transparency hinges on:

- Clarity of roles and responsibilities
- The public availability of information

- Open budget preparation, execution, and reporting
- Assurances of integrity (IMF, Fiscal Affairs Department, 2001)

Progress is being made. The accompanying information for budgets has improved. There are numerous consultations before the budget and some post-budget reviews as well. Yet, there still seems to be a "game" being played between the public and the federal government. "Innovations" are used to sequester funds out of public view (e.g., foundations). Forecasts of perfect budget balance end up as substantial surpluses, serving the purposes of delaying expenditures while reducing the debt *ex post*.

Recent Steps

In response to urgings by the Office of the Auditor General from the early 1980s, the Department of Finance finally made a commitment in 1995 to proceed with full accrual accounting. The change was introduced in the 2003 budget.

Full Accrual Accounting

The key elements of accrual accounting changes identified in the budget (Canada. Department of Finance, 2003, especially Annex 6, pp. 277–298) include:

- capital Assets on Balance Sheet,
- tax revenues when earned,
- recognize Environmental Liabilities,
- recognize Aboriginal Liabilities, and
- recognize Pension Liabilities.

It remains to be seen if departments will adopt capital budgeting with a real option to buy a capital asset instead of leasing or renting. The accrual accounting framework should make such considerations neutral.

Accounting Issues around Foundations

In 1997, the federal government introduced a new form of organization, a publicly-funded foundation, with an independent board of directors and an endowment appropriated by government. The advantage of this approach arises from the opportunity to set up a non-partisan, expert group to deliver something of public interest, with secure long-term funding. Examples include Canadian Institue for Health Information (CIHI), Canadian Institute for Health Research (CIHR), Africa Fund, the Strategic Infrastructure Foundation, and the Canada Foundation for Innovation (CFI).

The problems from a transparency viewpoint is that the funding is shown "as spent" when passed to foundation control, the audit of foundations is outside of the Auditor General's umbrella, and the fiscal impact is likely to be spread over many years, with little information on timing.

The federal government has taken steps to improve the transparency and accountability for foundations (ibid., pp. 179–181). However, it remains to be seen if these steps will satisfy the Auditor General and the public.

The Budget 2003 measures include: (i) Principles for such Public Foundations, (ii) Requirement for Parliamentary Approval, (iii) Improved public reporting, and (iv) Compliance with Funding Agreements.

Existing foundations will require agreements to introduce a regulatory oversight. Such steps will be likely if additional funding is sought at some point in the future.

Who Sets the Standards for Transparency?

The demand for transparency does not arise naturally. Nor is it seen as a desirable characteristic by most organizations, unfortunately. The main forces demanding transparency are those organizations charged with accounting standards, lenders, and "public opinion" as represented by the media and academics.

Domestic Organizations:
- Office of the Auditor General (OAG) and provincial Auditor Generals,
- Public Sector Accounting Board (PSAB) of the Canadian Institute of Chartered Accountants (CICA),
- Domestic Bond Rating Services, and
- Public Opinion.

International Organizations: United Nations, International Monetary Fund, and the Organisation for Economic Co-operation and Development:
- PSC/IFAC Public Sector Committee (PSC) of the International Federation of Accountants,
- International Bond Rating Services,
- Investors, and
- Other Governments (peer pressure).

Actions Suggested by International Monetary Fund

The International Monetary Fund (IMF) has put one of the more rigorous review processes in place. Although its principal purpose is to assist developing countries, the application of standards covers the developed countries as well. There is a strong demonstration effect if developed countries follow the standards. It also illustrates their feasibility.

The IMF publishes a *Report on the Observance of Standards and Codes* (ROSC) based on a review of a country's performance. The major elements from the ROSC on Canada, *Fiscal Transparency Module*, indicates a need for improvement, including:

- Current data on total government not available;
- No forward-looking calculations of Cyclically-Adjusted Balance (CAB) and Cyclically-Adjusted Primary Balance (CAPB);
- No within-year reports on program performance by departments;
- No analysis of fiscal risks or sustainability tests (e.g., public pensions);
- Publish procedures for budget and expenditure management;
- Reconciliation between Public Accounts and SNA — budget by Finance, historical by Statistics Canada;

                                        Michael C. McCracken

- Accounting for reserves (*ex post*) and identification of reserves (*ex ante*);
- Add information to budget and update documents to include:
  - functional and economic classifications,
  - tax expenditure summary,
  - fiscal risk, sustainability, reconciliations, and alternative budget measures.
- Publish estimates on quasi-fiscal activities (e.g., Canada Mortgage and Housing Corporation lending).

IMF members from the developed world set the standard by their behaviour. Failure does not mean that the IMF will refuse to take money from Canada!

OECD Shortfalls

The OECD (2001) has also published *Best Practices for Budget Transparency* with participation by Canadian officials in their development. The shortfall assessment below represents my interpretation of the current state in Canada.

OECD recommendations include: (i) budget three months prior to end of fiscal year; (ii) expenditures in gross terms; (iii) supplementary information on functional and economic categories (annual and monthly); (iv) long-term report at least every five years with range of plausible scenarios; and (v) disclose all key economic assumptions.

In addition, the OECD suggests a formal "sign-off" with the finance minister certifying that all government decisions with a fiscal impact have been included in the report, and the deputy minister certifying that best professional judgement was used in producing the report.

Suggested Areas for Improvement

Functional Breakdown

A call for a functional breakdown has been made to the National Accounts Advisory Committee (NAAC) for many years with little reaction and no support from Finance Canada. Canada has been deficient for at least 20 years within the OECD, resulting in a note in the OECD SNA publications about Canada. (See Minutes of NAAC in September 1995 for discussion.)

The current Statistics Canada plan is to produce a set of functional breakdowns by level of government in accord with the COFOG/SNA93/ GFS/IMF standards for 2005.

The adoption of accrual accounting may help, since one of the problematic areas has been the development of capital stock and capital cost allowance (CCA) estimates that could be allocated across functions. Recent spats about the shares of health spending are only a small reflection of this inadequacy.

Separate Education and Social Transfers

The intention to create a Canada Health Transfer (CHT) and Canada Social Transfer (CST) out of the Canada Health and Social Transfer (CHST) has been stated in the budget (Canada. Department of Finance, 2003, p. 183). Why not identify a Canada Education Transfer (CET) and CST, thereby moving back to the previous Canada Assistance Plan (CAP) plus Established Program Financing (EPF) framework? This would help in the discussion of education financing as well.

Common Federal-Provincial Framework

Auditor Generals from the various levels of government should agree on adoption of common standards and support of the FMS/SC role historically as well as encouraging Finance Departments to agree on publishing common accounts for forecast purposes.

                                                    Michael C. McCracken

Macroeconomic Budget Indicators

There has been discussion over the years about the output gap and the cyclically adjusted budget balance (CAB) and the measures of fiscal posture (CAPB) and fiscal thrust (first difference of CAPB). This measure is not available publicly at the time of the budget, no forecast is provided, and no sense of what is expected to happen because of the budget appears.

There should be regular and timely publication of historical estimates by Statistics Canada of the output gap, the CAB, and CAPB. Finance should provide projections of these measures as part of its budget. Illustrations of these measures are provided below.

Size of Output Gap

Figure 1: Output Gap

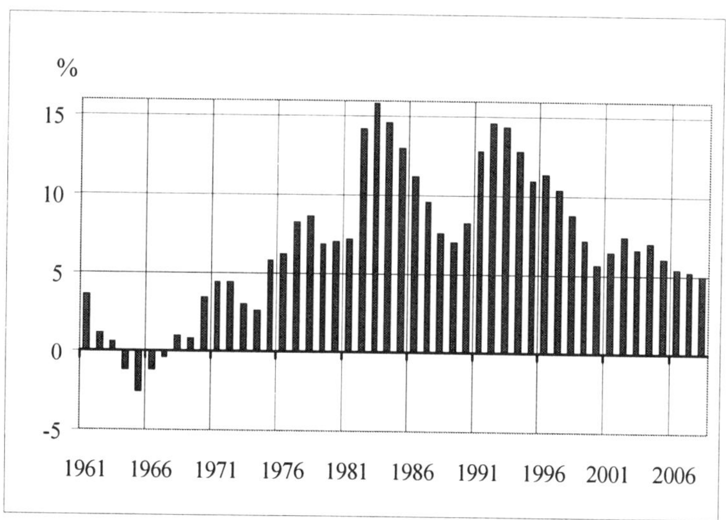

Size of output gap, based on a 4% unemployment rate for full employment (perhaps too high?) and application of Okun's Law to define potential.

Figure 2: Cyclically-Adjusted Primary Balances

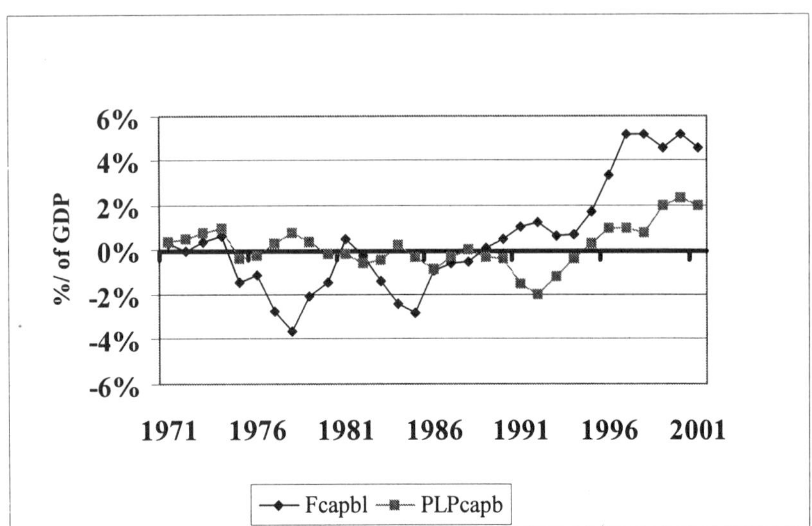

Note that federal government measure is about 5%, historically high, and sustained for a number of years (Canada. Department of Finance, 2002). Yes, there is restraint in the system!! There is no indication of their measure of "full employment", or the methodology employed here.

Provincial, Local, and Pensions combined sector is also running surpluses — about 2% of GDP.

Note that forecast values are not available. Nor are actual 2002 calculations provided in the budget documents. Statistics Canada should publish the historical data on a quarterly basis.

Figure 3: Fiscal Thrust

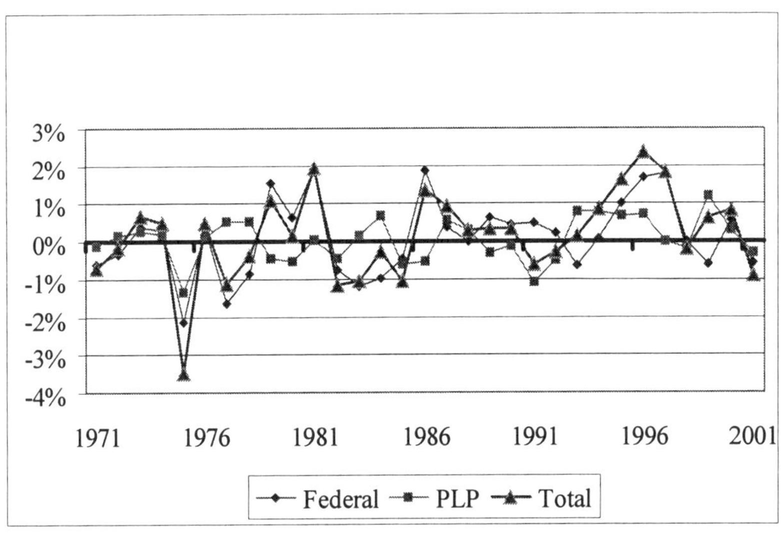

A similar story emerges here. There has been some apparent relaxation in 2001, but what about since then?

Conclusion

Progress has been made. Finance Canada has moved to full accrual accounting and appears to be improving the transparency of their foundations. There is room for more improvement, particularly with respect to measures of macroeconomic performance, functional breakdown of expenditures, and coordination of measures across governments.

Continuous pressure for more transparency is important. Without it, the natural tendency is to hide activities behind the opaque walls of bureaucracy.

References

Canada. Department of Finance (2002), *Fiscal Reference Tables* (Ottawa: Department of Finance).

__________ (2003), *The Budget Plan 2003*, February 18 (Ottawa: Department of Finance).

International Monetary Fund (IMF)(2001), *Manual on Fiscal Transparency*, Fiscal Affairs Department (New York: IMF).

__________ (2002), *Canada: Report on the Observance of Standards and Codes — Fiscal Transparency Module*, IMF Country Report No. 02/51, March (New York: IMF).

Organisation for Economic Co-operation and Development (OECD)(2001), *OECD Best Practices for Budget Transparency* (Paris: OECD).

Walker, Honorable D.M. (2003), "Truth and Transparency: The Federal Government's Financial Condition and Fiscal Outlook". Speech by Comptroller General of the US at the National Press Club, Washington, DC, September 17.

Wiersema, J. (2003), "Full Accrual Accounting", this volume.

BUDGETARY ACCOUNTING AND TRANSPARENCY: Lessons from Private-Sector Experience

Alan Macnaughton, University of Waterloo

Both the paper presenter, John Wiersema, and the commentator, Mike McCracken, have provided many fine comments on the introduction of full accrual accounting by the federal government. The only thing I wish to add, as a faculty member in a university school of accountancy, is that, since the private sector has been using accrual accounting for many years, this innovation brings private-sector financial accounting and government accounting closer together. Thus, it may be possible to learn something about pitfalls in future government accounting from the historical private-sector experience.

Perhaps the most important lesson is that no set of accounting principles can prevent the use of accounting choices to influence the financial bottom line (net profit or loss for a private firm and the surplus or deficit for a government). Just as private-sector firms sometimes want to please investors and shareholders at all costs, governments may go to great lengths to please voters by presenting attractive financial results. Changing actual expenditures or revenues is one way to achieve this result, but accounting choices provide another such means. In private-sector terminology, this can take the form of either earnings manipulation or earnings management.

Earnings manipulation, which is the use of accounting choices that violate generally-accepted accounting principles, attracts much public attention these days with the Enron and Worldcom scandals and the criminal convictions against prominent managers. While occurrences of fraud deserve the attention they are getting and merit shakeups in accounting regulation such as the recent Sarbanes-Oxley legislation in the United States, preventing earnings manipulation is hardly enough to ensure integrity in financial reporting. This is as true in government financial reporting as it is in private-sector financial reporting.

Earnings management complies with generally-accepted accounting principles but is still something less than unbiased financial disclosure. Earnings management is defined as "a purposeful intervention in the external financial reporting process, with the intent of obtaining some private gain" (Schipper, 1989).

Identifying earnings management is likely to prove to be as difficult in the public sector as it is in the private sector. For example, the paper cites the one-time deferral of corporate income tax instalment payments by small businesses as one example of an event that distorted financial reporting under the old modified accrual accounting regime. Was this an attempt to achieve a certain deficit/surplus result, a genuine attempt to help financially-troubled small businesses, or a mixture of both?

Under the new full accrual accounting regime, the estimates and judgements inherent in accrual accounting could be the instruments of earnings management. For example, suppose the government lengthens the estimated useful life of an asset to ten years from seven, thereby reducing depreciation expense and increasing the surplus (or reducing the deficit). This change may reflect the government's true belief about the wear-and-tear on the asset, but it could equally reflect an attempt to avoid reporting a government deficit or to increase a surplus (Cormier and Magnan, 1996).

Earnings-management research in private-sector financial accounting has focused on total accruals, measured as the difference between net income before extraordinary items and cash flows from operations. To identify the portions of these accruals resulting from "purposeful intervention", researchers attempt to break total accruals into non-discretionary and discretionary (i.e., managed) components. The non-discretionary component is predicted statistically by using such assumptions as that depreciation expense should move proportionately with the level of property, plant, and equipment. Whether the same method will work for governments remains to be seen.

                                          Alan Macnaughton

Another important lesson from the private-sector experience is that, where the auditor is less than vigilant, as in the case of the now-defunct accounting firm of Arthur Andersen in the Enron scandal, management has far too much freedom to "cook the books" (Wiedman, 2002). Thus, the Auditor General of Canada has much work to do in ensuring that the introduction of full accrual accounting actually improves financial disclosure. Since accrual accounting has been advocated by the Auditor General since at least the 1970s and the government announced its commitment to full accrual accounting as long ago as the 1995 budget, this is obviously a long-term project.

References

Cormier, D. and M. Magnan (1996), "Decisions, Decisions: What Motivates Managers to Choose Certain Policies and Methods", *CA Magazine* (September), 38–41.
Schipper, K. (1989), "Commentary on Earnings Management", *Accounting Horizons* 15(4), 91–102.
Wiedman, C. (2002), "The Power of Auditors", *CA Magazine* (December).

Session Four
THE TAX DIMENSION

THE CHRÉTIEN GOVERNMENT'S LEGACY: A Tax System for the 21st Century?

Bev Dahlby, University of Alberta

Introduction

In the weeks leading up to the federal government's budget on February 18, 2003, there was much speculation that it would contain a host of expenditure initiatives that would constitute Mr. Chrétien's "Legacy". But, as far as I know, none of the commentators referred to changes to the tax system as constituting a potentially important legacy. Is the tax system that Chrétien's government has put in place since 1994 a legacy for Canada? Has the foundation for a fair and efficient tax system which will finance the expenditure programs that are more frequently viewed as politicians' legacies, been put in place? Or does that task still fall to Chrétien's successor?

In this paper, I review the tax policy changes in the February 2003 federal budget as part of a larger assessment of the Chrétien government's tax policies since 1994. (It should be stressed that the tax system is not Chrétien's personal legacy because it is also the legacy of Mr. Martin, who

I would like to thank Jonathan Kesselman and Michael Smart for their comments on an earlier draft of this paper. The financial support of the Donner Canadian Foundation is gratefully acknowledged.

was minister of finance during most of this period, and to a lesser degree, John Manley, who delivered the February 2003 federal budget.) Many significant tax policy issues emerged during the Chrétien regime. Some of the more prominent issues are listed in Table 1 under four headings: funding social insurance programs, the personal tax system, the business taxation, and sales taxation. Note that under the last heading, the major

Table 1: Tax Policy Issues Under the Chrétien Government

Social Insurance Program Funding
- CPP/QPP contribution increases
- the ill-fated Seniors Benefit reform
- gradual reduction in UI/EI contribution rates
- backing away from benefit reductions for frequent EI claimants

The Personal Tax System
- enhancement of the Canada Child Tax Benefit (CCTB) program
- allowing provinces to levy tax on base instead of tax on tax
- reduction in federal personal income tax rates
- full indexation of personal tax system
- expansion in the RSP/RPP pension plan contribution limits
- expansion of education credits
- capital gains taxation changes

Business Taxation
- reduction in corporate income tax rates
- elimination of the federal capital tax
- elimination of the Resource Allowance
- increase in the small business deduction

Sales Taxation
- failure to eliminate the GST
- harmonization of sales taxes with the Atlantic provinces

issue — the elimination of the goods and services tax (GST) — was a non-event: the backing away from the 1993 election campaign promise and, in my view, a wise policy decision.

The paper is organized around some, but not all, of the policy issues listed under the other three headings. I will begin with a brief listing of the major tax policy changes in the February 2003 budget that are analyzed in more detail in the context of the overall tax policy performance of the Chrétien government since its election in 1993.

Major Tax Policy Initiatives in the February 2003 Federal Budget

The February 2003 budget was not a "tax budget". The spending initiatives announced in the budget will amount to $3.986 billion in 2003/04 and $4.969 billion in 2004/05, while the foregone revenues from the tax policy measures will only be $0.718 billion in 2003 and $1.548 billion in 2004. Perhaps to ward off criticism that there was too much emphasis on expenditure initiatives, the minister of finance reminded us that the personal income tax cuts announced in the October 2000 *Economic Statement and Budget Update* will amount to $8.282 billion in 2003/04, and the corporate income tax cuts will be $2.45 billion.

Table 2 lists six major tax policy initiatives in the February 2003 budget. I will not discuss each of these initiatives in detail at this point. They will be discussed in the context of the Chrétien government's tax policies since 1994. I will, however, note that all of these tax measures, except the reduction in the EI premium rate for 2004, will be phased-in over the next three to five years, and so the full revenue impacts and economic reper-cussions of these policy changes will not be felt until 2008 and beyond. One general comment about the Chrétien government's approach, which has been made by Jack Mintz and others, is that the government could have achieved a better balance between tax cuts and expenditure increases if it had sped up the implementation of these tax measures.

Table 2: Major Tax Policy Changes in the February 2003 Federal Budget

Measure	Details	Revenue Impacts (in millions of dollars)		
		2002/03	2003/04	2004/05
Employment Insurance premiums	• Employment and employer contribution rates reduced to $1.98 and $2.77 per $100 of insurable earnings in 2004 from $2.10 and $2.94 in 2003.		53	178
Canada Child Tax Benefit	• Increase the annual National Child Benefit supplement by $150 per child in July 2003, $185 in July 2005 and $185 in July 2006. The maximum CCTB benefit for the first child is projected to $3,243 in July 2007.		200	300
RRSP/RPP limits	• Increase annual RRSP contribution limits to $14,500 in 2003, $15,500 in 2004, $16,500 in 2005, $18,000 in 2006, and indexed to inflation in 2007. • Increase in maximum defined benefit pension per year of service increased to $1,833 in 2004, and $2,000 in 2005 and then index to inflation in 2006.	25	105	165
Small business deduction	• Increase in the small business deduction, which currently reduces the basic federal corporate income tax rate to 12% for the first $200,000 of income to $225,000 in 2003, $250,000 in 2004, $275,000 in 2005, and $300,000 in 2006.		60	110
Federal capital tax	• Scheduled reductions in the FCT rates to 0.225% in 2003, 0.200 in 2004, 0.175 in 2005, 0.125 in 2006, 0.0625 in 2007, and eliminated in 2008. • Elimination of the FCT for corporations with capital less than $50 million in 2004.		60	395
Resource Allowance	• Reduction in the federal CIT rate for mining and oil and gas companies to 27 in 2003 and by one percentage point a year until it reaches the general rate of 21% in 2007. • Elimination of the 25% resource allowance, but the deduction of provincial royalties permitted.	10	55	100
Other tax policy measures	• Child Disability Benefit, Mineral exploration tax credit, Film or video production services tax credit, and other measures.		130	300
Total		35	718	1,548

Source: Canada. Department of Finance (2003a, Table A1.2, p. 229).

Aggregate Trends in Taxation Since 1994

We will begin by examining the level and composition of federal tax revenues since 1994. Table 3 shows that while total federal revenues as a percentage of gross domestic product (GDP) declined slightly over the 1994–2002 period, personal and corporate income tax revenues rose in relation to GDP. The dramatic rise in corporate income tax revenues is a reflection of the rebound in corporate profits, from around 6% of GDP in 1994, back to its long-term average of 10% in 2002 (see Canada. Department of Finance, 2003a, p. 51). The growth of personal income tax (PIT) revenues is also related to the improved labour market conditions. The other major sources of federal tax revenues, consumption taxes (the GST and federal excise taxes) and social insurance contributions (largely EI

Table 3: The Level and Composition of Federal Revenues

		1994	*2002*
Personal Income Tax	Share of GDP	7.9	8.2
	Share of Total Federal Revenues	43.9	46.3
Corporate Income Tax	Share of GDP	1.3	2.3
	Share of Total Federal Revenues	7.5	12.9
Consumption Taxes	Share of GDP	4.1	3.7
	Share of Total Federal Revenues	22.7	20.6
Contribution to Social Insurance	Share of GDP	2.8	2.0
	Share of Total Federal Revenues	15.8	11.2
Total Federal Revenues	Share of GDP	17.9	17.7

Source: Calculations based on Cansim II series V156320, V156323, V156324, V156328, V156347, and V498906.

premiums) declined relative to GDP and as a share of total tax revenues. And so over this period, the federal government became more reliant on personal and corporate income taxes. This raises the question of whether this tax mix, with its heavy reliance on personal and corporate income taxes, is the appropriate tax mix for a modern twenty-first century.

We begin our review of the tax policies of the Chrétien government by examining the funding of the social insurance system, specifically the public pension and unemployment insurance systems. Then we will turn our attention to the personal and business taxation systems.

Funding the Social Insurance System

In 1994, the combined employee and employer contribution rate for the Canada and Quebec Pension Plans (CPP/QPP) was 5.6%. It had been slowly increasing from 3.6%, the initial rate set back in 1966. In 1998, the federal and provincial government agreed to a series of reforms to the CPP that included ramping up the combined employee and employer contribution rates from 5.85% in 1997 to 9.9% in 2003. The reforms have placed the CPP on a financially sustainable path till the end of this century, although unforeseen economic or demographic changes may require further adjustments to contribution rates or the benefits.[1] As a result of these premium increases, total contributions to the Canada and Quebec Pension Plans have mushroomed from $11.7 billion or 1.6% of GDP in 1994 to $29.7 billion or 2.7% of GDP in 2002. An employee's maximum contribution has increased from $806 in 1994 to $1,673.2 in 2002, a very substantial increase. As shown in the following section, the CPP/QPP premium increases have largely offset the other tax reductions for low-income, single individuals.

While actions had to be taken to address the fiscal sustainability of the CPP/QPP — it is regrettable that the federal and provincial governments delayed the implementation of the fiscal adjustment for so long — it can be

---

[1]See Robson (2000) on the sensitivity of the current funding arrangements to changes in demographic and economic variables such as the rate of inflation.

                                                    Bev Dahlby

argued that too much of the adjustment occurred through contribution increases. Other measures, such as eliminating disability benefits and gradually raising the eligibility age for a full pension from age 65, would have reduced the magnitude of the contribution increase.

Old Age Security is the federal government's largest expenditure program. Total expenditure on the Old Age Security (OAS) pension, the Guaranteed Income Supplement (GIS), and the Spouse's Allowance was $25.3 billion in 2001/02, almost twice as much as Employment Insurance spending. The first wave of the baby-boom generation will be 65 in 2011, and OAS expenditures will rapidly increase after that date.

The attempted reform of the OAS was one of the policy disasters of the Chrétien government. The ill-fated Seniors Benefit would have combined the OAS pension and the GIS into a single benefit program with a 50% clawback rate at low income levels (as under the GIS) and a 20% clawback rate that would have reduced the benefits paid to seniors in the middle and upper income ranges. This reform was sold to the public as part of the Chrétien government's deficit-reduction strategy, not as a necessary adjustment to avoid pension funding problems after 2011. The government's justification for the reform evaporated when the federal deficit abruptly declined and surpluses emerged. There were also serious concerns about the effect that the relatively high clawback rate would have on retirement savings incentives for lower and middle-income individuals. More ominously, the public debate over the Seniors Benefit revealed the strength of the "gray power" lobby in this country and their unwillingness to accept any reduction in "entitlements" under the OAS program, even though the Seniors Benefit would not have reduced the benefits of any current OAS recipient, and it would have increased transfers to low-income seniors in the future.

It is likely that we will have to re-address the reform of the OAS in coming years. Certainly one of the lessons from the Seniors Benefit debacle is that it should be sold on the basis of addressing the long-term viability of the public pension system and that the impact on savings incentives will have to be satisfactorily addressed by the reform proposal. Further discussion of this point will be taken up when we consider the Kesselman and Poschmann (2001) proposal for a tax-prepaid savings plan in the next section.

The reform of the funding of the Employment Insurance (EI) program (formerly Unemployment Insurance) was also a missed opportunity by the Chrétien government. In 1994, the UI premium rate was $3.07, and the employer rate was $4.30, per $100 of insurable earnings. After 1994, the unemployment rate declined, but the Chrétien government did not lower premiums in line with the reduction in EI expenditures. The EI premiums contributed to the reduction in the federal government's deficit, even though there is a notional EI account for surplus contributions. In 1998, under pressure from businesses and the public, the Chrétien government started to reduce the EI premium rate at a more rapid rate, but in my view it missed a golden opportunity to introduce an element of experience-rating in setting EI premiums, as recommended by the Technical Committee on Business Taxation (a.k.a. the Mintz committee of which I was a member) in 1998. At that time, it would have been possible to introduce partial experience-rating of the EI premiums in a way that would have reduced the premiums for employers with low layoff rates, while not raising the premium for employers with high layoff rates, thus making this reform as palatable as possible. The fact that the Mintz committee proposal received virtually no support in either the government or the business community has convinced me that EI financing cannot be reformed in a way that would improve employers' incentives with regard to laying off workers, and thus lower the equilibrium unemployment rate.

As noted in Table 2, a reduction in the EI premium rate for 2004 was announced in the budget, but no other structural changes to EI funding were announced. Instead, the minister of finance indicated that a committee would be set up to review EI financing. A review of EI funding is certainly desirable, and given the political reality — there is no support for even a limited form of experience-rating — we need to carefully consider our limited options. In my view, it makes less and less sense to have an ear-marked payroll tax with a maximum contribution limit to fund an income redistribution program that also includes social programs (the expanded parental leave program) and labour market training. Such programs would normally be funded out of general revenues, not from ear-marked payroll taxes. Thus, the relevant questions are: Should we have a general federal payroll tax? And, what form should it take? It is not possible to have a full discussion of these questions in this paper, but I will briefly argue that, especially in the context of moving toward a tax system that places greater emphasis on consumption taxation, it would be useful to have a general

                                                   Bev Dahlby

payroll tax with no upper bound on "contributions". Ideally, such a tax would only be levied on employees, to avoid any possible disincentives to employ workers, although international experience with general payroll taxes suggests that they are almost always levied on employers.[2] A reform along these lines would improve the fairness of the current tax-transfer system whereby low- and middle-income employees wind up financing income redistribution and social programs that should be financed through more progressive taxes.

The Personal Taxation System

In this section, I will examine how tax policy changes have affected earnings and savings incentives and the progressivity of the tax-transfer system since 1994. As noted in the introduction, there have been a number of significant tax policy changes, including reductions to the federal and provincial statutory tax rates, the enhancement of Canada Child Tax Benefit, and the switch from the tax on base to tax on income in levying provincial taxes, and the changes in the financing of the social insurance programs, which could potentially affect the earnings incentives of Canadian workers through changes in their marginal and average tax rates. These changes are examined in the first subsection.

I entitled this section the "Personal Taxation System", not the "Personal Income Tax System" because our system is a hybrid income-consumption tax system. The increase in the contribution limits under the RSP/RPP programs, announced in the February 2003 budget, will shift the balance of the personal tax system even more toward a consumption tax system — a direction that I support. In the last subsection, I discuss the best way to move toward a consumption tax system.

---

[2]See Kesselman (1997) on the design and international experience with general payroll taxes. While a payroll tax on employers will usually be shifted to employees, minimum wages may prevent this and cause a reduction in employment of minimum wage workers. Hence my preference for levying the payroll tax on employees.

In assessing the federal policies, we need to take into account the combined effects of federal and provincial taxes. There have been important differences in the provincial governments' taxation policies in recent years, and space does not permit the analysis of the changes in all ten provinces. Instead, I focus on the changes in Ontario because it is the largest province, and it is where the mythical "median" voter, whose preferences determine federal fiscal policies, lives. Actually, she lives in Mississauga, and federal tax policies, at least in their general form, are designed to suit the gal from Mississauga.

Marginal tax rates are the additional taxes paid on an additional dollar of earnings. For the purposes of this study, they include:

- the employee's EI and CPP/QPP contributions (net of the tax credits earned under the personal income tax),
- federal and provincial income tax payments,
- federal and provincial transfers, such as sales tax and child tax credits, that are delivered through the tax system. (These programs impose an implicit marginal tax on earnings to the extent that these transfers decline when an individual earns an additional dollar of income.)

First, I offer a few words about this measure of the marginal tax rate.[3] It has been adopted in order to measure the earnings incentive effects of the tax system. It is not a comprehensive measure of the marginal tax wedge — the gap between the value of the additional output from an additional hour of work and the net increase in real income that the worker receives for that hour of work. The marginal tax wedge is useful to measure the degree of tax distortion in the system. For example, the marginal tax wedge is used in measuring the marginal cost of public funds (Dahlby, 1994). It includes a wider range of taxes, such as the employer payroll taxes and employer contributions to EI and CPP/QPP, but they are not included in the marginal tax rate in this study because they do not directly affect an employee's incentive to earn income. (Employer payroll taxes reduce the incentive to earn income only to the extent that they are shifted back to workers through lower wages.)

---

[3]On the measurement and trend in marginal tax rates in Canada, see Davies and Zhang (1996); Davies (1998); and Macnaughton, Matthews and Pittman (1998).

                                                      Bev Dahlby

The marginal tax rate used in this study is more limited than the marginal tax-wedge measure because I want to focus on earnings incentive and in particular on the changes in earnings incentive over the 1994–2002 period. It can be argued that sales tax rates should be included in the marginal tax rate because sales taxes reduce the real return from working by increasing the prices of consumer goods. However, I compare the marginal and average tax rates of individuals with same real income in 1994 and 2002, and this makes it difficult to incorporate the sales tax rate in the measured marginal tax rate. In any event, the federal GST rate and the Ontario retail sales tax rate did not change over this period, so neglecting the sales tax rates does not affect our measure of the changes in average and marginal tax rates between 1994 and 2002.

In addition, some might question the inclusion of EI and CPP/QPP contributions in the measure of the marginal tax rate by arguing that these are not taxes, but the price that taxpayers pay for these benefits. I feel that this argument carries little or no weight with regard to the EI premium because an individual's expected EI benefits generally bear little or no relation to their EI contributions. Contributions are not experience rated, and a significant portion of the EI program funds general social programs or labour market programs. In addition, throughout the 1994–2002 period, EI premiums exceeded the amount necessary to fund the program. Therefore, it is best to think of the EI premium as a general federal payroll tax.

The case for viewing the CPP contributions as a payment for a benefit, and not a tax that distorts incentives, is stronger because there is a stronger linkage between contributions and CPP pensions. However, this link is not one-to-one for several reasons. First, roughly a third of the current contributions of a young worker pays for the unfunded liability of the Canada pension plan, that is, the pensions of previous generations of workers when the plan was under-funded. Second, for workers with low lifetime earnings, higher CPP contributions and therefore CPP pensions will be partially offset by lower federal and provincial transfers, such as GIS, in retirement. Third, significant numbers of young people may have serious doubts about whether they will receive their CPP pension. They may still think that there is a crisis in public pensions, in spite of the 1998 reforms making the CPP financially viable. For these reasons, I think that a strong case can be made for treating employees' CPP/QPP contributions as a tax that reduces a worker's net return from earning income.

In measuring the marginal and average tax rate changes, I have assumed that the taxpayer has the same real income in 1994 and 2002. I have chosen to measure the marginal tax rates holding real income constant because, with a progressive rate structure, a reduction in real incomes lowers a taxpayer's average tax rates. If we compared the taxes paid by two taxpayers with the same nominal income in 1994 and 2004, then it would be comparing a taxpayer in 2002 whose real income is 14% lower than the taxpayer in 1994. Under a progressive tax system, we would expect average tax rates to be lower in 2002 if the tax system is indexed for inflation. In the absence of full indexation, which was the case from 1994 to 2000, average tax rates will increase even if real earning remains constant. To sort out these effects, it seems best to compare the taxes imposed at the same real income level over time, and this is the procedure adopted in this paper.

The Tax Treatment of Single Individuals

Figure 1 shows the marginal tax rates on earnings faced by a single individual in Ontario in 2002. The marginal tax rates exceeded 30% for earnings above $10,000 and exceeded 40% for incomes of $65,000. At the $110,000 level, the 46.4% marginal tax rate is based on the federal marginal tax rate of 29% and a provincial marginal tax rate of 17.4% that results from a combination of a top provincial statutory rate of 11.16% and the provincial surtaxes.

The marginal tax rate is higher in the $35,000–40,000 range than in $45,000–60,000 range because taxpayers in this region are subject to the EI and CPP/QPP levies as well as the clawback of the GST credit, which adds 5% to their marginal tax rate, while taxpayers at higher income levels pay the maximum contributions and do not receive the GST credit and therefore their marginal tax rates are reduced.

Figure 2 shows the change in the marginal tax rates on a single individual with the same real (inflation-adjusted) earnings between 1994 and 2002. For example, an individual with $8,571 in 1994 had the same real earnings as an individual with $10,000 in earnings in 2002. The marginal tax rate of an individual earning $8,571 in 1994 has been calculated and compared with the marginal tax rate of an individual earning $10,000 in 2002. The figure shows that marginal tax rates have declined at all income levels,

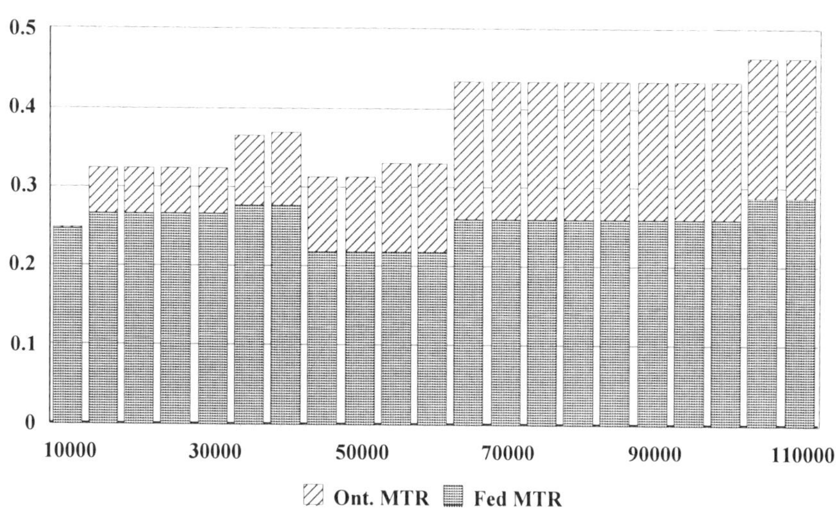

Figure 1: Marginal Tax Rates on a Single Individual in Ontario in 2002

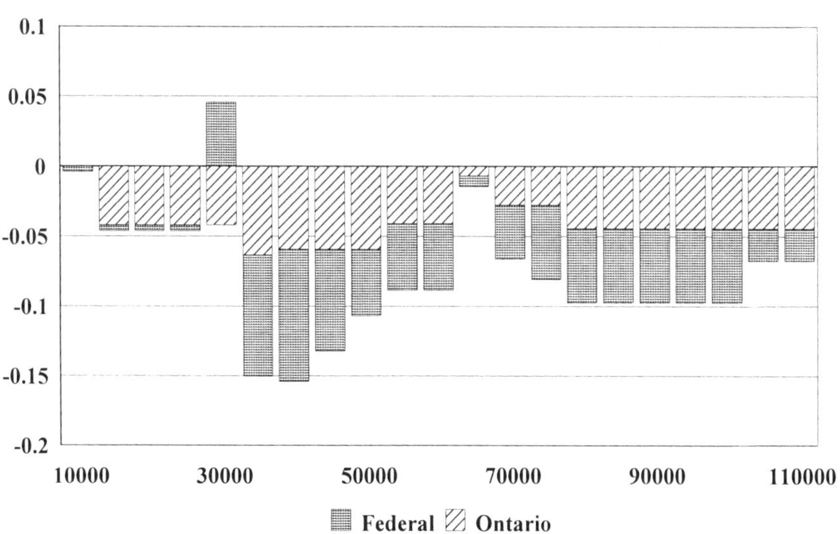

Figure 2: Changes in the Marginal Tax Rates on a Single Individual in Ontario Between 1994 and 2002

except at the $30,000 level in 2002 where it is only slightly increased. The figure shows that Ontario was primarily responsible for the decline in the marginal tax rates in the under $35,000 income range. The federal government's tax policies had little net impact on the marginal tax rates in the low-income range because reductions in income tax rates were offset by higher EI and CPP contributions. Overall, the largest marginal tax rate reductions of 11 to 15 percentage points occurred in the $35,000 to $50,000 income range.

So far, I have focused on the marginal tax rates on earnings under the personal tax system. It is also important to consider the changes in the average tax rates in order to assess the redistributional effects of the tax policy changes over the 1994–2002 period. In addition, average tax rates affect labour supply responses through income effects. Figure 3 shows the average tax rates under the tax-transfer system in 1994 and 2002. It should be stressed that this is only a partial view of the redistributional effect of the government taxes and expenditures because this measure does not include the tax burden from other types of taxes, such as sales and excise tax, property taxes and corporate income taxes. It also assumes that all income is fully taxable labour income. The latter may be shifted to workers through lower wage rates. To the extent that those at higher incomes would have a higher proportion of capital income (e.g., capital gains), other tax changes may have worked to their comparative benefit. Our purpose here is to assess the redistributional effects and earning incentive effects of the tax-transfer system on wage earners and not to consider the impact of the entire fiscal system.

In both years, the tax-transfer system is progressive — average tax rates increase with earnings. Figure 4 shows the change in average tax rates between 1994 and 2002. Average tax rates have fallen at all income levels except the $10,000 level where there was an increase in federal taxes, again because of the increase in CPP/QPP contributions. The declines in average tax rates were higher at the higher income levels, especially average federal tax rates. The Ontario average rate reductions reached a maximum of 2.5 percentage points at the $65,000 level and then declined slightly at higher income levels. Overall, the largest reduction, almost five percentage points, occurred at $105,000 earnings level. While there is no consensus on how to measure changes in the progressivity of the tax system because it involves value judgements about the willingness to trade off gains and

                                                        Bev Dahlby

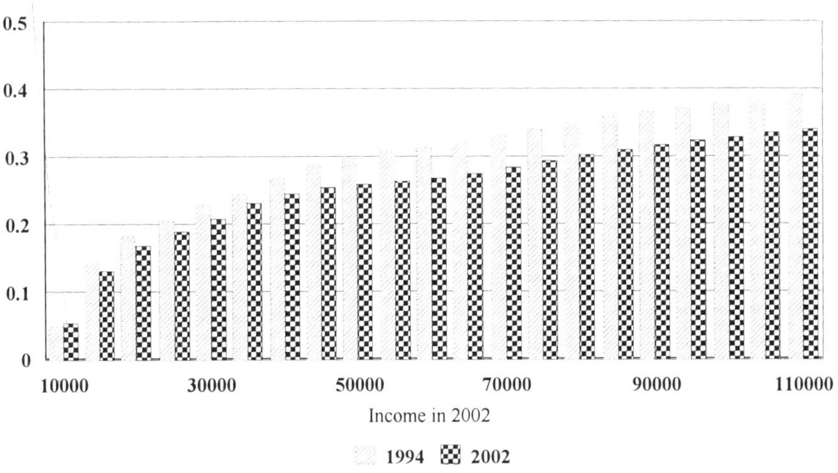

Figure 3: Average Tax Rates on a Single Individual in Ontario in 1994 and 2002

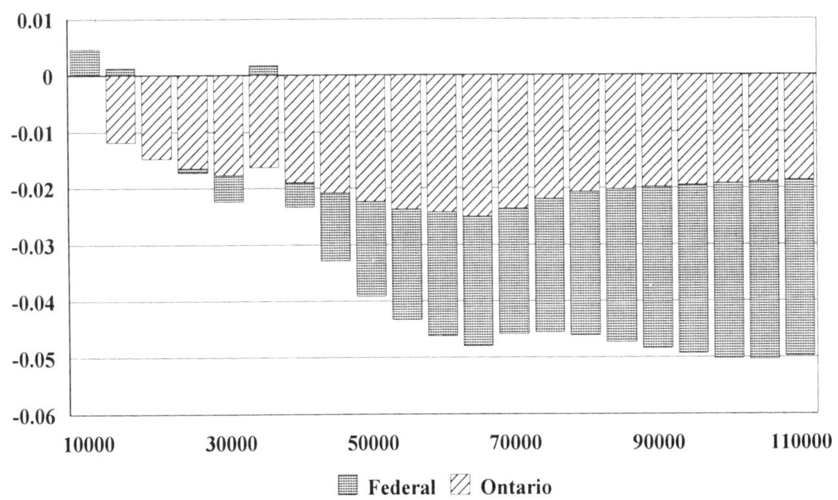

Figure 4: Changes in the Average Tax Rates on a Single Individual in Ontario Between 1994 and 2002

losses to individuals at different income levels, I think that most people would regard the changes in average tax rates depicted in Figure 4 as regressive, that is, the tax-transfer system became less progressive in 2002. Thus, the overall effect of the tax policy changes since 1994 was to make the personal tax system for single individuals less progressive in 2002.

The overall effect of the tax changes on labour supply incentives is ambiguous (except at the $30,000 income levels), because while the marginal tax rates declined so did average tax rates, leading to offsetting income and substitution effects. The overall impact on earnings incentives depends on the relative strengths of the income and substitution effects, which is an empirical matter. At the $30,000 level, a slight increase in the marginal tax rate on earnings was combined with a reduction in the average tax rate. The standard labour supply model predicts that an increase in the marginal tax rate combined with a reduction in the average tax rate would lead to reduced earnings because both the income and substitution effects would lead to reductions in labour supply.

Tax Treatment of Families

The expansion of the Canada Child Tax Benefit (CCTB) program has been one of the most important tax policy initiatives undertaken by the Chrétien government. The CCTB was instituted in order to improve the incentives for poor families with children to leave welfare and to provide income transfers to low-income working families with children. In the early 1990s, there were more children than seniors living in poverty. The decline in the poverty rate among seniors was a laudable achievement of the Liberal governments of the 1960s, and the task of enhancing the social safety net for Canadian children fell to the Chrétien government. The CCTB seems to have helped achieve these objectives because the proportion of children living in poverty decreased from 16.7% in 1996 to 12.5% in 2000 and "the employment rate among low-income families rose by 4 percentage points" (Canada. Department of Finance, 2003a, p. 97). Of course, the improvement in labour market conditions over this period also contributed to this achievement.

The CCTB has two components: the base CCTB and the National Child Benefit (NCB) supplement. From July 2002 to June 2003, the base CCTB

                                                         Bev Dahlby

was $1,150.92 for the first two children and $1,231 for each additional child with an extra $228 for each child under seven years old. The NCB supplement, which provides additional benefits to low income families, was $1,293 for the first child, $1,087 for the second, and $1,009 for the third and subsequent children.

As shown in Table 4, the total transfer under the CCTB/NCB was $7.50 billion in 2001/02, and it provided support for 5.35 million children. Over 70% of the total benefits were paid to the 44% of children who live in

Table 4: The Distribution of Benefits Under the CCTB in 2001/02

	Children		Benefits	
Net Family Income	*Average Number*	*Percent*	*Total Paid (1000s)*	*Percent*
Under $30,000	2,377,660	44.4	$5,314,711	70.9
30,000–40,000	687,530	12.9	$791,880	10.6
40,000–50,000	663,700	12.4	$595,705	7.9
50,000–60,000	628,150	11.7	$419,830	5.6
60,000–70,000	545,070	.10.2	$239,846	3.2
70,000–80,000	285,140	5.3	$91,171	1.2
80,000–90,000	88,820	1.7	$30,671	0.4
90,000–100,000	51,940	1.0	$11,130	0.1
100,000 plus	22,030	0.4	$5,210	0.1
Total	5,350,040	100.00	$7,500,154	100.0

Source: Canada Customs and Revenue Agency Web site <www.ccra-adrc.gc.ca/tax/individuals/stats/gb00/pst/final/pdf/gb00cctb.pdf>.

families with net family incomes under $30,000. The concentration of the benefits among low-income families with children was achieved by imposing a benefit phase-out or clawback. The basic CCTB benefit in 2002 was reduced by 2.5 cents for every dollar of net family income in excess of $32,960 for a one-child family and by 5 cents for a family with two or more children. The NCB supplement was reduced for families with incomes in excess of $22,397, by 12.2 cents for one child, 22.5 for two children, and 32.1 cents for three or more children. Table 5 shows the income ranges for these benefit clawbacks. The NCB supplement phase-outs place a significant marginal tax on earnings in the $22,750 to approximately $33,325 range and the CCTB phase-out boosts the marginal tax rate by 2.5% for

Table 5: The Marginal Tax Rates under the CCTB in 2002 and 2007

		NCB Supplement		Basic CCTB
Number of Children	MTR	Income Range (2002 dollars)	MTR	Income Range (2002 dollars)
			2002	
1	0.122	$22,397 to $32,995	0.025	$32,960 to $88,117
2	0.225	$22,397 to $32,975	0.05	$32,960 to $83,557
3	0.321	$22,750 to $33,955	0.05	$32,960 to $108,356
			2007	
1	0.122	$18,297 to $32,995	0.025	$32,960 to $88,117
2	0.225	$20,175 to $32,975	0.05	$32,960 to $83,557
3	0.321	$20,839 to $33,955	0.05	$32,960 to $108,356

Notes: Calculations based on the assumption of one child under seven years and a 2% annual rate of inflation until 2007. The assumed values of the NCB supplement in 2007, based on information contained Table 4.1, page 94 of the budget are $1,972 for the first child, $1,745 for the second child, and $1,651 for the third and subsequent children. This implies that the inflation-adjusted NCB supplement will increase in real $500 per child. All other parameters are assumed to be fully indexed to inflation.

single-child families and by 5.0% for two-child families in roughly the $33,000 to $85,000 range. For a family of three children, the marginal tax rate is increased by 5%, up to $108,356.

The marginal tax rates implicit in the CCTB program, combined with the marginal tax rates from the rest of the personal tax system and social insurance financing system, may significantly weaken earning incentives. Figure 5 shows that the NCB supplement phase-out was the largest component of the federal marginal tax rates faced by a single-earner family with two children at the $25,000 and $30,000 income levels in 2002. The total federal marginal tax rates at these income levels are in the 45 to 50% range. Figure 6 shows that the combined federal and Ontario marginal tax rates on a single-earner family with two children in Ontario were 60% at $30,000 and 55% at $35,000. On incomes of $65,000 and over, the marginal tax rates in Ontario exceeded 45%.

Are the marginal tax rates on low-income families too high? Should the marginal tax rates increase or decrease as income rises if we want to achieve redistribution with a minimal distortion to individuals' labour supply decisions? These are complex issues that have been the subject of many research papers.[4] Basically, a tax-transfer system that achieves a significant amount of redistribution to lower income households can either impose high marginal tax rates on low-income households through "targeted" benefits with high clawback rates or with high marginal tax rates on high-income households that finance "universal" benefits. The optimal tax rate structure depends on the responsiveness of earnings to marginal and average tax rates at different income levels. The simulations in Slemrod, Yitahaki and Mayshar (1994) suggests that if labour supply elasticities are constant across income groups, then marginal tax rates should decline with income because the distortions in labour supply decisions by high-income individuals are more costly than similar percentage distortions by lower-income individuals. If earnings by high-income individuals are more responsive to marginal tax rates than they are for lower-income individuals, as a study of US taxpayers by Gruber and Saez (2002) indicates, than the case for declining marginal tax rates is even stronger. Thus, the existence of high marginal tax rates at relatively low income levels does not necessarily imply we have a perverse marginal tax rate

---

[4]A summary of the issues is contained in Smart (2000).

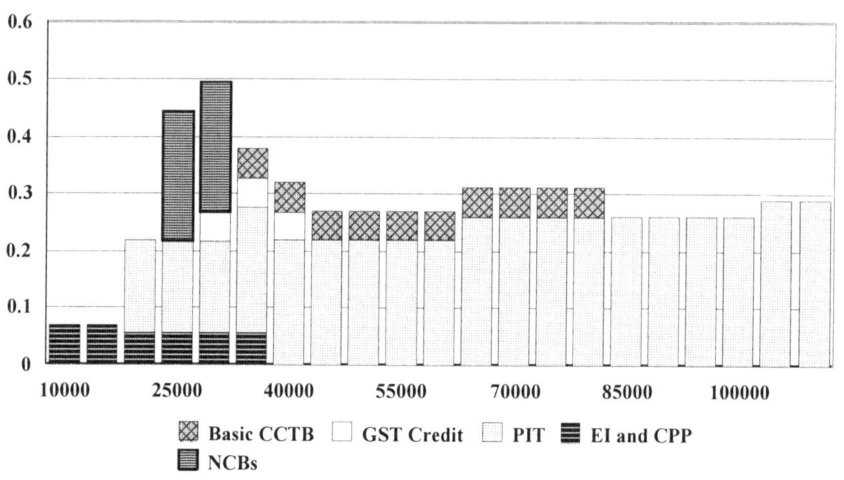

Figure 5: Federal Marginal Tax Rates on a One-Earner Family with Two Children in 2002

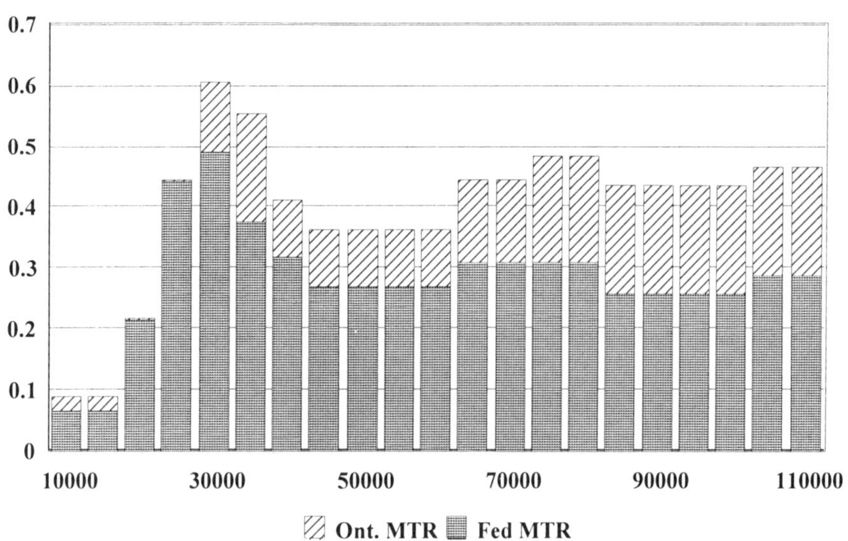

Figure 6: Marginal Tax Rates on a One-Earner Family with Two Children in Ontario in 2002

   Bev Dahlby

structure. But how high is too high? This question can only be answered by econometric studies of the degree to which labour market choices (hours of work, retirement, labour force participation, occupation, and fringe benefits) are being distorted. We certainly need more empirical studies on these issues in order to assess whether the current marginal tax rate structure is out of whack.

How have the earnings incentives faced by single-earner families with children in Ontario changed since 1994? As in the previous section, we compare the marginal tax rate in 2002 with the marginal tax rate faced by a family in 1994 with the same real (inflation adjusted) income. Figure 7 shows that marginal tax rates went down at most income levels between 1994 and 2002, but they increased for families in the $25,000–30,000 income range. This uptick in marginal tax rate was mainly due to the increase in the phase-out rate of the NCB supplement from 10% to 22.5%. However, the federal increases in the marginal tax rates in this income range were to a large degree offset by reductions in the marginal tax rates imposed by the Ontario government. The figure also shows that for incomes above $50,000 marginal tax rates have fallen by just under ten percentage points and that the federal government and the Ontario government were equally responsible for the reductions in the marginal tax rates.

Figure 8 shows that average tax rates on a family in Ontario under the tax-transfer system were lower in 2002 than in 1994 at all income levels and that a family earning less than $30,000 in 2002 had negative average tax rates, that is, they received more in transfers than they paid in personal taxes and social insurance contributions. Figure 9 shows that the largest reductions in the average tax rates were at the bottom and at the top of the income distribution. This is different from the pattern we saw for single individuals in Ontario. The main reason for the difference was the enhancement in the NCB supplement.

Thus, the federal government was largely responsible for the reduction in the average tax rates for low-income families, and the Ontario government was largely responsible for the reductions in the average tax rates for high-income families. Average federal tax rates increased at the $35,000 income level, largely because of the increase in total social insurance contributions, and the reduction in average federal tax rates increased slightly as income

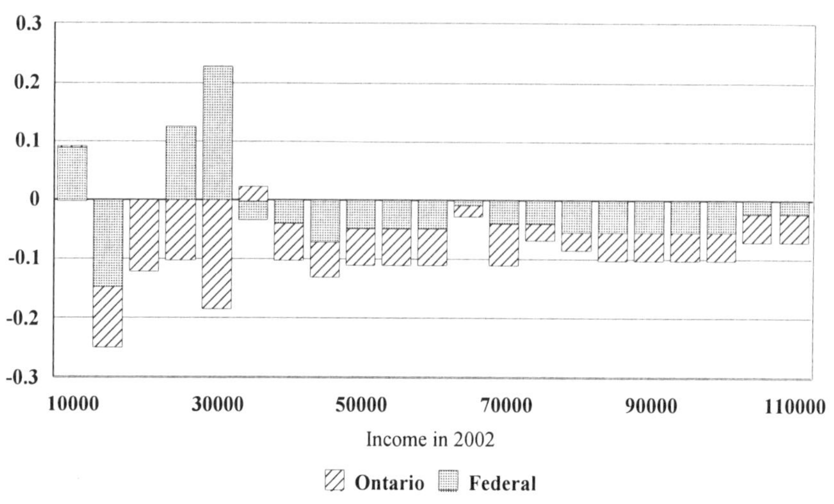

Figure 7: Changes in the Marginal Tax Rates on a Single-Earner Family with Two Children in Ontario Between 1994 and 2002

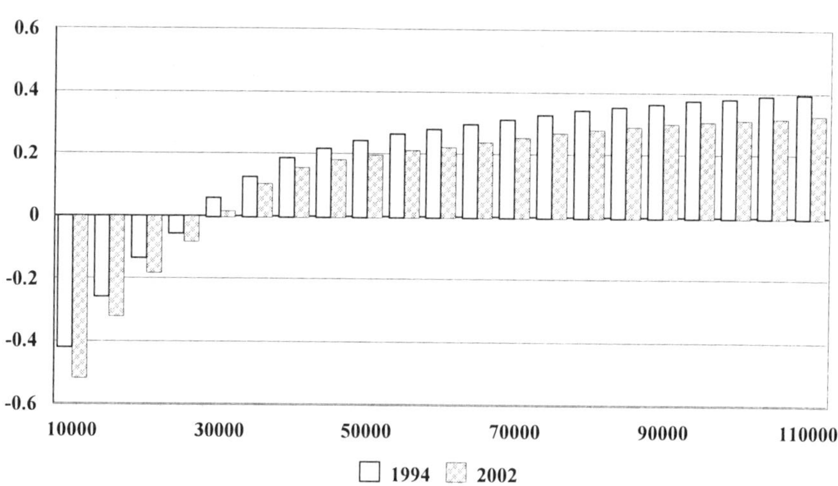

Figure 8: Average Tax-Transfer Rates for a Single-Earner Family with Two Children in Ontario in 1994 and 2002

Bev Dahlby

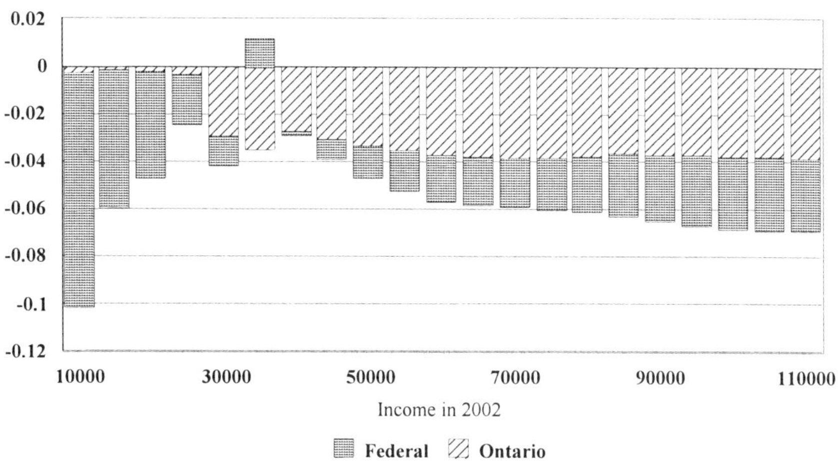

rose above this level. Therefore the impact of federal tax policies over this income range could be considered regressive. Overall, the combined effects of the tax policies of the two levels of government had an ambiguous effect on the progressivity of the tax-transfer system.

Turning to the future, a significant increase in the NCB supplement was announced in the February 2003 budget, and the total cost of the program is projected to increase by $965 million by 2007. Based on information contained in Table 4.1 of the budget, the NCB supplement will increase by 2007 to $1,972 for one child, $1,745 for a second child, and $1,651 for the third and subsequent children assuming a 2.0% annual rate of inflation. These changes represent an inflation-adjusted increase in the NCB supplement of about $500 per child.

Table 5 shows the projected phase-outs ranges for the NCB supplement will increase in 2007, assuming that the other parameters of the system are fully indexed to inflation. The increase in the NCB supplement by approximately $500 will mean that the phase-out income level for the NCB will have to be reduced to avoid an overlap in the phase-out NCB supplement and basic CCTB phase-out ranges. The reduction in the phase-out income level will be approximately equal to 500/cbr where cbr is the clawback rate.

In other words, for a family with one child, the phase-out income level will decline by $4,100 to approximately $18,297. For a family with two children, the phase-out income level will decline by $2,222 to approximately $20,175. For families with three or more children the phase-out income level will decline by $1,558 to $20,839. This means that more families at lower income levels will be subject to higher marginal tax rates, which will lower their earnings incentives. Whether or not the NCB will change in this way, or whether there will be some other parameter changes, is unclear because there is a call for a general review of the phase-out rates and income levels in view of the increase in the NCB supplements.

Those responsible for redesigning the NCB supplement will face tough choices. If they maintain the current income levels at which the phase-outs start (in real terms), then more higher income families will be eligible to receive the NCB supplement, and there will be an overlap in the NCB supplement and basic CCTB phase-out ranges so that families between $36,388 to (roughly) $41,600 income range will be subject to a combined marginal tax rate under the CCTB/NCB of 14.5%, 27.5%, or 37.1%, depending on the number of children. To avoid the overlap and maintain the current income phase-out range, the phase-out rates for the NCB supplement would have to increase to 16.9% for one child, 31.9% for two children and 46.0% for three or more, but the cure would be worse than the disease. Alternatively, the income level at which the basic CCTB is phased out could be increased to around $41,250, but this would be a costly measure because more families would qualify for the full benefit and more high-income families would receive partial benefits. For example, a family with two children with an income of $97,120 in 2007 would receive some basic CCTB, and be subject to the additional 5.0% marginal tax rate on earnings.[5]

These calculations illustrate the basic dilemma in designing negative income tax programs: if the benefit level is increased, holding the phase-out rate constant, more families will qualify for benefits, the total cost of the program will increase, and marginal tax rates will increase. Alternatively, if the phase-out rates are increased to restrict recipients to the same income range, the marginal tax rates for current recipients will increase sharply,

---

[5]Moreover, since the income test is based on family earnings, both parents will be subject to this additional marginal tax rate.

                                                          Bev Dahlby

lowering their earnings incentives. Designing income transfer programs requires tough choices.

Savings Incentives

In the February 2003 budget, the government announced that the limits on RRSP contributions will increase to $14,500 in 2003, $15,500 in 2004, $16,500 in 2005, and $18,000 in 2006. In subsequent years, the limit will be indexed to average wages. The maximum pension benefit per year of service for defined benefit Registered Pension Plans (RPPs) will increase to $1,833 in 2004 and $2,000 in 2005, and then will be indexed to average wages in subsequent years.

As noted above, the Canadian personal tax system has elements of both a consumption and a classical income tax system. It is a consumption tax system to the extent that the return to savings is not taxed if savings is in the form of contributions to RRSPs or RPPs, (where the contributions are tax deductible, no tax is levied while investment returns accumulate in the fund, and withdrawals are taxed), or if it is used to purchase assets, such as housing, out of after-tax income where the return on the asset is not taxed. In the case of housing, mortgage and principal payments are made out of after-tax income while the return on owner-occupied housing (the implicit rental income and capital gains on a principal residence) are not taxed. Housing is the largest single component of most individuals' net worth. On the other hand, the return on savings that are held outside RRSPs and RPPs is taxed, and therefore the system retains some of the characteristics of a classical income tax where labour earnings and investment income are both taxed.

We are already three-quarters of the way to a consumption tax system (Poddar and English, 1999). Increasing the RRSP/RPP contribution limits, which have been maintained at $13,500 and are now lower in real terms than they were in the mid-1970s, will shift the system even further in the direction of a consumption tax system. Many Canadian economists have endorsed this shift toward a consumption tax system on both equity and efficiency grounds. The arguments for moving toward a consumption tax system cannot be fully discussed here. See, for example, Mintz (2001); Kesselman and Poschmann (2001); and Dahlby (2003).

Given that we want to shift the personal tax system more toward a consumption tax system, is increasing the RRSP/RPP contribution limit the best way to achieve this goal? While the increase in the contribution limits is overdue, and some increase is necessary to restore the real contribution limits, it may not be the best way to expand retirement savings incentives in the future. The reason is that RRSP/RPPs have two shortcomings. First, when the tax rate at which contributions are made is different from the tax rate at which withdrawals are taxed, the return on savings can be either taxed or subsidized. For example, if contributions are deducted at a 30% marginal tax rate and withdrawals of contributions and accumulated investment income are taxed at a 40% marginal tax rate, then the RRSP system can impose a very high rate of tax on savings because the individual's assets are taxed at a 10% rate. The opposite, of course, occurs when the tax rate on withdrawals is less than the tax rate at which contributions were deducted. Most people seem to assume that their tax rates will be lower when they withdraw their savings because of the progressivity of the current tax system and the anticipated expected decline in their income in retirement. But, who can predict what tax rates will be 20 or 30 years in the future? In any event, under a consumption tax system the return to savings should not be taxed, but it should also not be subsidized.

The second problem is that individuals who save for their retirement in the form of an RRSP/RPP may lose some income-tested benefits in retirement, such as GIS or seniors housing benefits. This problem would have been even more severe under the Seniors Benefit. Less than 17% of individuals with incomes under $20,000 contributed to RRSPs in 1999, and less than 50% of individuals with incomes below $40,000 contributed (see Statistics Canada, 2003, Table 4–7, p. 90). The low participation rate in RRSPs by individuals in these income ranges is in part due to the difficulty that low-income people have in saving for retirement, but also due to their recognition that any retirement savings will be subject to a high clawback rate. So the RRSP/RPP contains some serious flaws with regard to the implementation of a consumption tax system.

How should tax policy proceed in this area? Kesselman and Poschmann (2001) have proposed an alternative savings instrument that would overcome the problems that afflict the RRSPs. They call their mechanism a tax-prepaid savings plan (TPSP). Basically, a TPSP would extend our current treatment of owner-occupied housing to other assets. Contributions to a TPSP would be made out of after-tax income. Investment income earned within the plan and withdrawals would not be taxed. The return on savings would not be affected by variations in the tax rates that an individual faces over time, and an individual's eligibility for income-related retirement pensions and benefits would not be affected because withdrawals would not be recorded as income. Another advantage of the TPSP is that it does not involve any immediate loss of tax revenue for governments because con-tributions are made out of after-tax income. Tax revenues might decline in the future, to the extent that TPSPs increase the amount investment income that is not subject to tax, and the system would retain some of the vestiges of a classical income tax system to the extent that there are limits on contributions to TPSPs and RPPs/RRSPs.

The TPSP proposal is a potentially useful addition to our personal tax system, and it seems to have caught the attention of the government. In the 2003 budget, the government indicates that it will "examine whether tax pre-paid savings plans could be a useful and appropriate mechanism to improve the tax treatment of savings and to provide additional savings opportunities for Canadians" (Canada. Department of Finance, 2003a, p. 140). I anticipate that that review will produce a favourable assessment of TPSPs and that they will be introduced to supplement the RRSP/RPP mechanism for providing savings incentives for Canadians.

Business Taxation

In the October 2000 *Economic Statement and Budget Update*, the federal government started a gradual reduction in corporate income tax rates for non-manufacturing and processing activities, from 28% in 2000 to 21% in 2004. These reductions, combined with corporate rate reduction at the provincial level, have dramatically reduced average statutory corporate tax rates in Canada.[6] See Figure 10. Our average corporate tax has gone from

---

[6]However, the federal corporate surtax equivalent to 1.12 percentage points still applies.

Figure 10: Corporate Tax Rates in Canada and the United States

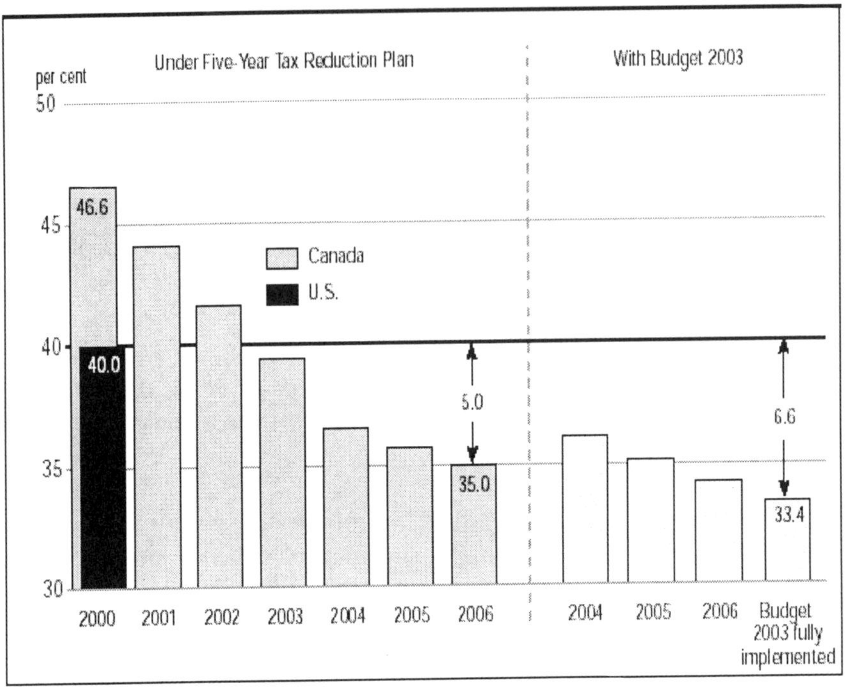

Source: Canada. Department of Finance (2003a, p. 145).

being more than six percentage points above the US average in 2000 to slightly below the US rate in 2003. By 2006, it is projected to be five percentage points below the US rate. The elimination of the federal capital tax on non-financial institutions, announced in the 2003 budget, will help to widen this competitive advantage vis-à-vis the United States.

The federal rate reductions will bring the corporate income tax rate on the service sector down to the same level as the manufacturing sector. This "levelling of the playing field" will be further enhanced by the announcement in the February 2003 budget that the federal government will reduce the tax rate on the resource sector to 27% in 2003 and to 21% in 2007.[7] As

---

[7]The rate is scheduled to decline to 26% in 2004, 25% in 2005, 23% in 2006, and 21% in 2007.

Bev Dahlby

part of this restructuring of resource sector taxation, the 25% Resource Allowance will be phased-out and deductibility of provincial resource royalties will be phased-in.

Thus, by 2007, the federal government will have re-shaped the corporate income tax rate structure in line with two themes for business tax reform articulated in the 1998 Mintz committee report — a corporate income tax structure that is internationally competitive and that provides a level tax playing field for investments across the sectors of the Canadian economy. In that report, we argued that Canada needs a competitive statutory rate because the level of direct investment by foreign multinationals in Canada is very substantial, and Canadian-based multinationals now have significant direct investments in foreign countries. The reduction in the statutory rate reduces the marginal effective rate of tax on real investments, which helps to stimulate real investment in Canada. In addition, it helps prevent the erosion of the Canadian corporate income tax base through debt placement, transfer pricing, and other strategies that can be pursued by corporations in order to minimize their global tax bill. Levelling the playing field by imposing a common rate of taxation on corporations in the manufacturing and processing, service, and resource sectors will lessen the tax-induced distortions in investment across these sectors and greatly reduce the compliance and administration costs that arise when different forms of income are taxed at different rates. While these reforms will help to level the playing field, further reforms are still needed, especially with regard to the taxation of the financial sector.

Capital Taxes

The elimination of the federal capital tax on non-financial institutions by 2008 is a particularly welcome reform because capital taxes increase the cost of capital, thereby reducing incentives to invest. A study of the capital tax by Ernst & Young (2002a) showed that the federal and Ontario capital taxes on a $1 million investment in a pipeline is equivalent to a 5.32% excise tax on the purchase price of the pipeline. No one, to my knowledge, advocates imposing excise taxes on capital goods. Indeed, one of the advantages of the GST is that it eliminated the taxation of business inputs that occurred under the old federal sales tax (the Manufacturers Sales Tax). Imposing a capital tax reverses some of the efficiency gains that we obtained by adopting the GST. Capital taxes also place a particularly heavy burden on the capital-intensive sectors of the economy. Another Ernst & Young (2002b) study found that 40% of the capital tax burden fell on the resource and manufacturing sectors, even though they account for less than 25% of GDP. Finally, capital taxes are independent of a firm's profitability, and firms have to pay the tax even if they are in a loss position when their financial resources are already stretched. The Ernst & Young study found that 55% of capital taxes were collected from firms that were in a loss position in 1998.

While elimination of the federal capital tax is welcome news, two further reforms are required — elimination of the provincial capital taxes and elimination of the capital taxes imposed on financial institutions by the federal and provincial governments. Figure 11 shows that six provinces levied general capital taxes in 2003, at an average rate of 0.425%, almost twice the federal capital tax rate of 0.225%; and that all of the provinces, except Alberta, imposed special capital tax rates on financial institutions. In Ontario and Quebec, these rates are 0.90% and 1.45% respectively, (or two to three times the provincial general rate) and in the other provinces the rates on financial institutions vary between 3 and 4%, well in excess of the 1.25% federal capital tax rate on financial institutions capital (the Large Financial Institutions Capital Tax). The relative importance of provincial capital taxes on the financial institutions is illustrated by the following revenue figures. In 2002, the six largest banks paid $769.8 in provincial income taxes and $469.6 million in provincial capital taxes.[8] They also paid $1,948.9 million in federal income taxes, but only $69.5 million in federal capital taxes.

The federal government has long argued that the provinces have imposed high capital taxes (and payroll taxes) because they are deductible under the federal corporate income tax whereas provincial corporate income taxes are not deductible under the federal corporate income tax. Thus, part of the cost of imposing a provincial capital tax is shifted to the federal government and therefore to taxpayers across the country. Indeed, Jacques Parizeau admitted, during a lecture that he gave in one of my classes at the University of

---

[8]Calculations based on data in Table DB248B available from on the Canadian Bankers Association Web site.

                                                          Bev Dahlby

Figure 11: Provincial Capital Tax Rates in 2003

Percent

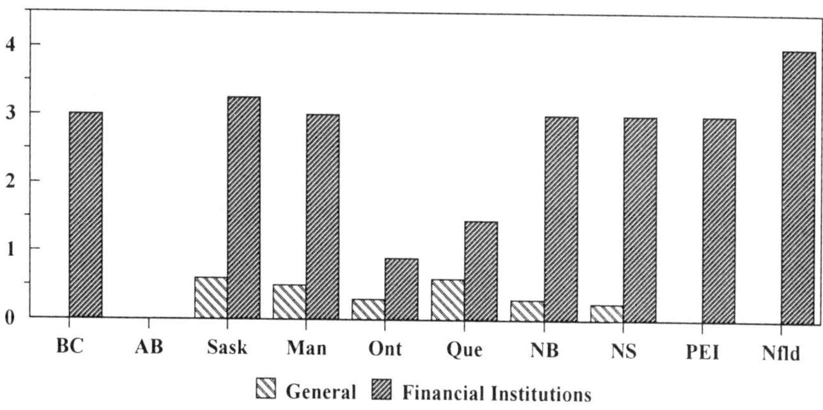

Source: Canada. Department of Finance (2003a, p. 59).

Alberta, that the primary reason why he increased capital and payroll taxes in Quebec when he was the provincial finance minister was their deductibility under the federal CIT. The federal government has for a number of years warned the provinces that it would not allow the deductibility of any further capital or payroll tax increases.

The provincial capital taxes create the same disincentives for investment as the federal capital taxes by raising the cost of capital to the firm. Provincial variations in capital tax rates distort investment patterns across provinces, leading to a less efficient allocation of capital for the country as a whole. In addition, because there are significant differences in the way the capital tax bases are defined in different provinces, provincial capital taxes impose large compliance costs on corporations that operate in several provinces (see McQuillan and Cochrane, 1996).

It would have been desirable to have both the federal and provincial governments eliminate their capital taxes. In its March 27, 2003 budget, the province of Ontario announced that it planned to reduce its capital tax so that it will be eliminated in 2007 when the federal capital tax is also eliminated. While this coordinated elimination of the capital tax is good news it is not clear that the other provinces will follow suit. In its June 12, 2003 budget, Quebec suspended a previously announced reduction in the provincial capital tax. (Instead, the Quebec budget cut a wide range of business tax subsidies.) Achieving a coordinated reduction in the provincial capital taxes may require leadership on the part of the federal government, and it may need to compensate the provincial governments for the loss of provincial tax revenues, perhaps by giving them greater access to other shared tax fields, such as the personal income tax or the consumption taxes.[9] An agreement along these lines should be pursued by both levels of government.

Taxing the Banks

The banks are one of the least popular institutions in Canada. The public views them as large, uncaring institutions that make huge profits because they are part of a cozy oligopoly that limits competition in retail banking services, credit cards, and other financial services. Whether or not it is deserved, this perception makes imposing high taxes on banks politically popular. But, is it wise? Over the period, 1992–98 (the longest period for which comparable data can be obtained), income taxes as a percentage of positive adjusted profits were 28.2% for the financial sector and 26.2% for the non-financial sector.[10] While the rate of taxation for the financial sector as a whole does not seem to be terribly out of line, the average tax rate on banks, 37.9%, is significantly above the tax rates imposed on the non-financial sector. McKenzie (2000) has shown that the marginal effective tax rate on the cost of intermediating an incremental loan is over 70%. The economic consequences of the high rate of taxation on the Canadian banking sector needs to be carefully considered.

High taxes on the Canadian banking industry likely reduce investment and ultimately the banking services that are provided to the Canadian public. Even if the banking industry is an uncompetitive oligopoly, it is likely that a significant portion of the tax burden is shifted forward to borrowers or

---

[9]An alternative to provincial capital and corporate taxes proposed by Bird and McKenzie (2001) is a provincial business value-added tax.

[10]Calculations are based on data from Cansim II Table 180–0001.

                                                        Bev Dahlby

backward to depositors. In others words, high capital taxes on the banking sector likely increase the interest rate spread between loans and deposits, reducing domestic savings and investment. The distortionary effects of taxes are even greater for a non-competitive industry because taxes cause the sector, where too few resources are employed in the absence of taxation, to shrink even further. For this reason, non-competitive industries should be taxed at relatively low rates, not high rates. Thus, on efficiency grounds, but perhaps also on equity grounds, a strong case can be made for removing the relatively high tax burden that we currently impose on the banking industry. The implications of our current tax regime on the banking industry need to be thoroughly researched, and if the conclusions of that research support the simple analysis that I have outlined here, then public finance economists are going to have to take on the difficult task of convincing the public that it is in their interest to reduce the taxes on banks.

Taxing the Non-Renewable Resource Sector

The February 2003 budget signalled the end of the Resource Allowance, the reintroduction of the deductibility of provincial royalties on the mining and oil and gas sector, and the reduction in the federal corporate income tax rate to 21% for the mining and oil and gas sector. These measures will only have their full effect in 2008. The Resource Allowance is a deduction equal to 25% of "resource profits", which are defined as revenues derived from the extraction and basic processing of minerals, crude oil, and natural gas minus operating costs and capital cost allowances for these activities. The Resource Allowance has been provided in lieu of the deductibility of provincial royalties on oil and gas and mining taxes since 1975. The federal government at the time argued that the deductibility of resource royalties encouraged the provincial governments to increase their royalties because part of the cost of a royalty increase was borne by the federal government. Over the last decade, the total Resource Allowance provided to the oil and gas sector has been slightly higher than the provincial royalties, and in 2001 they were virtually identical —$10 billion (see Canada. Department of Finance, 2003b, p. 16). (However, within the industry some firms are better off with the Resource Allowance, while others would be better off with royalty deductibility.) In the mining sector, the Resource Royalty has been considerable higher than provincial royalties and mining taxes. For example, in 1998, the Resource Allowance was just over $600 million while provincial royalties and mining taxes were just under $400 million. Over the period, 1990 to 1998, the differential varied between $200 million and $600 million. Thus, the Resource Allowance has lowered the effective rate of tax in the mining sector for a number of years.

In addition to providing an effective tax subsidy to the mining sector, the Resource Allowance also distorted decisions in both the mining and oil and gas sectors because resource profits (on which the Resource Allowance is based) are calculated before the deduction of exploration and development expenditures and interest on debt. This meant that while resource revenues were taxed at a 21% rate, exploration and development expenditures and interest on debt are deducted at a 28% rate, providing a tax subsidy for these types of expenditures. Furthermore, the Resource Allowance mechanism undoubtedly raises administration and compliance costs because a "ring fence" for exploration, development, and basic refining activities has to be defined and enforced so that the Resource Allowance does not apply to the manufacturing and processing activities, such as oil refining, of integrated resource firms.

The phased elimination of the Resource Allowance and the reduction in the corporate income tax rate on the mining and oil and gas sector to the 21% rate that will apply in the other sectors of the economy in 2004 is a beneficial reform that will reduce the administration and compliance costs, reduce inter-industry tax distortions in allocation of capital, and increase the competitiveness of the oil and gas sector. Calculations provided by the Department of Finance indicate that the marginal effective tax rate on investment in the oil and gas sector will decline from 13.6% to 8.7%, which will be below the marginal effective tax rate on a similar investment in Texas (see Canada. Department of Finance, 2003b, p. 23).

Will deductibility induce the provinces to increase their royalty rates? This seems unlikely given that the provinces have to ensure that their royalty regimes maintain the competitiveness of the mining and oil and gas industries. In addition, the royalty regimes are now more likely to automatically increase the share of resource revenues going to the provinces as oil and natural gas prices increase. So it is unlikely that the return to deductibility will lead to escalation of provincial royalties.

                                                  Bev Dahlby

Because the Resource Allowance was more generous than the royalty deductibility for the mining sector, these reforms would increase the level of taxation on the mining sector. However, to soften the blow, the federal government has introduced a new 10% tax credit for qualifying mineral exploration. (This is in addition to the already generous tax treatment of the mining industry's exploration and development costs.) The marginal effective tax rate on investment in the mining sector is also projected to decrease as a result of these reforms.

The overall thrust of this reform is positive and satisfies the two principles which guided the recommendations for tax reform in the Mintz report: it lowers effective tax rates to make Canadian industries internationally competitive, and it provides a more uniform tax treatment of business income across the sectors of the Canadian economy.

An Overall Assessment

The overall direction of the tax reform measures of the Chrétien government has been the right one. The CPP/QPP has been put on a financially viable path, although too much of the adjustment was made on the tax side. Marginal tax rates have been reduced for most taxpayers, and while low-income families with children now face higher marginal tax rates, they receive more financial support from the state. Full indexation of the personal income tax system, to prevent bracket creep, has been restored. Long overdue increases in the contribution limits to RRSPs and RPPs will soon be implemented. The business tax reforms have made the corporate tax regime in Canada more competitive vis-à-vis the United States and have produced a more uniform taxation of investment across the various sectors of the Canadian economy. There have been no major policy blunders, such as the introduction of mortgage interest deductibility that is being touted by Ernie Eves, former premier of Ontario, but there have been policy failures — the Seniors Benefits — and missed opportunities — experience-rating of EI premiums. The pace of tax policy change was understandably slow in the early part of the Chrétien government because of the necessity of getting the deficit under control, but in its recent budgets the government could have been more aggressive, implemented the tax cuts more quickly, and put less emphasis on expenditure enhancements. Overall, I would give the Chrétien government's tax policy performance a solid B.

While the foundations for a fair and efficient tax system have been put in place, much more work needs to be done. The funding of the EI program has to be addressed, perhaps through a general payroll tax. The clawback rates and income ranges for the Canada Child Tax Benefit and Old Age Security will have to be reassessed. There is still the need to bring marginal tax rates on earnings down at all income levels. Alternatives to the RRSP/RPPs to promote savings for retirement have to be explored. The tax-prepaid savings plan is a promising option. While corporate income tax rates have come down, they are still somewhat above the rates imposed by other countries, such as the United Kingdom, Mexico, and Australia. The new international "norm" for the corporate income tax seems to be around 30%, with some countries such as Ireland significantly below this norm. Thus, there will be further pressure for corporate income tax rate reductions. The high rates of capital taxation imposed by the provinces, especially on the banking industry, need to be rectified.

A tax system is always a work in progress. In that sense, it can never be someone's legacy.

References

Bird, R. and K.J. McKenzie (2001), *Taxing Business: A Provincial Affair?* C.D. Howe Institute Commentary No. 154 (Toronto: C.D. Howe Institute).

Canada. Department of Finance (2003a), *The Budget Plan 2003* (Ottawa: Department of Finance).

___________ (2003b), "Improving the Income Taxation of the Resource Sector in Canada", background paper to budget (Ottawa: Department of Finance).

Dahlby, B. (1994), "The Distortionary Effect of Rising Taxes", in R. Robson and W. Scarth (eds.), *Deficit Reduction: What Pain; What Gain?* (Toronto: C.D. Howe Institute), 44–72.

___________ (2003), "Restructuring the Canadian Tax Mix by Changing the Direct/Indirect Tax Mix", in H. Grubel (ed.), *Tax Reform in Canada: Our Path to Greater Prosperity* (Vancouver: Fraser Institute), 77–108.

Davies, J.B. (1998), *Marginal Tax Rates in Canada: High and Getting Higher*, C.D. Howe Institute Commentary No. 103 (Toronto: C.D. Howe Institute).

Davies, J.B. and J. Zhang (1996), "Measuring Marginal Income Tax Rates for Individuals in Canada: Averages and Distributions over Time", *Canadian Journal of Economics* 29(4), 959–975.

Ernst & Young (2002a), "Capital Taxes: Penalizing Investment in Canada", *Tax Policy Bulletin* (Fall).

__________ (2002b), "Who Pays the Capital Tax?" *Tax Policy Bulletin* (Spring).

Gruber, J. and E. Saez (2002), "The Elasticity of Taxable Income: Evidence and Implications", *Journal of Public Economics* 84(1), 1–32.

Kesselman, J. (1997), *General Payroll Taxes: Economics, Politics, and Design* (Toronto: Canadian Tax Foundation).

Kesselman, J. and F. Poschmann (2001), *A New Option for Retirement Savings: Tax-Prepaid Savings Plans*, C.D. Howe Institute Commentary No. 149 (Toronto: C.D. Howe Institute).

McKenzie, K.J. (2000), "Taxing Banks", ATAX Discussion Paper No. 1 (Sydney: Australian Taxation Studies Program, Faculty of Law, University of New South Wales).

Macnaughton, A., T. Matthews and J. Pittman (1998), " 'Stealth Tax Rates': Effective versus Statutory Personal Marginal Tax Rates", *Canadian Tax Journal* 46(5), 1029–1066.

McQuillan, P.E. and E.C. Cochrane (1996), "Capital Tax Issues", Working Paper No. 96–8 (Ottawa: Technical Committee on Business Taxation, Department of Finance).

Mintz, J.M. (2001), "Taxing Future Consumption", in P. Grady and A. Sharpe (eds.), *The State of Economics in Canada: Festschrift in Honour of David Slater* (Kingston: John Deutsch Institute for the Study of Economic Policy, Queen's University).

Poddar, S. and M. English (1999), "Canadian Taxation of Personal Investment Income", *Canadian Tax Journal* 47(5), 1270–1304.

Robson, W. (2000), "Precarious Pyramid: The Economics and Politics of the CPP", in P. Boothe (ed.), *A Separate Pension Plan for Alberta*, Western Studies in Economic Policy No. 5 (Edmonton: University of Alberta Press), 1–22.

Slemrod, J., S. Yitahaki and J. Mayshar (1994), "The Optimal Two-Bracket Linear Income Tax", *Journal of Public Economics* 53(2), 269–290.

Smart, M. (2000), "How Do Recent Tax Reforms Affect the Behaviour and Welfare of Families?" in P.A.R. Hobson and T.A. Wilson (eds.), *The 2000 Federal Budget: Retrospect and Prospect*, Policy Forum Series No. 37 (Kingston: John Deutsch Institute for the Study of Economic Policy, Queen's University).

Statistics Canada (2003), *Canada's Retirement Income Programs: A Statistical Overview (1990-2000)*, Cat. No. 74–507–XIE (Ottawa: Supply and Services Canada).

UNFINISHED BUSINESS: A Tax System for the 21st Century

Jonathan R. Kesselman, Simon Fraser University

Introduction

The 2003 federal budget continues the tax cuts and reforms undertaken in a series of budgets under the Chrétien government. When viewed individually, these changes may not appear very significant, but taken together and in combination with provincial tax changes, they amount to the first stage of a major transformation of the Canadian tax system. Bev Dahlby has provided a skillful analysis of the key changes and insightful assessment of their strengths and shortcomings. Tax policy undeniably involves complex judgements and often hidden personal values, yet I find agreement with much more of Dahlby's findings than dissent. However, my comments here will focus on areas of tax policy where I offer a different or supplemental perspective. Then I shall briefly sketch my vision of the tax design needed to complete the cuts and reforms initiated thus far by the federal and provincial governments in order to create a tax system truly attuned to the needs of the twenty-first century.

Over the past eight years, tax cuts and reforms at the provincial level have been as important as federal tax moves. This can be seen in several of Dahlby's figures, with Ontario used to show the provincial changes in personal taxes along with the federal changes. The provinces have in fact played a leading role

---

I thank Bev Dahlby for useful suggestions on an earlier draft. This paper reflects tax developments as of Spring 2003.

in major respects. Pressures by the provinces for greater flexibility in their personal tax rate structures led to the TONI system, and Ontario planned to cut its capital gains inclusion rate to 50% before the federal government acted. Ontario and Alberta began their personal tax rate cuts well before the federal government. Cuts in and abolition of the corporate capital tax for non-financial institutions were led by British Columbia and Quebec and followed by the feds in their 2003 budget. Moreover, most provinces moved ahead of the feds in cutting tax rates and raising the deduction level for small corporations. Federal cuts in the general corporate tax rate have also been equalled in the plans of several major provinces.

Alternative Views on Recent Policy

Financing Employment Insurance

Employment Insurance (EI) has been used by the federal government as a large source of general revenue since the mid-1990s, as the premium revenues have consistently outstripped program benefit costs. The EI surpluses have continued despite a gradual lowering of premium rates and some benefit enhancements in recent years. Dahlby argues that the linkage between a worker's premium costs and his or her expected EI benefits is so weak, and the program so highly redistributive, that the pretense of social insurance should be abandoned in EI finance.[1] This situation might support either general revenue financing of EI benefits or converting the EI premiums into a general payroll tax. The latter would be consistent with a desired shift of the tax system toward greater reliance on consumption and labour income bases. Dahlby expresses a preference for removing the earnings ceiling from EI premiums and using it as a general payroll tax; he further suggests that levying the tax solely on employees would avoid any potential hiring disincentives for employers.

Some practical and perceptual problems would arise if the EI premiums were converted to a general payroll tax on all earnings of all employees. First, this

---

[1]Note that similar arguments were used by the federal government in the late 1980s in converting the tax deduction for employee EI premiums to a non-refundable tax credit.

                                                    Jonathan R. Kesselman

approach would exclude from tax liability the self-employed, entrepreneurs, and investors, many at higher incomes. Since one goal supported by Dahlby is to improve the progressivity of EI finance, this approach would fall short. Why should only higher-earning employees be shouldered with more of the program's financial burden but not other higher income individuals? Second, without a ceiling on taxable earnings, it would be difficult to justify a system of EI benefits that also imposed a maximum (currently 55% of maximum insurable earnings of $39,000). Third, public support for the EI program might diminish over time if there were not at least a plausible linkage between the insured worker's previous earnings level and period and the prospective benefit entitlement. Moreover, without the premium financing and a nominal benefit linkage, stronger pressures might emerge for new redistributive provisions in the EI program. While more redistribution may be supportable, the EI program is not necessarily the best delivery framework.

A better solution to EI finance — and there may never be a politically acceptable perfect solution — would be one proposed over 20 years ago by industry groups.[2] That is, the overtly social functions of the EI program should be financed out of general revenues. However, the federal government is constitutionally constrained in its ability to pursue some of these functions outside the EI program. As far as politically practicable, the regular jobless benefits should be tied more closely to the individual worker's previous contributions and work spell. This could entail such contentious reforms as attenuating regionally redistributive elements of the benefit structure. The experience rating of the premiums themselves might be, as Dahlby suggests, a political non-starter even though supported consistently by economic analysts over the years. Still, it might be possible to proceed by separating the fishing benefits from the regular EI program, since they are the most regionally concentrated and pose the greatest resistance to reform. The industries that consistently receive the largest EI subsidies — construction and resources — are much more regionally dispersed and might not muster effective opposition to experience-rating. Alternatively, it might be feasible to introduce premium differentials by industry sector. This would at least reduce the cross-industry *and* cross-regional subsidies of the program, even if it would not achieve

---

[2]See Kesselman (1983) for discussion of financing of "special benefits" under the UI program (pp. 75–76) as well as experience rating premiums (chapter 9), the UI account operations (chapter 4), and premium rate setting (chapter 8).

incentives for reduced layoffs at the individual firm level. Differential rating of premiums is common in provincial workers' compensation programs.

The 2003 federal budget announced that, "The Government will consult on a new EI rate-setting regime for 2005 and beyond, based on the principles of transparency and of balancing premium revenues with expected program costs" (Canada. Department of Finance, 2003, p. 26).[3] One wonders whether this exercise is mainly to allow the government to bury forever the large cumulative surplus of the EI account that has greatly assisted budgetary balance in recent years. The 2003 budget sets EI premiums for 2004 at a rate that will balance forecast program revenues and costs for that year; it does not choose a lower rate that would allow the program's massive cumulative surplus to decline to a more realistic level. Future provisions should have EI premium rates set by a fully independent body based on projections over a sufficient span to minimize pro-cyclical impacts. It might also appear attractive to revert to separate EI program accounting, like that before the 1986 merger with the federal budget (and current CPP practice). However, the merged treatment presents a more accurate view of the overall federal fiscal stance.

Financing Public Pensions

Canada Pension Plan (CPP) premium rates have been raised sharply over the past six years to ensure long-term financial viability of the program. The combined employee-employer rate reached its ultimate peak of 9.9% just this year. Nevertheless, the maximum total premiums paid by a higher earner for CPP are less than one-fourth the corresponding maximum paid in the United States for social security and medicare by a high earner, even when the exchange rate is computed by purchasing power parity. This difference is a combination of a higher total US rate (15.3%) and a much higher taxable ceiling (US$87,000 versus C$39,900 less a C$3,500 exemption). Nevertheless, the US program is widely agreed to be facing chronic unfunded future liabilities that will require still higher premium rates (or benefit cuts) in future years. Indeed, Canada's premiums for public pensions are among the lowest of

---

[3]Further criteria for the new regime were detailed as relative stability of premium rates, counter-cyclical impact, and the use of independent expert advice (Canada. Department of Finance, 2003, p. 183).

 Jonathan R. Kesselman

the advanced economies, and the raising of rates to a long-run sustainable level was, as Dahlby states, an important achievement of the Chrétien and Martin administration.

The hidden weakness in funding Canadian public pensions arises for Old Age Security (OAS), a general-revenue-financed demogrant program for seniors. The United States has no counterpart program; its social security retirement benefit structure embodies a comparable redistributive element. The impending explosion of the elderly population in Canada, in conjunction with a declining workforce, will pose heavy burdens for future public finances. Dahlby discusses the Chrétien government's failed attempt to address this problem through its Seniors Benefit plan, which would have placed a steeper clawback on OAS from middle-income seniors. He asserts that "we will have to re-address the reform of the OAS in coming years". While I agree that the OAS is likely to pose a significant burden for future governments, it is not clear that a strengthened clawback on benefits is necessarily the best solution. So long as current working-age individuals can expect to receive the OAS, they can save less privately for their retirement. The problem from the economy's standpoint is that a failure to pre-fund future OAS liabilities will reduce aggregate savings, thereby retarding growth, and shift the burden to future workers.

One solution to financing future OAS liabilities would be for the feds to establish a special fund, perhaps as an adjunct to the CPP, financed by current taxes. It is true that these incremental taxes would exert some disincentive effects and efficiency costs. But they would put the burden of future OAS on those future beneficiaries during their working years rather than on a still later generation of workers. This would avoid the need for significant increases in future tax rates, with the associated inefficiencies. Moreover, it would avoid the incentive and efficiency costs of a steeper clawback on OAS benefits, as would have arisen with the Seniors Benefit scheme. This solution thus accepts more tax distortions from current workers in order to reduce the tax distortions on future workers *and* retirees, which includes the distortion to savings decisions by current workers as they anticipate their fiscal treatment during retirement. This trade-off is something like the one described by Dahlby in terms of the use of a more universal benefit (with higher gross tax revenues and tax rates) versus a more selective benefit (requiring lower tax rates but more tax-like distortions of clawbacks) for the National Child Benefit. Even without a formal fund to cover future OAS and health-care costs, the federal strategy of running surpluses and reducing the debt-to-GDP ratio will serve the same purpose.

Still further policy actions will likely prove necessary and prudent in dealing with public finances for the growing elderly population. Dahlby's suggestion that the normal retirement age for a full CPP benefit be raised from 65 years is appealing and one that follows actions in other countries. A similar adjustment would be justified for eligibility to receive the OAS and the Spouse's Allowance. Moreover, a recent study reporting that the CPP benefit discount for early retirement was too generous, and thus a drain on the system with the increasing popularity of retiring early, should be addressed. Changes of these kinds in the public pension system need to be reinforced with other policies making it easier for individuals to choose later retirement. The federal government should relax mandatory retirement in federally regulated industries, and it should encourage the provinces to take similar actions. It is ironic that the Supreme Court of Canada upheld the right of provinces to enforce mandatory retirement at age 65 (including professors), when the justices whose work is most like that of other professionals (such as professors) can work to age 75.

The National Child Benefit

The evolution of the Child Tax Benefit into the National Child Benefit (NCB) program over the past decade has been one of the most notable fiscal developments in Canada, which Dahlby rightly gives close scrutiny. The repeated expansion of the low-income component of benefits, the NCB supplement, in recent federal budgets has accounted for large increases in spending. Because the NCB is delivered via the tax system and classified as a tax expenditure, these spending increases are misleadingly counted as tax cuts.[4] The key "innovation" of the NCB program was to reduce the differential in benefits paid for children in families on welfare and in lower-income working families. This goal has been achieved by paying a federal benefit to all children in low-income families regardless of welfare status, offset by a reduction in the welfare benefit for children. It also has been facilitated by many provinces using their welfare savings to extend in-kind benefits to children in non-welfare families.

---

[4]It is interesting to see the documents for the 2003 federal budget present figures that show both ways of counting the NCB program — as a tax cut and as expenditures (Canada. Department of Finance, 2003, p. 222).

                                                      Jonathan R. Kesselman

One explicit goal of the NCB program has been to reduce the "welfare wall" of high effective marginal tax rates (EMTRs) on welfare families that inhibit their return to work. But as Dahlby points out, the NCB cannot avoid the inexorable arithmetic of any negative income tax or guaranteed income type of program. Raising the benefits and avoiding high EMTRs (via benefit phase-outs) means extending the benefits higher up the income scale and thus expanding the budgetary cost; raising the program's gross budgetary cost means that the reduced EMTRs for some beneficiaries are offset by higher MTRs on taxpayers to finance a larger program; and reducing the high EMTRs at lower incomes necessitates raising the EMTRs at higher incomes. It is the last of these possible avenues that has plagued the NCB program. The EMTRs on labour force entry for welfare beneficiaries with children have been reduced, but the total EMTRs on families have been significantly raised as the benefits are phased out. The disincentives are most severe in the $25,000 to $35,000 earnings range but are more widely dispersed. Hence, "getting the kids off welfare" — as proponents call their strategy — is also putting the kids on another program that happens not to be called "welfare". That other program is called the NCB supplement, and while its disincentives are less extreme than those of welfare, with its 100% clawback, the NCB disincentives apply to many more workers and greater earnings.[5]

In assessing the NCB program, and especially the NCB supplement, it is important to recall a basic lesson from taxation economics. The efficiency cost or deadweight loss of a tax or tax-back rate is proportional to the *square* of the EMTR. One of the figures compiled by Dahlby shows that, for families with two children and income in the $25,000 to $35,000 range, their EMTRs are virtually doubled by the NCB program. That means that the efficiency costs for that group of workers is *quadrupled* from what it would be in the absence of the program. The base Canada Child Tax Benefit, which extends to much higher incomes, has tax-back rates of 2.5% (for one child) and 5% (for two or more children). While these may seem like small additions to the EMTRs of higher earning families, they too exert disproportionate damage to the

---

[5]For recent analysis of how the optimal design of income-transfer programs hinges on the relative labour force versus hours-worked responsiveness of individuals, see Saez (2002). With high labour force responsiveness, and high valuation on labour force participation, policies should incorporate features like the Working Income Supplement which was abolished with the creation of the NCB program, but retained in some provincial programs.

economy's efficiency because they are added to already high MTRs from the personal tax and apply to larger amounts of earnings. The high EMTRs of the NCB program are typically associated with work disincentives, but they also distort a wide range of other behavioural incentives such as education, training, savings, investment, and tax compliance.

If the disincentives and efficiency costs of enlarging income-tested benefits are of concern, what is a sensible course for policy action? Since increasing the NCB supplement does raise living standards for low-income families, this is a classic trade-off between greater vertical equity and greater efficiency. Some proponents would like to see the NCB enriched until all child-related benefits, including their part of housing costs, are removed from welfare programs; others would like it enriched even further to eliminate child poverty. In my judgement, the program has already been extended as far as prudent, and perhaps too far, relative to the balancing of distributional and efficiency goals. More fundamentally, I believe that public policies related to child development should put less stress on income support and more focus and funds on universally provided in-kind services and supports for children. By providing these services to children with special needs irrespective of family income and by targeting special facilities to communities at greatest risk, one can avoid the efficiency costs of raising EMTRs.[6]

The Goods and Services Tax

The first major tax policy decision of the Chrétien administration was to retain the goods and services tax (GST) with only minor reforms, thus reversing its electoral pledge to replace the tax. Dahlby deems this "a wise policy decision" and simply notes that the GST eliminated the burden on business inputs arising under the previous federal sales tax. As one of the few tax economists who favoured fundamental federal sales tax reform at the "panel of tax experts" for the House of Commons Finance Committee in 1994, I believe that the decision to retain the GST warrants greater scrutiny. While the GST was an advance in some respects over the manufacturers sales tax, it has significant deficiencies

---

[6]For further exposition of this approach and also for an early analytical critique of the "getting kids off welfare" argument, see Kesselman (1994). For a recent analysis with similar conclusions, see Lefebvre and Merrigan (2003).

                                                  Jonathan R. Kesselman

of its own. First, it is relatively costly to administer and places major compliance burdens on business, especially small firms, as well as on consumers. Second, its base is far from comprehensive, necessitating a higher rate, creating consumer inefficiencies, and introducing numerous practical complexities. Third, the GST adds an entirely new layer of difficulties for operation of the tax system, such as for employee fringe benefits and services sourced abroad. Fourth, the input tax credit mechanism is open to abuse, such as the recently reported evasion by fictitious exporters costing millions of dollars in revenues.

Two attractive alternatives — both discussed in the 1994 deliberations over replacing the GST — are the business transfer tax (BTT) and the direct consumption tax (DCT).[7] Either of these approaches to taxing consumption would greatly simplify the operation of the tax and sharply reduce the costs of administration and compliance. Both the BTT and DCT would involve a much more comprehensive base than the GST, since they would be applied to all business value-added (the BTT) or to all payrolls and business cash flows (the DCT). The BTT would operate on each business's accounts rather than each transaction, and it could be applied as an adjunct to corporate and personal taxes. The DCT would apply to all labour compensation as a general payroll tax on employees plus a business cash-flow tax. The BTT might be preferred for its greater simplicity than the DCT, but the BTT is confined to a single tax rate and hence is not suitable for harmonizing with subnational sales taxes. The DCT can be harmonized through employee payroll tax rates differentiated by province, if this were desired. Politicians who prefer reduced visibility of taxes would welcome the hidden nature of the BTT, while public finance economists inclined toward tax visibility might prefer the DCT.

The attractions of replacing the GST with a more direct form of consumption tax are further enhanced when one considers the prospect of Canada entering a customs union with the United States. The open borders of a customs union would yield major benefits to the Canadian economy through lowered trading costs and increased efficiency and competitiveness. However, this prospect would be thwarted by Canada's existing high indirect consumption tax rates, which require border controls to enforce. Sales tax rates are only about half as high in most of the United States, where 45 states impose a retail sales tax, but

---

[7]Detailed discussion of the operation, merits, and deficiencies of the BTT and DCT, and comparisons with the GST, are provided in Kesselman (1997, chapter 8).

where there is no federal counterpart to the Canadian GST. To overcome this obstacle would require eliminating or changing the format of either the federal or provincial sales taxes in Canada. Changing the GST to a more direct form would raise the tax-paid price of goods and services produced in Canada, but the exchange rate would adjust to restore the nation's international trade competitiveness.

Even if it were not replaced with a more direct taxing method, the GST could benefit from several reforms that were not pursued by the government in 1994. For example, the land component could be excluded from the taxable base for sales of new buildings, as it is neither newly created output nor value-added. This change would make the tax less burdensome on buyers in cities where housing and business building prices are above average on account of high land prices, thus stimulating business expansion. The GST should also be removed from various snack foods, baked goods, and soft drinks. The distinctions now drawn between salted and unsalted peanuts, and between two cookies and half a dozen, for example, are not only arbitrary but silly, and they tarnish the tax's public image. The only reason to retain tax on any food items would be if the federal government wanted a precedent for expanding the tax to more such items. In yet another example, the registration threshold of $30,000 should be substantially increased to at least $75,000. This change would exclude from tax most self-employed workers who do not have employees, including most in the home repair and renovation sector for whom the GST can be used to bargain for cash payments and thereby facilitate income tax evasion.

Personal Taxation

The 2003 federal budget's planned hikes in the contribution limits for tax-deferred plans (RPPs and RRSPs) is a long-overdue change in the personal tax treatment of savings. It joins a series of tax policies in recent years that are shifting the personal tax base further from income and toward consumption.[8] Yet, even when fully implemented in 2006, these higher limits will still leave Canada far behind competitors like the United States and the United Kingdom in taxing personal savings. Those countries allow much larger sums to be

---

[8]Dahlby (2003) provides an excellent economic analysis of various paths to pursuing greater consumption taxation.

                                                        Jonathan R. Kesselman

treated on a tax-deferred consumption basis, and both also have schemes for tax-prepaid savings. This feature of the personal tax is important for efficiency, growth, and horizontal equity as well as for making Canada's tax internationally competitive for higher earners. In a hopeful note, the 2003 budget also announced that the federal government will consult on the possible introduction of tax-prepaid savings plans (TPSPs) in Canada. It is instructive that the US administration (United States. Department of Treasury, 2003) proposed to convert existing tax deferred schemes (standard IRAs, analogous to RRSPs) into tax-prepaid schemes (Roth IRAs). Being a TPSP proponent (Kesselman and Poschmann, 2001a,b), I will not reiterate here the many advantages offered by tax-prepaid schemes, which Dahlby has commendably described.

A medley of other tax changes in recent federal budgets have also reduced the personal tax burden on various forms of capital, financial, and entrepreneurial incomes. In 2000 there were two cuts in the capital gains inclusion rate, better tax provision for flow-through shares, deferral of tax on capital gains from small business shares when the proceeds are reinvested, and deferral of tax on exercising certain employee stock options. The 2003 budget extended the capital gains rollover for small business investors and reduced taxes on venture capital and qualified limited partnerships. While each of these changes needs to be evaluated for its equity, efficacy, potential avoidance, and additions to tax complexity, they jointly serve to make the Canadian personal tax more consumption-oriented and more conducive to business. Note that TPSPs apply zero tax to capital gains, interest, and dividends on assets held in the plan; and tax-deferred schemes have an effective zero tax rate on the normal return to capital on plan assets.

Among the most significant recent policy developments for personal taxation in Canada is a change in the Federal-Provincial Tax Collection Agreement allowing provinces to shift from "tax on tax" to "tax on income". This change has encouraged several provinces to reduce their tax progressivity, but Dahlby's use of Ontario as the representative province to chart changes in the distribution of taxes obscures this outcome. Ontario has even raised its MTR progressivity by applying steep surtax rates; the province's 2003 budget raises the surtax threshold and offers a vague promise of eventually removing the surtax. Yet, Alberta has gone to a fully flat MTR above an enhanced exemption level, and Saskatchewan has greatly flattened its tax schedule to rates of 11, 13, and 15%. British Columbia has reduced its MTRs more at higher than lower incomes, with some rate flattening. One might expect this tendency for rate flattening to continue at the provincial level, given competitive pressures to attract and retain high value-added industries that employ highly skilled workers. To the extent that this process continues, it may at some point induce the federal government to increase its personal tax rate progressivity, and even its top-bracket rate, to maintain a semblance of vertical equity in the country's overall revenue system.

Business Taxation

The 2003 federal budget completes some important changes for business taxation that were begun in the 2000 budget update. The 2000 measure set in force a phased reduction of the general corporate income tax rate from 28% to 21%, which will be completed in 2004. However, the 2000 measure excluded the non-renewable resource sector, and the 2003 budget begins cutting that sector's 28% rate next year and ends with the same 21% rate in 2008. The budget additionally will terminate the Resource Allowance for this sector but restore its deductibility of provincial royalties for federal tax purposes. Dahlby provides a useful analysis of these changes and how they achieve the most central goals of the Mintz committee, which were to make Canadian corporate income taxes more neutral across industries and assets and more competitive internationally. He raises interesting issues about the possible effects of the changes in tax provisions for the resource sector. Of course, the total decline in corporate income tax rates over this period is at least half explained by provincial cuts, assuming that Alberta and Ontario deliver on their targeted 8% rates and that British Columbia follows.

A major item for business taxation in the 2003 federal budget is the plan to phase out the corporate capital tax on non-financial institutions by 2008. This follows the abolition of BC's non-financials capital tax in 2002 and Quebec's 2002 budget pledge to cut both of its capital taxes by more than half by 2007. And Ontario has pledged in its 2003 budget to phase out its non-financials capital tax by the same time as the federal government. Taken together, these changes imply an even larger cut in the effective total tax burden on corporate income and capital than was anticipated in the 2000 budget update. The federal budget documents express the capital taxes in terms of their corporate income tax equivalents. In fact, relatively little has been explored about the economics of capital taxes either at the theoretical level or in empirical studies. Can one

                                          Jonathan R. Kesselman

state with any confidence whether a marginal dollar of revenue is raised with less efficiency costs and distortions by a tax on capital or one on capital income? Dahlby (2002) has provided one of the first economic analyses of this issue, and under certain assumptions he finds that the optimal rate of a source-based capital tax should be low relative to the rate of capital income tax. His present discussion suggests possibly costly distortions on the banking industry from capital taxes.

A salient question in the coming years is whether Canada's cutting its total corporate tax rates below counterpart rates in the United States will sub-stantially stimulate business expansion in Canada. Some policy analysts are already calling for further cuts in corporate income tax rates, presumably to pursue an economic strategy similar to Ireland's success with very low corporate tax rates.[9] In addition to the issue of whether this policy would yield commensurate economic gains, one must ask whether it would provoke some form of retaliation from the United States. The Irish tax policies provoked other members of the European Union, which called Ireland a "tax pirate" and have recently induced Ireland to raise its corporate tax rates somewhat. Corporate tax rates that were significantly lower in Canada than the United States could lead multinationals to engage in transfer pricing and debt shifting that favoured the Canadian revenue base. To the extent that foreign investment in Canada originates in the United States and other countries with higher corporate tax rates, there are also limits to this strategy on account of the operation of foreign tax credits.

Future Tax Policy

At the outset of my commentary I indicated my judgement that the Chrétien-era tax policy changes amounted to the *first stage* of a major remaking of the Canadian tax system. But more steps are needed to complete the transformation of Canadian taxes into an efficient and growth-promoting revenue system to

---

[9]Mintz, Poschmann and Robson (2003) propose an additional four percent-age point cut in the federal general corporate income tax rate by 2008, plus removal of the 1.1 percentage point corporate income surtax, to bring the total federal rate to 17%.

advance the economy into the twenty-first century. Some of these further needs for reform were suggested in my comments about the financing of public pensions and EI and issues to be faced with the National Child Benefit program. I have also presented a case for reform of the GST and further expansion of tax-recognized treatment for personal savings. Now I would like to complete the picture by painting my view of the remaining needs for Canada to create a world-beating tax system. In this presentation, I shall be drawing on my forthcoming study titled "Tax Design for a Northern Tiger", which develops all these points in greater detail.

Any big-picture thinking about future Canadian tax policy should consider the possible formation of a customs union between Canada and the United States. The removal of border controls on the free passage of tangible goods between the two countries whether by rail, truck, car, post, or courier would greatly improve the competitive position of Canadian business. It would eliminate significant costs to transacting business and trading with the United States — preparation of export documents, import brokerage, wasted time at the border, differential postage and courier fees, and faster transport and shipments. To facilitate such an arrangement, Canada would need to reduce its comparatively large reliance on consumption taxes that are collected in an indirect manner, on the sale and purchase of goods and services. An economically efficient consumption base can be maintained, while shifting to a more direct method of tax collection, such as the BTT or the DCT noted earlier as possible replacements for the federal GST.

If either the federal or the provincial sales taxes has to be shifted to a more direct means of collection, a case can be made for doing this with the provincial taxes. The remaining retail sales taxes place substantial burdens on business inputs, have restricted, albeit growing, bases, and add complexity to tax administration because of their varying coverages. Hence, a BTT or DCT would serve as an attractive replacement for the provincial sales taxes. Either form of tax could be administered as an adjunct to the personal and corporate income taxes, and this change would be eased by Canadian Customs and Revenue Agency administration. The strain of Canada's heavy reliance on indirect taxes on the formation of a customs union might be partially relieved if the United States fully implements its Streamlined Sales Tax Project (to aid cross-state tax collection on mail-order and Internet sales for out-of-state deliveries), but the pressure of big tax rate differences on cross-border shopping would remain in the absence of Canadian tax reforms. Provincial excise taxes

                                                      Jonathan R. Kesselman

would also be under pressure from their lower US counterparts if the borders were opened, but random vehicle inspections could partially control the flow of alcohol and cigarettes.

Provincial tax policy could reap further benefits if a BTT enacted to replace sales taxes were also used to subsume some other taxes.[10] Such a tax could easily encompass the provincial corporate income and capital taxes, provincial payroll taxes, and part of the non-residential property tax. Compared with the taxes it could replace, the BTT has important advantages for investment and economic growth. A BTT would eliminate the tax burden on the normal return to capital, thus making the effective marginal tax rate on investment zero. It would shift more of the tax burden to labour income, which is economically efficient. It would remove the tax bias, at the provincial level, in corporate finance that favours debt over equity. It would eliminate the distortions of measuring depreciation on a firm's capital stock, since capital purchases would be expensed. And it would reduce incentives for debt-shifting by firms across provinces.

Personal taxation would also benefit from reforms going beyond those of recent years or slated for the next several years. Further moves of the personal tax base toward consumption for higher earners would be desirable, if this can be done in a way that does not undermine total revenues or vertical equity. As noted earlier, tax-prepaid savings plans offer a more attractive option than expanding tax-deferred plans beyond what is already scheduled. There is little justification for keeping high earners from saving enough, on a tax-recognized basis, to maintain their accustomed living standards when retired. To achieve this, the dollar limit on contributions (mostly to TPSPs) should be entirely removed. At the same time, the allowable contributions on earnings above $100,000 should be limited to 15%, which equates to about 23% of post-tax earnings. These changes would make Canada competitive with the tax treatment of high earners in the United States and the United Kingdom in its ability to attract and retain the most talented workers.

---

[10]See Bird and Mintz (2000) and Bird and McKenzie (2001) for detailed analysis of a "business value tax" to replace provincial corporate income and capital taxes. Their BVT is an income-type value-added tax, whereas the BTT is a consumption-type value-added tax; both use the "subtraction method" rather than taxing individual transactions.

Other reforms of a more housekeeping nature should also be pursued for the personal tax. The base should be expanded where that makes sense for equity, efficiency, and incentives. For example, union dues are tax deductible, but the strike pay financed out of dues is non-taxable. That treatment is inconsistent and provides an undue incentive for more and longer work disruptions. Employer-paid health and dental extended insurance plans are not deemed a taxable fringe benefit, which causes inefficient over-expansion of such plans relative to taxable pay. This is also horizontally inequitable and likely vertically inequitable too. In moving the base further toward consumption, it might make sense to reinstate a modest annual exemption on interest and dividend income. This would allow average earners to obtain consumption tax treatment of precautionary savings without the bother of using a tax-recognized savings plan.

The rate structure for personal taxes bears monitoring as the process of rate flattening at the provincial level likely continues. That might at some point suggest an increase in the progressivity of the federal rate structure or even a hike in the top federal marginal tax rate. At present, the overall Canadian personal tax rate structure is reasonably in line with that of the United States, with federal rates lower for those at middle and higher incomes, while provincial rates are mostly well above their US state counterpart rates. Lower personal taxes paid by many Americans are attributable to economically inefficient base-eroding provisions in the US tax, such as tax-free municipal bonds and the deductions for mortgage interest and property taxes. The much heavier rates of payroll tax on earners at middle and upper-middle incomes in the United States than Canada compensates for most of the differential. If any aspect of the current rate structure in Canada warrants remedy, it is likely the width of the income brackets for the upper tax rates. The income threshold for the top federal tax rate should be sharply raised from the current $104,600 level; most provinces are even more constrained in their top-bracket income thresholds.

Perhaps the most intriguing and unresolved question about Canada's future tax strategy is whether to pursue the path of the Celtic Tiger — still lower corporate income tax rates than those that will result from current plans of the federal and provincial governments. The potential payoff in terms of investment, productivity, and economic growth could be enormous, if the Canadian results were anything like those in Ireland. Of course, Ireland also had other major factors at play, such as low initial wages, convergence with more prosperous economies, and large subsidies from the European Union. Alternatively,

                                              Jonathan R. Kesselman

Canada might benefit handsomely from being a pioneer in replacing the corporate income tax with a corporate cash-flow tax or some variant of the BTT. Priority should be given to research about the economic, design, operational, and legal aspects of these approaches to business tax reform. Based on the findings, Canada should complete the business of recent budgets in creating a tax system for the twenty-first century.

It is important to understand that pursuing a more efficient and growth-oriented tax system for Canada does not need to constrain public services and benefits. The policy goal is to maximize the real living standards of Canadians, which includes both their private consumption (net-of-tax incomes) and their public consumption (financed out of their taxes). If Canadians wish to continue having more of their consumption in the public sphere, with higher taxes as a percent of GDP than the United States, an efficient tax system does not stand in their way. To the extent that higher taxes enter into business costs, the exchange rate will adjust to offset any adverse impact on trade competitiveness. Choosing higher or lower taxes is entirely an issue of how best to optimize domestic living standards, not a matter of being competitive. Nevertheless, the mix and structure of taxes must be optimally tuned for efficiency and growth in order to provide Canadians with a tax system for the twenty-first century that will maximize their well-being.

References

Bird, R.M. and J.M. Mintz (2000), "Tax Assignment in Canada: A Modest Proposal", in H. Lazar (ed.), *Canada: The State of the Federation 1999/2000: Toward a New Mission Statement for Canadian Fiscal Federalism* (Montreal and Kingston: McGill-Queen's University Press), 263–292.

Bird, R.M. and K.J. McKenzie (2001), *Taxing Business: A Provincial Affair?* C.D. Howe Institute Commentary No. 154 (Toronto: C.D. Howe Institute).

Canada. Department of Finance (2003), *The Budget Plan 2003* (Ottawa: Department of Finance).

Dahlby, B. (2002), "Globalization and the Optimal Taxation of Capital in a Small Open Economy". Unpublished paper (Edmonton: Department of Economics, University of Alberta).

__________ (2003), "Restructuring the Canadian Tax System by Changing the Mix of Direct and Indirect Taxes", in H.G. Grubel (ed.), *Tax Reform in Canada: Our Path to Greater Prosperity* (Vancouver, BC: The Fraser Institute), 77–108.

Kesselman, J.R. (1983), *Financing Canadian Unemployment Insurance* (Toronto: Canadian Tax Foundation).

___________ (1994), "Public Policies to Combat Child Poverty: Goals and Options", in K. Banting and K. Battle (eds.), *A New Social Vision for Canada? Perspectives on the Federal Discussion Paper on Social Policy Reform* (Kingston: School of Policy Studies, Queen's University), 73–97.

___________ (1997), *General Payroll Taxes: Economics, Politics, and Design* (Toronto: Canadian Tax Foundation).

___________ (2004), "Tax Design for a Northern Tiger", *Choices* 10(1) (Montreal: Institute for Research on Public Policy).

Kesselman, J.R. and F. Poschmann (2001a), "Expanding the Recognition of Personal Savings in the Canadian Tax System", *Canadian Tax Journal* 49(1), 40–101.

___________ (2001b), *A New Option for Retirement Savings — Tax-Prepaid Savings Plans*, C.D. Howe Institute Commentary No. 149 (Toronto: C.D. Howe Institute).

Lefebvre, P. and P. Merrigan (2003), "Assessing Family Policy in Canada: A New Deal for Families and Children", *Choices* 9(5) (Montreal: Institute for Research on Public Policy).

Mintz, J.M., F. Poschmann and W.B.P. Robson (2003), *Focus on the Future: A Shadow Federal Budget for 2003*, Backgrounder No. 69 (Toronto: C.D. Howe Institute).

Saez, E. (2002), "Optimal Income Transfer Programs: Intensive Versus Extensive Labor Supply Responses", *Quarterly Journal of Economics* 117, 1039–1073.

United States. Department of the Treasury (2003), "President's Budget Proposes Bold Tax-Free Savings and Retirement Security Opportunities for All Americans", Press Release KD–3816 (January 31).

FISCAL ASPECTS OF KYOTO

BUDGET '03 AND THE KYOTO PROCESS

Ross McKitrick, University of Guelph

Background

The Issue, and the Lead Up to Kyoto

In 1992, Canada joined other countries around the world at the Rio Conference on Sustainable Development and signed a document called the UN Framework Convention on Climate Change (UNFCCC). This included a non-binding commitment to reduce carbon dioxide emissions and other infrared-absorbing (or greenhouse) gases in response to the concerns about their possible effect on climate.[1] The "Rio target" asked signatories to reduce emissions to 1990 levels by the year 2000. The target was collective; individual countries were not given differentiated obligations. In Canada's case a cut of this size was forecast at the time to require emission cuts of about 12.5%. The target was not legally binding on signatories to the UNFCCC.

Total greenhouse gas emissions in Canada actually rose about 20% over the decade (Figure 1) and stood at 726 Megatonnes (MT) as of the year 2000. By the mid-1990s it was clear that the participating countries would not

---

[1]For a review of the scientific and policy debates behind the Kyoto Protocol, see Essex and McKitrick (2002).

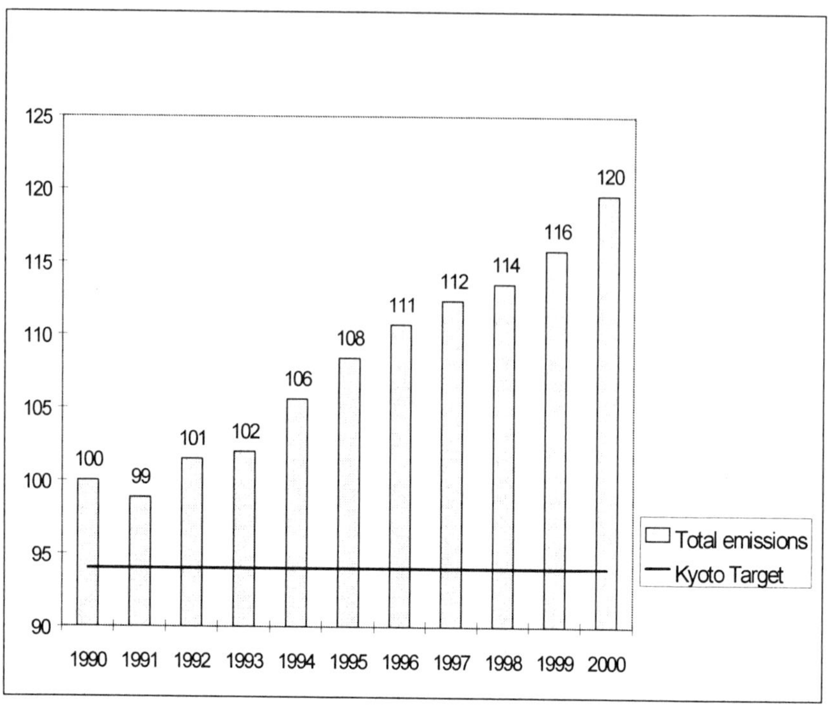

Notes: Emissions in 1990 are indexed to equal 100. The actual level was 607 MT. Source: Environment Canada, *State of the Environment Infobase*, at <http:// www.ec.gc.ca/soer-ree/English/indicator_series/techs.cfm?tech_id=15&issue_id= 4&supp=1#data>.

achieve the Rio target. A series of meetings were held to develop country-specific targets which would form the basis of a protocol to be added to the UNFCCC. This process culminated at a meeting at Kyoto, Japan in December 1997 at which the participants agreed to a set of legally-binding targets.

Ross McKitrick

Kyoto 1997

The Kyoto Protocol binds its signatories to reduce greenhouse gas (GHG) emissions to, on average, 5.2% below 1990 levels over the period 2008–2012. Canada's specific target is to get emissions to 6% below 1990 levels, which works out to 571 MT (see Figure 1). The intent of the treaty is that these targets are legally binding, though it is ambiguous what this means since there are no penalties for non-compliance. As of 2000, Canada was 27% above the Kyoto target.

Situation re Entering into Force

Kyoto is not currently in force. In order for it to become law, it must pass the so-called 55/55 rule. Participants are divided into two groups, Annex I and Annex II. The Annex I nations, comprising Organisation for Economic Co-operation and Development (OECD) and former Soviet Union countries, agreed to emission reductions, whereas Annex II nations were not asked to reduce emissions. To enter into force, Kyoto must be ratified by 55 nations, including enough Annex I countries to account for 55% of 1990 Annex I emissions. At present, 106 countries have ratified, accounting for 43.9% of Annex I emissions. The United States and Australia have indicated they will not ratify. Of the remaining Annex I nations, Russia is the largest, with 17.4 % of Annex I emissions. If Russia ratifies, the treaty will enter into force. If Russia decides not to, the treaty cannot enter into force as the remaining Annex I countries cannot muster the required 11.1% of emissions to reach the 55% threshold.

Russia's decision is therefore pivotal. It has been postponed and indications are that it may not enjoy sufficient support in the Duma to pass (see Box 1). A decision will likely not be made before the end of this year. In the fall of 2003 the Russian government will host a large gathering of scientists and policy advisors to debate the rationale for Kyoto. Standing against Russian ratification are two factors. First, with the withdrawal of the United States, the potential value of emission permits that Russia might sell on the international market has fallen considerably, limiting the financial incentive to join the treaty. Second, Russia is actively trying to encourage international investment in its eastern oil and gas fields, and potential developers are cautioning the Russian government that Kyoto targets may discourage the long-term financial commitments that are needed.

Box 1: Russia and Kyoto

Russian stalling could kill Kyoto consensus

By MARK MacKINNON

Moscow — Russia has delayed ratification of the international Kyoto Protocol on climate change, and two of its top scientists have begun to question the science underpinning it, developments that environmentalists say could kill the painstakingly crafted deal.

Although Russian Prime Minister Mikhail Kasyanov said last year that the Russian parliament would ratify the accord, a bill to begin that process has not yet been put to the Duma. The original schedule was to have the accord ratified by the end of last year.

One cabinet minister said recently that Russia no longer has a set timetable for ratification, a stall that could put the entire deal in jeopardy. Under a series of complex mechanisms, the accord will come into force only when countries representing 55 per cent of global emissions sign the pact.

The 100-plus countries that have ratified account for just 44 per cent. Russia, with 17.4 per cent of the global total, is the only remaining country that could make the pact binding on its own, since the United States has dropped out of negotiations.

The wait may be long. At a recent climate-change conference in India, two members of the Russian parliament told their international colleagues that only about half the Duma backs ratification of the Kyoto accord, and that its passage is by no means certain.

More troubling to some environmentalists, the two leading Russian scientists on the file, Alexander Bedritsky and Yuri Israel, have been questioning whether the deal is scientifically sound, even suggesting Russia might benefit if global warming makes its colder regions more productive.

(*Globe and Mail*, March 1, 2003)

Size of Canada's Commitment

Canada's target works out to 571 MT CO_2 equivalent. As of 2000, our emissions were 726 MT, or 27.2% over the Kyoto target. The current estimates from the federal government regarding the costs of Kyoto compliance (see below) assume emissions will be just over 810 MT as of 2010, implying a reduction of about 30% will be needed. Some of this will be covered by so-called "sinks credits": Canada can claim that our forests and grasslands absorb 30 MT annually. Canada had also hoped to claim 70 MT in "clean energy credits", on the grounds that our natural gas exports to the United States displace coal consumption and thereby reduce world emissions. This argument was rejected by the other Kyoto participants as it conflicts with the national emissions accounting system negotiated in Kyoto.

The potential costs of Canada's commitment are illustrated in Figure 2. Picture a "demand" curve for emissions, arising from the fact that the activity that generates emissions is beneficial. A plot of the total emissions generated at each marginal value shows the demand curve. If there were a market for emission permits this would indicate the total demand for permits at each price. Because the current price of emissions is effectively zero, the unregulated emissions level is the horizontal intercept (here assumed to be 809 GtC). The demand curve is also called the Marginal Abatement Cost curve, as it shows the marginal cost of emission reductions (defined as foregone net benefits of emissions) for each emissions level. This construction assumes emission reductions are occurring sequentially from lowest- to highest-cost measures, and that the equi-marginal criterion applies. Hence the demand curve is a lower-envelope of emission reduction costs.

The Kyoto target is 571 MT, implying a reduction of 238 million tonnes. For cuts of this magnitude economic models have typically estimated marginal costs of at least $100 per tonne (see Wigle, 2001). If the demand curve is linear and the marginal cost of emission reduction rises to $100 this defines a triangular social cost area of $12 billion (one-half x 238 million x $100). There is also a rectangular area of magnitude $57 billion. These are scarcity rents which will be transferred from some people to others, with the losers and winners determined by the policies implemented.

Figure 2: Social Costs and Scarcity Rents Associated with Domestic Emissions Abatement

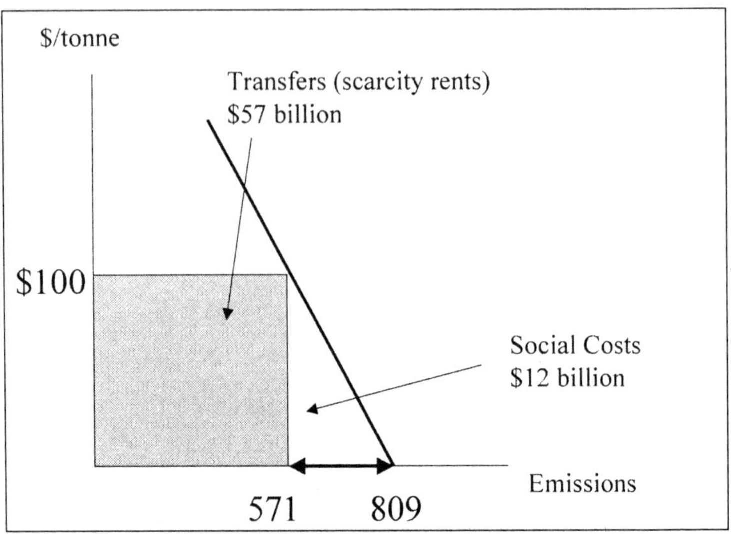

Some of these rents will be dissipated by rent-seeking behaviour as people and firms lobby to get "winner" status.

These are, of course, non-trivial amounts. Even if all the rents are captured through a carbon dioxide tax the social costs of the policy are $12 billion annually. These are unrecoverable regardless of the form the policy takes. If the emissions control policy takes the form of a cap-and-trade permit system the rents will constitute a massive wealth transfer to the permit recipients at the expense of energy consumers, that is, the general public (in part through increases in consumer prices and reductions in real wages). If the policy apparatus relies on command-and-control (or "targeted measures") these transfers and social costs are at least as large, and the amounts involved may be considerably higher since the demand curve is a lower envelope that assumes equi-marginal abatement costs across all sources, an assumption that does not hold up in a command-and-control system.

Estimates of the cost of reducing CO_2 emissions vary widely because of different assumptions about the nature of the policy regime, as well as

                                                              Ross McKitrick

methodological differences; $12 billion is about 1% of gross domestic product (GDP). This is an annual cost. Estimates can go higher by assuming inefficient policy choices, such as sectoral exemptions and over-reliance on command-and-control (see, e.g., Wigle, 2001; Beauséjour, Lenjosek and Smart, 1992). They can go lower by assuming international trading of permits at a lower marginal cost than $100 per tonne, or by assuming that some technological innovations will reduce the marginal abatement cost.

The federal government presented cost estimates in May 2002 which relied heavily on an assumption that permits will be available internationally at $10 per tonne. This would reduce the implementation costs considerably. There are reasons to doubt the feasibility of such a market forming in the foreseeable future, however (see, e.g., McKitrick and Wigle, 2002; Victor, 2001).

The Kyoto Process in 2002

Commitments of the Federal Government

The federal government has long maintained that there will be no carbon dioxide tax. In March 2002, the prime minister responded to concerns of industry by promising that ratification would only happen once a workable plan was in place (see Box 2).

There were four policy proposals released in May 2002 that focused on combinations of domestic permits trading, international permits trading, and command-and-control (Government of Canada, 2002). In this discussion paper the federal government reiterated a commitment to consultation and avoided presupposing ratification (see Box 3).

May 2002 Discussion Paper

The discussion paper presented four packages of options for achieving the Kyoto commitment. Each package presupposed that the measures announced in the *Action Plan 2000* would reduce emissions by 45 MT, and

Box 2: Prime Minister's Letter to Canadian Council of Manufacturers and Exporters, March 26, 2002

PRIME MINISTER / PREMIER MINISTRE

March 26, 2002

Dear Mr. Beatty:

Thank you for your letter of February 26, 2002, regarding the Kyoto Protocol and the recent report entitled *Pain Without Gain: Canada and the Kyoto Protocol.*

The Government of Canada believes that Canada should do its part to address the global challenge of climate change. I have stated that the Government would like to ratify the Kyoto Protocol, but we will only do so once we have a workable plan for meeting our target. Our goal is to make a ratification decision in 2002. The precise timing will depend on progress in our discussions internationally on clean energy exports and our consultations with provinces, territories, stakeholders and other Canadians. I assure you that there is no artificial deadline for a ratification decision.

I agree with your position that Canadians should have a full understanding of how meeting the Kyoto target could affect their lives before a ratification decision is made. We are working on updated modelling estimates for this reason.

---

that Canada could claim 34 MT worth of emission credits through biomass sinks. The discussion paper also claimed that measures in budget 2001 would reduce emissions by 5 MT. Neither *Action Plan 2000* nor budget 2001 gave project-specific emission reduction numbers. Budget 2001 allocated $100 million to the "Sustainable Development Technology" program, $150 million to the Climate Change Action Fund and $60 million for "energy efficiency and renewable energy programs".

Box 3: Extract from Page 1 of Federal Climate Change Discussion Paper, May 2002

In determining how to meet its climate change commitments, the Government of Canada established two important conditions. First, there must be a workable plan. And second, such a plan must be developed in full consultation with provinces, territories, stakeholders and Canadians.

This Discussion Paper is a step towards meeting those objectives. It explains what we know about climate change and what we have concluded. It presents four options for addressing Canada's climate change commitments and the analytical results that are currently available and seeks input on a number of key issues.

Some have expressed reservations about Canada's ability to achieve its target without U.S. participation in the Kyoto Protocol. Canada's challenge is to see whether there is a workable plan for achieving our Kyoto target — a plan that is affordable, a plan where no region of the country is asked to bear an unreasonable burden, a plan that promotes innovation and addresses issues related to the competitiveness of Canadian industry and a plan that takes into account the complexity and long-term nature of climate change.

This Discussion Paper will be considered in depth by federal, provincial and territorial energy and environment ministers at their meeting on May 21, 2002. There will be consultations with some 900 stakeholders in mid-June, with day-long sessions planned in every jurisdiction in Canada — 14 meetings in all. The views of Canadians everywhere are welcome.

Following consultations based on this document, a preferred approach will be identified and a draft plan developed in greater detail and analyzed over the summer. Consultations on that plan will take place in the fall.

The assumptions above leave 166 MT of emission reductions to be accounted for with new measures. The four options assume a minimum of 72 MT to be controlled with targeted measures at marginal costs that were never published. In the simulations done by Informetrica, a permit price of $10 per tonne only yielded about 16–24 MT emissions reduction domestically, depending on the range of emitters covered. This implies the emission demand curve has a slope of about –0.4 (see Figure 3). The rest of the gap would have to be covered by command-and-control, purchases of international permits, sinks credits or other credit-earning mechanisms such as the Clean Development Mechanism.

Figure 3: The Demand for CO$_2$ Emissions in Canada

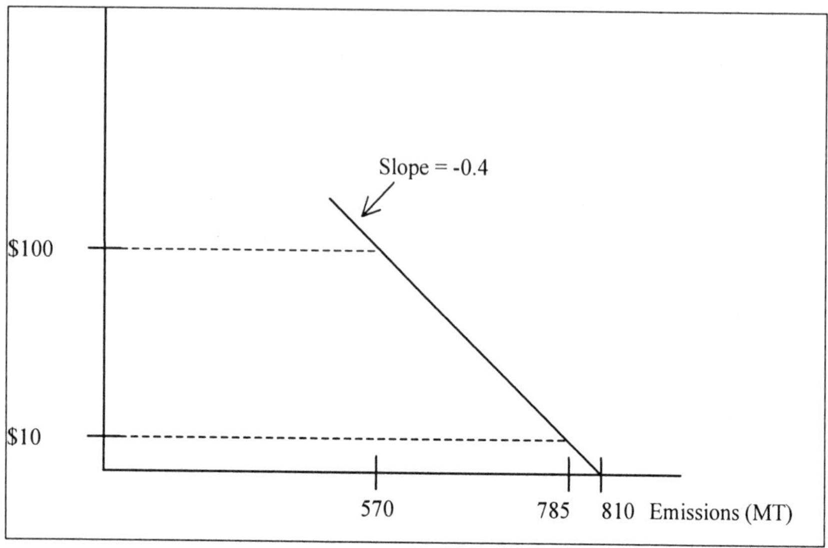

Note: A price of $10 per tonne yields about 25 MT reduction.

Following consultations over the summer of 2002 a new plan was devised. Released in November 2001, the "Climate Change Plan for Canada" assumes that pre-existing programs will achieve 80 MT emission reductions. New measures were proposed that will achieve about 100 MT cuts, and a future phase will identify another 60 MT reductions.

The actions described by this plan were those that came out of the earlier Issues Tables process. The language describing them is extremely vague, lacking clear timetables, mechanisms, and cost measures. For instance, one plan is to retrofit a fifth of the national building stock. It is explained in the plan as follows:

Ross McKitrick

Energy efficiency retrofit of 20 percent of housing by 2010 (1.5 MT)

This Plan proposes the goal of energy efficiency retrofits for 20 percent of housing by 2010. Cost shared audits and information for homeowners under the Energuide for Houses initiative will be expanded. Financial incentives for retrofits will also be explored.

Energy efficiency retrofit of 20 percent of buildings by 2010 (1.2 MT)

This Plan proposes the goal of retrofitting 20 percent of the commercial and institutional buildings stock to higher energy efficiency levels by 2010. This could be achieved through collaboration between provincial/territorial governments, municipalities, Aboriginal people, non-governmental organizations, trade associations and the private sector. Commercial and institutional building owners would be consulted on how to encourage retrofits. They can contribute, for example, through the formation of buyers groups to reduce price and risk in the acquisition of new technologies and products.

(http://www.climatechange.gc.ca/plan_for_canada/plan/chap_3_2.html)

Note that these ambitious undertakings would yield only 2.7 MT emissions cuts, or about 1% of the estimated Kyoto target.

Households are challenged to reduce emissions by one tonne per person, through measures such as:

‐

On the Road

Transportation accounts for half of individual greenhouse gas emissions. The kind of vehicle and the number of kilometres driven can have a huge impact on greenhouse gas emissions. Canadians can take many actions to reduce emissions from transportation.

- Buy a fuel-efficient vehicle – A 25 percent more fuel-efficient vehicle could reduce emissions by more than one tonne per year and save $360 on an average annual gasoline bill of $1440.
- Use ethanol blend gasoline – Current vehicles can use up to 10 percent ethanol blended gasoline without any adjustment to or effect on the engine.
- Use the car less – Driving 10 percent less, by walking, cycling, carpooling, or taking public transit, can reduce greenhouse gas emissions by 0.2 to 0.8 tonnes per year, depending on the vehicle.
- Reduce idling – If every Canadian motorist avoided idling their vehicles for just five minutes a day, all year, more than 1.6 million tonnes of carbon dioxide, along with other toxic substances, would not enter the air.

(http://www.climatechange.gc.ca/plan_for_canada/plan/chap_4.html#a)

December: Ratification

In the view of the federal government this qualified as a workable plan and the prime minister ratified Kyoto on December 16, 2002.

Pre-Budget Clues about Strategy Post-Ratification

Auto Sector Exemption

Prior to ratification, in a confidential agreement later reported by *The Globe and Mail*, Ottawa agreed to exempt the automotive sector from direct obligations under Kyoto (see Box 4).

Box 4: Auto Sector Exemption

Ottawa exempts auto makers on Kyoto

By STEVEN CHASE

Ottawa — Ottawa has quietly dropped auto makers — a powerful engine of the Ontario economy — from the list of industries whose factory emissions it proposes to regulate under the Kyoto Protocol.

Government sources say the exemption for car-assembly plants was granted several months ago amid heavy lobbying by Liberal MPs and cabinet ministers from Ontario, where more than half of Prime Minister Jean Chrétien's caucus is based.

"Political pressure was an important factor in deciding to remove them from the list of covered sectors," a senior federal official said.

(*Globe and Mail*, January 3, 2003)

Oil and Gas Sector, 15/15 Rule

Shortly after ratification, the federal minister of natural resources wrote to John Dielwart, chairman of the Canadian Association of Petroleum Producers, and offered two significant promises: the industry would not have to pay more than $15 per tonne for abatement costs, and the industry's target would be limited to getting emissions intensity (CO_2 emissions per unit of output) down by 15% compared to the business as usual level by 2010 (see Box 5). While a letter from a Cabinet minister is not necessarily a binding contract, oil and gas industry planners report that this cost commitment is being reiterated in current discussions with the federal government, and short-term project planning is going ahead on the basis of this promise (Vitello, 2003). The charge of $15 per tonne implies a relatively small effect on the cost of producing refined fuels, even in the emissions-intensive oil sands sector: some estimates are as low as 3 cents per barrel.

Box 5: The 15/15 Promise

outstanding issues. Earlier this month at a speech in Edmonton, the Prime Minister committed to provide certainty regarding the price and volume of emissions reductions that industry will be required to make as part of our climate change plan. I am therefore very pleased that I am able to make a specific commitment on both of these issues.

On the price of carbon credits, the Government will ensure that, during the first commitment period, Canadian companies will be able to meet their emission reduction responsibilities at a price no greater than $15 a tonne. The Government will work with industry and others to develop appropriate mechanisms to meet this commitment in a manner that is affordable to industry and responsible for all Canadians.

Canada

With respect to the volume of emissions, the Government will set the emissions intensity targets for the oil and gas sector at a level not more than 15 percent below projected business-as-usual levels for 2010.

The Government recognizes such clarity on the cost and volume issues is important for industry to be able to plan and make the investments which will create jobs and increase incomes for Canadians. In providing this clarity, we believe we have addressed a very significant concern for industry and set the stage for a cooperative approach to implementing Canada's Climate Change Plan.

I look forward to working with you and your members to this end in the coming months.

Yours sincerely,

The Honourable Herb Dhaliwal, P.C., M.P.

The other promise is significant in that it refers to an emissions *intensity* target, rather than a level target. Using an intensity rule allows emissions to grow in step with output. According to Statistics Canada (Harchaoui, Kabrelyan and Smith, 2002) emissions intensity in oil and gas-related sectors grew annually from 1981 to 1996 roughly as follows:

Crude petroleum and natural gas	+0.5%
Refined petroleum and coal products	+1.4%
Pipeline transport	+1.8%

If we take the average for the whole sector to be about 1% annually this implies the business-as-usual increase in emissions intensity from 2003 to 2010 will be about 7%. Hence, the letter asks the sector to get emissions intensity down by about 8% from current levels. If output grows by 8%, that implies sectoral emissions can remain roughly constant.

The two promises taken together imply the oil and gas sector will likely not have to reduce its emissions overall, and in any case will not have to pay more than $15 per tonne. At that price, relatively little abatement occurs. As mentioned above, the simulations for the April 2002 discussion paper suggest about 25 MT of abatement will occur at $10 per tonne, bringing emissions down to 785 MT. If the demand curve slope is –0.4, a $15 emissions price would yield a further reduction to 773 MT, assuming everyone gets the $15 price cap. In order to get emissions down to 570 MT, the federal government would have to cover the costs in excess of $15 per tonne, implying a subsidy burden of over $17 billion (see Figure 4).

The question therefore is what spending measures would accompany this 15/15 rule. If the large final emitters are expected to do more than 20 or 30 MT of emission cuts, then their expenses in excess of $15 per tonne will have to be borne by the federal government.

Ontario Power Sector

In November 2002, the Ontario government froze electricity rates at 4.3 cents/kilowatt hour for households, small businesses and farmers. Coverage has since been extended. Power is therefore being sold at below market rates (the average price is about 5.5 cents/kwh). This means the large stationary power plants have no financial ability to invest in emissions control, such as conversion to natural gas. It also means advertisements and other measures to control domestic energy consumption (thus far the main tools in the federal climate change plan) are being actively undermined by the Ontario subsidies to electricity prices.

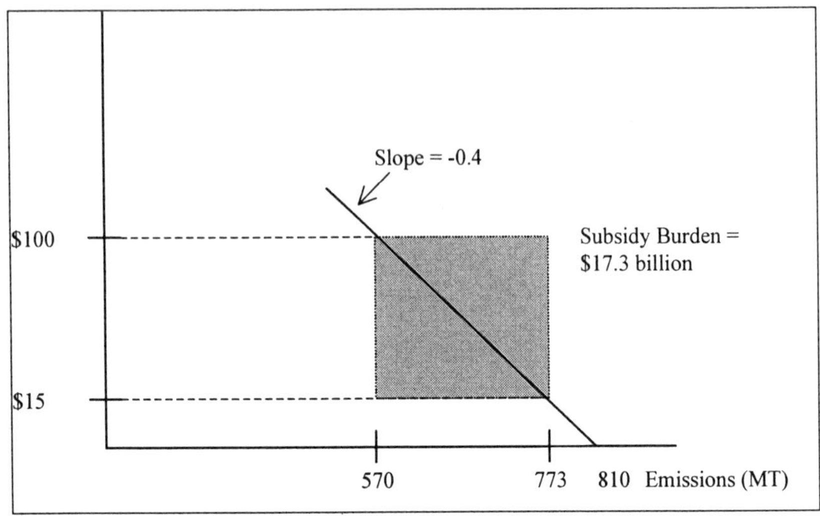

Note: If a subsidy of $100 per tonne is paid, but industry repays the first $15 per tonne the total cost is $85 on 203MT, or $17.3 billion.

Alberta Bill 37

The Alberta government (as well as British Columbia, Newfoundland, and others) strongly opposed ratification of Kyoto. It has recently introduced Bill 37 in the provincial legislature which enacts (Section 3(1)) a target of a reduction in emissions intensity of 50% by 2020.

Jurisdiction over CO_2 emissions is ambiguous under Canadian constitutional law. While the federal government is within its rights to enter into the Kyoto treaty, management of the energy sector is a provincial responsibility. Also, air emissions regulation is primarily a provincial matter, but the federal government can invoke the "peace, order and good government" provision of the constitution to claim national jurisdiction. However, where jurisdiction is ambiguous the courts have sometimes assigned authority based on which level of government enters the area first. The intent of Bill 37 is, in part, that by regulating emissions before the federal government

                                                            Ross McKitrick

does, the courts will grant constitutional jurisdiction to the province. The other intent is to make it difficult for the federal government to ask Alberta to enter into any emissions control agreements. Section 8 authorizes the provincial environment minister to enter into agreements with the federal government, but only subject to

> **(2)** The Minister may not enter into any agreement under subsection (1) unless the Minister is satisfied that the agreement will be consistent with this Act and with the specified gas emission target for Alberta established by section 3(1).

Budget '03

Spending to Date

$1.7 billion has been spent to date, including $1.53 billion on abatement efforts since 1997. As GHG emissions data are only released with a lag of several years we cannot say if they have continued to increase after 2000 as quickly as up to that point (see Figure 1). Energy demand fell in 2001, in part due to higher prices, reduced industrial consumption and the warm winter of 2001–02. Recent estimates from Environment Canada say that GHG emissions fell by 3% in 2001. But StatsCan reports natural gas sales rose 10% in 2002 due to the cold temperatures. Coal produced for domestic consumption in Canada rose 49% from 2000 to 2002,[2] suggesting CO_2 emissions have probably continued to rise.

2003 Budget Plan: A Five-Year Plan

The budget (pp. 149–152) promises spending of $2 billion over five years, or $400 million annually, on average. The announcement of a five-year plan is significant since it takes us to 2008, the start of the Kyoto compliance period. There is no time thereafter for a significant change in plan if these measures do not work.

---

[2] See <http://www.statcan.ca/english/Pgdb/prim22.htm>.

Budget Table

There are three entries for climate change (Annex 1, p. 226):

- Sustainable Development Technology: $250 million in 2003/04.
- Canadian Foundation for Climate and Atmospheric Science: $50 million in 2003/04.
- Other climate change measures: $200 million in each of 2003/04 and 2004/05.

Total spending in the first two years is $700 million, indicating that spending plans are loaded onto later years. This conflicts with the recognition that an approach based on technological innovation requires an early start.

Subsidies Predominate

The budget identifies a number of areas that will be targeted for subsidies. A recurring theme is technology. Money will be spent on *sustainable development* technology ($250 million), *longer-term climate change* technology ($200 million), and miscellaneous "other measures" ($1.7 billion) including technologies like fuel cells. There are no specific examples given to explain how the miscellaneous measures are different from sustainable development technologies or longer-term climate change technologies.

- Sustainable Development Technology:
    - $100 million in 2001, additional $250 million in 2003/04.
    - It should be noted that this program is not exclusively concerned with CO_2 reduction, instead it covers climate and clean air generally.
- Longer-Term Climate Change Technologies:
    - $200 million earmarked in future, on cost-sharing basis with project partners.
- $1.5 billion worth of other measures "will be considered", but only $200 million is actually budgeted for the next two years. This must cover:
    - actions to promote energy efficiency
    - renewable energy
    - sustainable transportation

                                                             Ross McKitrick

- new alternative fuels
  - building retrofits
  - wind power
  - fuel cells
  - ethanol.
- Other programs (including Technology Partnerships Canada, granting councils, regional development agencies) will be asked to report on how their contributions to Canada's climate change objectives can be improved within existing resource levels.

One problem with a subsidy-based approach is that it cannot guarantee overall emission reductions. While individual sources may reduce emissions on existing operations, subsidies increase the rate of return to activities in the emitting sectors, and may thereby attract new entrants or expansion of existing operations, shifting the demand curve in Figure 4 to the right.

Minor Fiscal Measures

There are two small tax changes that affect the climate plan.

- The ethanol component of diesel fuel is to be exempted from fuel excise tax, as already happens for ethanol in gasoline.
- The tax depreciation is accelerated for some alternative and renewable energy equipment.

Research

- $60 million was given to the CFCAS in the 2001 budget. This budget adds $50 million to that.

Notably Absent

- Permits
  - There is nothing set aside to buy permits on the international market. Of course, no such market exists but there are demonstration projects. Also, no money has been specifically designated to help create the infrastructure to support such a market. The annual $200 million for general climate measures may be intended to cover this.
- Fiscal measures
  - There are, as expected, no charges on emissions.
- Funds to cover expenses above $15/tonne
  - There are no specific funds to cover abatement costs in excess of $15/tonne; however, the annual "other measures" budget may be intended to do this. If emissions reduction costs rise to $100 per tonne, budget '03 will be able to cover 2 MT worth of reductions annually. If the entire amount is spent on foreign credits at $10 per tonne, this will cover 20 MT worth of permits.
- Specific funding for the November 2002 "Plan"
  - Considering the amount of work that supposedly went into producing the November 2002 Plan, it is strange that there is no mention of it in the Budget Tables. In particular, there is no list of the major plan items with funds specifically allocated. For instance, a major component of the plan is to retrofit 20% of the national building stock: an enormous physical undertaking that would surely rank as the largest public building program in at least a generation. There are about ten million homes in Canada. If two million are to be rebuilt at a cost of, say, $2,000 each, this amounts to $4 billion. And this is just the residential building stock: there are also commercial and institutional buildings. Yet there is no specific item in the federal budget for any of this. There is only a general (and rather cryptic) suggestion that building retrofits "will be considered".

In sum, it is hard to see any evidence that actually implementing the November 2002 Climate Change Plan in the next few years was seriously in mind when this budget was written. This would not be surprising since the November 2002 Plan cannot be taken seriously. It is a hodgepodge of comically bad ideas, and the lack of any specific cost estimates cannot disguise the fact that it would be ruinously expensive while at the same time accomplishing no significant public good.

                                             Ross McKitrick

The Next Steps

Russia

Of course, all discussion of implementing Kyoto is premature and potentially moot until and unless Russia ratifies.

Possible Effects of Current Policy Framework

The policy formation process to date has been characterized by ad hoc improvisation, the absence of understanding of the consequences of inefficient policy design, and a basic contradiction between commitments and actual policy pronouncements. It is highly unlikely that the measures introduced to date have reduced or even slowed down CO_2 emissions. Since the current "plan" merely expands on the existing portfolio of ineffectual measures, the future initiatives will not likely have any effect either, regardless of their cost. In terms of energy production, a large-scale switch to "renewables" or hydrogen is simply not going to happen in the next five years, no matter how much public money disappears into programs categorized under an ever-expanding list of adjectives for the word "technology". Neither can it realistically be expected that moral suasion will radically alter Canadian household energy consumption. If the federal government seriously opposes price-based incentives for emission reductions they will not succeed in getting Canada's GHG emissions down to anywhere near the Kyoto target (nor even likely anywhere near the optimistic business-as-usual target).

Possible Outcomes of this Process

It will be apparent within about two years that Canada cannot meet its Kyoto target.[3] If Kyoto is in force at the time, the options will be either large-scale purchases of Russian and/or Ukrainian credits (if available),

---

[3]My discussant, Chris Green, disagrees — he says it is already quite apparent, and after seeing his presentation of the Kaya Identity I think he is right.

non-compliance, or withdrawal from the treaty. I consider the most likely outcome to be a multilateral approach to the second option.

References

Beauséjour, L., G. Lenjosek and M. Smart (1992), "An Environmental CGE Model of Canada and the United States", Working Paper No. 92–04 (Ottawa: Department of Finance).

Essex, C. and R. McKitrick (2002), *Taken By Storm: The Troubled Science, Policy and Politics of Global Warming* (Toronto: Key Porter).

Government of Canada (2002), "A Discussion Paper on Canada's Contribution to Addressing Climate Change", Ottawa, May.

Harchaoui, T.M., D. Kabrelyan and R. Smith (2002), "Accounting for Greenhouse Gases in the Standard Productivity Framework", Cat. No. 11F0027MIE - No. 007 (Ottawa: Statistics Canada).

McKitrick, R.R. and R.M. Wigle (2002), *The Kyoto Protocol: Canada's Risky Rush to Judgment*, C.D. Howe Institute Commentary No. 169 (Toronto: C.D. Howe Institute).

Victor, D. (2001), *The Collapse of the Kyoto Protocol and the Struggle to Slow Global Warming* (Princeton, NJ: Princeton University Press).

Vitello, C. (2003), "Like Oil and Vinegar", *Hazardous Materials Management* 15(2), 6–10.

Wigle, R.M. (2001), "Sectoral Impacts of Kyoto Compliance", Industry Canada Working Paper No. 34, March, Industry Canada, at <http://strategis.ic.gc.ca/SSG/ra01796e.html>.

CANADA'S KYOTO COMMITMENT:
Fiscal and "Real" Aspects

Christopher Green, McGill University

Introduction

The session is entitled the "Fiscal Aspects of Kyoto". Ross McKitrick has said as much as I think can be said about the "fiscal aspects" of Canada's joust with the Kyoto windmill, and he has said it well. I agree with McKitrick that it will become apparent that Canada will not meet its Kyoto target. In fact, I will show that it is already apparent that Canada will not meet its target, even a modified one. If meeting the Kyoto target is the *raison d'être* for Canada's budgetary expenditures on climate change, the federal government is indeed throwing money away. But if so, it is aiming at a real problem. The increased concentration of greenhouse gases (GHGs) in the atmosphere will pose a very real problem for subsequent generations. I have no dispute with climate science.

Canada's climate policy is another matter, altogether. Our attempt to meet, by an arbitrary date, a meaningless, and unattainable, GHG emission target comes uncomfortably close to fitting the description of throwing money away. While I trust the climate science, I do have a bone to pick with climate policymakers and their non-governmental organization (NGO) sidekicks; with rent-seeking-renewables companies and their pseudo-technologist apologists; and with those economic modellers who predict low abatement costs by using models with unjustifiably high substitution elasticities and/or the assumption of a generic carbon-free backstop energy technology. The high substitution elasticities eventually run afoul of the laws of physics, including thermodynamics; assuming a generic carbon-free backstop overlooks the fact that there does not now exist a carbon-free backstop technology(ies), and that developing one or more will require a conscientious and long-term commitment, one that will have to overcome major engineering and physical hurdles. In short, the foundations of Canadian, as well as global, climate policy in contrast to climate science have serious weaknesses. As a result, Canada's Climate Change Plan, and the funding of it, run the serious risk of both failure and waste.

My commentary proceeds as follows. After a very brief review of past and prospective federal government spending on climate change, I will turn to two key issues:

- The federal government's estimate that a 240 million tonne (MT) reduction in CO_2 will achieve Canada's Kyoto commitment.
- Whether Canada can even come close to meeting its Kyoto commitment, even at a cost substantially above what the federal government modelling group has estimated.

Budget Expenditures

The federal government's environmental spending distinguishes between monies in the budget plan that are directed to climate change and those for all other environmental programs. Table 1 presents information on Canada's "investment" in climate change and other environmental spending. Climate-change spending (investment) not only dominates the budget plan spending on the "environment" for 2003–2007, but did so as well for 1997–2002.

The question is what spending on climate change has or will accomplish. Presumably, the $3.7 billion in climate-change spending over the decade 1997–2007 has helped, or will help prepare the way for: (i) a reduced trend growth in greenhouse gas emissions in the next several years; and (ii) substantial reductions in GHG emissions below trend. In fact, if the spending in 1997–2002 does not contribute to future emissions reduction, then not only is the federal government's estimated decline in the trend rate of growth of GHGs for 2000–2010 in jeopardy (see below), but so is the government's estimate that achieving our Kyoto commitment requires a 240 MT CO_{2e} reduction from the reference, or business as usual (BAU) emission level of

                                                    Christopher Green

Table 1: Federal Government Budgetary Expenditure on Climate Change and Environment (billions of $)

	1997–2002	*2003–2007*	*2003–2004*
Climate Change	1.7	2.0	0.505
Environment	0.6	1.0	0.274
Total	**2.3**	**3.0**	**0.779**

Source: Canada. Department of Finance (2003, ch. 5).

810 MT CO_{2e} in 2010. If the federal government's expenditure on climate change in 1997–2002 does not do its work in the first decade of the twenty-first century, achieving our Kyoto commitment will require more than the 240 MT CO_{2e} that is the target of Canada's climate-change plan.

Targeted Reductions

The federal government Climate Change Plan calls for an approximately 240 MT CO_{2e} reduction in GHG emissions from the BAU or reference level of 810 MT. A 240 MT reduction from 810 MT would meet Canada's Kyoto commitment of a 6% reduction below the 1990 level of emissions of 607 MT CO_{2e}. Figure 1 illustrates this. By 2000, the last year for which there is data, Canada's GHGs had risen to 726 MT CO_{2e}, and may now, in 2003, exceed 750 MT. The most striking aspect of Figure 1 is the predicted change in the BAU rate of growth of carbon emissions for 2000–2010, from the 1.8% average annual rate of growth in emissions that prevailed from 1990 to 2000, to 1.1% for 2000–2010. The federal government's estimate that the trend (or BAU) rate of growth of GHG emissions will decline to approximately 1.1% in 2000–2010,

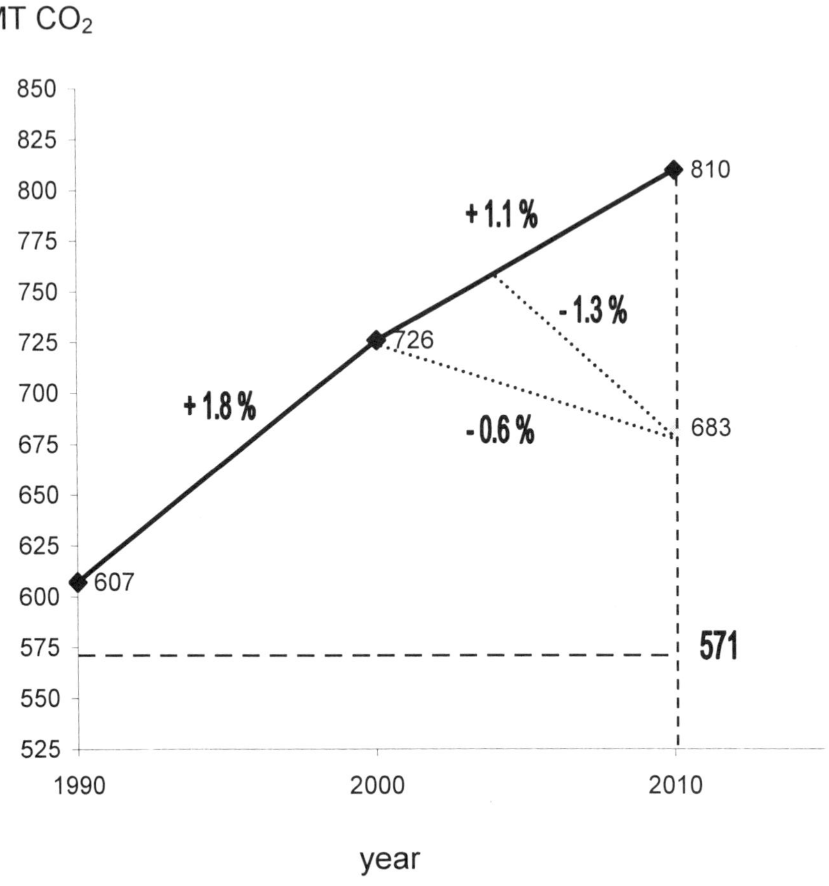

is apparently based on two assumptions:[1] (i) that Ontario's nuclear plants will soon be back on line, allowing coal-fired plants brought into commission in the late 1990s to be shut down; and (ii) that the "voluntary challenges" to industry contained in the 1996/97 federal budget will begin to impact the GHG emissions growth rate in the next several years, over and above the mandated

---

[1]Based on a telephone conversation with Dr. Neil McIlveen, Natural Resources Canada, who is a member of the federal government's Climate Change Analysis and Modelling Group.

                                                                                   Christopher Green

cuts in emissions called for in the Climate Change Plan. If either (or both) of these assumptions turn out to be incorrect, emissions could be tens of MT CO_{2e} higher in 2010 than the currently estimated 810 MT CO_{2e} reference (BAU) level.

On the assumption that BAU GHG emissions will in fact be 810 MT CO_{2e} in 2010, how does Canada plan to achieve a 239 MT CO_{2e} reduction to its Kyoto target of 571 MT CO_{2e}? According to the federal government's Climate Change Plan (2002), the called-for reductions fall into the following categories.

- Large Industrial Emitters: 80 MT, of which 55 MT would be via domestic emission trading (DET). At least some of the remaining 25 MT could be achieved via "offsets" purchased from reductions made voluntarily by entities not covered by emissions limits.
- Other Industrial Emitters: 16 MT
- Individuals and Governments: 28-33 MT
- Land cover and use: 38 MT, of which 30 MT are credited to Canada for land and forestry *sinks* granted under the Kyoto agreement.
- "Other potential actions": 60 MT, currently unplanned for, but which apparently includes the possibility that Canada will eventually gain credit for clean(er) energy exports to the United States.
- Purchases of emission permits on the international market: 12 MT +

There is no space here to analyze, much less question, the plausibility of each of the targeted sectoral reductions. But I do wish to briefly assess the plausibility of the *overall* exercise. I will do so by employing a thought experiment, one that I think will show that, even under the best of conditions, attaining a reduction in net emissions to 571 MT via a combination of credits, purchases and real emission reductions, is highly implausible. In what follows, I will assume that to achieve its Kyoto commitment by 2010, Canada need only reduce actual emissions to 683 MT CO_{2e}. The remaining 112 MT reduction, to nominally achieve the Kyoto target, would consist of the following: (a) the 30 MT credit for agricultural and forestry sinks; (b) 12 MT of international purchases of emission permits; and (c) credit for 70 MT of clean energy exports to the United States — credit for which, has to date been denied to Canada by the gatekeepers (chiefly EU-based) of Kyoto rules and regulations.

Is Canada's Kyoto Commitment Achievable?

To assess whether Canada's Kyoto commitment is achievable, let me review elements of the "thought experiment" to follow. Canada is committed to reducing, by 2008–2012, GHG emissions to an average 571 MT CO_{2e}, or 6% below the 607 MT CO_{2e} that prevailed in 1990. As shown in the previous section, emissions were 726 MT CO_{2e} in 2000, and now may exceed 750 MT. To ease the task of meeting its commitment, Canada negotiated a 30 MT credit for land-forest sinks. Further, it is assumed that Canada will get, or take, a 70 MT credit for clean(er) energy exports, a piece of "low hanging fruit" created by the US decision not to ratify Kyoto. Finally, the federal government will follow through on its planned purchase of (at least) 12 MT of permits from countries with an excess of permitted over actual GHG emissions, such as Russia. The resultant target for CO_{2e} reductions is 683 MT CO_{2e}. Even this increase in target level of emissions is not costless. The price of a permit to emit 1 tonne of CO_{2e} is likely to be at least \$20 US in 2010. To purchase 12 MT would cost Canada US\$240 million — or at least \$320 Canadian, even on the optimistic assumption that the Canada-US exchange rate rises to \$0.75 US per Canadian dollar. (Note that if Canada does not get, or take, credit for all or any of the 70 MT of clean(er) energy exports to the United States, it would have to purchase more international permits and/or reduce domestic emissions commensurately.

What will it take to get to the 683 MT net domestic emission target? The dashed lines in Figure 1 illustrates, and Tables 2 and 3 provide some relevant calculations. To reach 683 MT CO_{2e} by 2010 would require an 0.6% average annual rate of *decline* in carbon emissions for the decade 2000–2010. A 0.6% average annual rate of *decline* in GHG emissions is in stark contrast to the approximately 1.8% rate of *increase* for 1999–2000, and the predicted BAU rate of *increase* of 1.1% for 2000–2010. As we are now well into 2003, the rate of decline in carbon emissions between now and 2010 is perhaps more relevant. On the optimistic assumption that the growth rate of emissions since 2000 has conformed to the BAU estimate of 1.1%, emissions in 2003 are 750 MT CO_{2e}. Figure 1 shows that a decline from 750 MT in 2003 to the 683 MT target in 2010, implies an average annual rate of *reduction* in GHG emissions of 1.3%.

Table 2 provides further perspective. The first three rows of Table 2 present historical rates of increase for GHG emissions, gross domestic product (GDP), and the rate of decline in the carbon intensity of output, that is, the rate of

Table 2: Average Annual Rates of Change in GHGs, GDP, and the Carbon (GHG) Intensity of Output

	% Δ GHG	=	% Δ GDP	+	% Δ GHG/GDP
1 1970–1980	2.1		4.1		–2.0
2 1980–1990	0.9		2.7		–1.8
3 1990–2000	1.8		2.4		–0.6
4 2000–2010 (BAU)	1.1		2.3		–1.2
5 2000–2010 (683 MT target)	–0.6		2.3		–2.9
6 2003–2010 (683 MT target)	–1.3		2.3		–3.6
7 2000–2010 (613 MT target)	–1.7		2.3		–4.0
8 2003–2010 (613 MT target)	–2.9		2.3		–5.2

Sources: For rows 1 and 2, *Canada's Emissions Outlook: An Update*, National Climate Change Process, Analysis and Modelling Group, December 1999, Chart 4.15. Rows 3 and 4 are based on updated emission estimates (1990–2000) and the Federal Government's reference emissions of 810 MT for 2010. Rows 5–8 are author's calculations.

decline of GHG emissions per unit of GDP. Row 4 is based on the federal government's estimates of BAU emissions and GDP growth rates for 2000–2010. Rows 5 and 6 are the author's calculations of what it would take, in terms of rates of reductions in GHG emissions per unit of GDP, to achieve the modified (683 MT) GHG emission targets. Rows 7 and 8 assume a 613 MT emission target, one that would apply if Canada were not to get, or take, credit for 70 MT of clean(er) energy exports to the United States.

Rows 5 to 8 of Table 2 are predicated on the highly unrealistic assumption that Canada maintains its estimated 2.3% "trend" rate of GDP growth 2000–2010, while still attaining the GHG emission targets. Before assessing the implications of more realistic assumptions about the GDP growth rate, if Canada attempts to reduce net domestic emissions to 683 (or 613) MT, it is useful to examine the Kaya Identity on which Table 2 is based.

The Kaya Identity links GHG emissions to the factors that drive these emissions: population (P); growth in GDP per capita (GDP/P); the energy intensity of GDP (E/GDP) and the GHG intensity of energy (GHG/E).

$$(1) \quad GHGs \equiv Px\left(\frac{GDP}{P}\right)x\left(\frac{E}{GDP}\right)x\left(\frac{GHG}{E}\right)$$

The Kaya Identity can be transformed into a rate of growth form (by converting to natural logarithms and taking time derivatives).

$$(2) \quad \%\Delta GHG = \%\Delta P + \%\Delta\frac{GDP}{P} + \%\Delta\frac{E}{GDP} + \%\Delta\frac{GHG}{E}$$

The first two right-hand terms are expected to be positive. The last two terms have been negative in industrialized countries in the past few decades, as a result of improvements in energy efficiency, sectoral shifts toward less energy-intensive activities, and a growth in the relative role of less carbonaceous (natural gas) or carbon-free (nuclear, hydro) forms of energy.

Equation (2) can be further simplified by cancelling the P and E (population and energy) terms, thereby allowing us to focus on the relationship between GHG emissions and two drivers, one economic (GDP) and one largely technological (GHG/GDP), of GHG emissions. Equation (2) also helps us to see why it is unrealistic to assume that the trend rate of GDP growth will remain constant, or largely so, while sharply reducing the rate of growth (or facilitating a decline) in GHG emissions. A constant GDP growth rate in the face of a lower growth rate of GHG emissions, to say nothing of an absolute decline in emissions, implies that all of the required adjustment comes from the largely technological variable, the rate of change of GHG emissions per unit of GDP. As a comparison of rows 5–8 with rows 1–3 in Table 2 indicates, to achieve the 683 (or 613) MT target would force the $\%\Delta(GHG / GDP)$ far outside the range of historical rates, and could even be outside the bounds of what could be physically achieved over a seven-to-ten-year period.

                                                    Christopher Green

Let me pursue the historical perspective a bit further. The rates of decline in GHG/GDP experienced in the 1970s and 1980s arguably suggest what an upper limit might look like in the 2000–2010 decade. The 1970s and 1980s were to some extent special so far as the rates of change in energy intensity (E/GDP) and carbon per unit energy (GHG/E) are concerned, the two variables that comprise the $\%\Delta$ in GHG/GDP (see the last two components in equation (1)). What is "special"? The run up in fossil fuel prices, especially oil and natural gas, following the OPEC oil embargo of 1973, and then again as a result of the Iran-Iraq war in 1979–80, squeezed out a lot of inefficiency in energy use attributable to the low and declining real prices for energy that the world experienced in the two previous decades. There is, of course, some room for further, relatively costless improvements in efficiency, and perhaps a repeat, in 2000–2010, of the amount of energy efficiency improvement experienced in the mid- and late 1970s and early 1980s.

But the picture is different for the other component of the rate of change in carbon intensity of output (GHG/GDP), the carbon intensity of energy (GHG/E). In the 1970s and 1980s, the rate of decline in GHG/GDP was materially affected by the large expansion in carbon-free electricity generation in Canada, as a result of the virtually simultaneous appearance of huge new hydro-electric facilities, especially in Quebec, Manitoba, and Saskatchewan, and of the CANDU nuclear reactors in Ontario. The displacement of fossil fuel-generated electricity by hydro-electric and nuclear electricity, contributed importantly to a substantial decline in GHGs per unit of energy generated, and thereby to GHG per unit of output. To my knowledge, there is no similar capability for a large-scale displacement of fossil fuels by carbon-free energy in the next decade.

Table 3 presents the results of the thought experiment. It indicates what might be the GDP costs of attempting to achieve, by 2010, the 683 MT target. The thought experiment is predicated on the assumption that there are more or less stringent upper limits on the attainable ten (or seven) year average annual rate of decline in the carbon-intensity output, that is the rate of decline in GHGs per unit of GDP. In Table 3, the calculations are based on the unrealistic assumption that there are firm upper limits to the rate of decline in the carbon intensity of output. While unrealistic, and will be modified below, the results are nevertheless suggestive. Also presented (in brackets) are the percentages by which actual GDP would fall below the BAU level in 2010. Although the assumed upper limits on the near term rates of decline in GHGs per unit of GDP that are

Table 3: Potential GDP Costs of GHG Reductions for Specified Limits to the Rate of Decline in GHG/GDP

Average annual rate of decline in GHGs to reach 683 MT target in 2010	*Average annual GDP growth rates (top rows) and % GDP [cost] in 2010 for maximum attainable rates of decline in GHG/GDP[a]*		
	−2.5%ΔGHG/GDP	*−2.0%ΔGHG/GDP*	*−1.5%ΔGHG/GDP*
−0.6 (2000–2010)	+1.9	+1.4	+0.9
GDP cost in 2010	[−3.8%]	[−8.4%]	[−12.8%]
−1.3 (2003–2010)	+1.2	+0.7	+0.2
GDP cost in 2010	[−7.3%]	[−10.5%]	[−13.5%]

Note: [a]Rate of decline in GHG/GDP is a measure of the rate of decline of the carbon intensity of output.
Source: Author's calculation.

indicated in Table 3, are only illustrative, they serve to make an important point. If more or less firm limits to the average annual rate of decline in GHG/GDP do exist, even if only because it takes time to make the necessary adjustments to capital equipment and the energy capital stock, and to human behaviour, as well, then the economic (GDP) costs of attempting to achieve even the 683 MT, to say nothing of the (613) MT, net emission target could be very substantial indeed.

To summarize, the bracketed figures in Table 3 are the outcome of a thought experiment in which the GDP growth rate is made to adjust to targeted decline in GHGs and maximum rates of decline in GHG/GDP. The bracketed figures indicate the percent by which GDP falls below the BAU level of GDP in 2010, as a result of limiting domestic GHG emissions to even modified targeted levels, if there are limits on the maximum achievable rate of decline in GHGs per unit of GDP. I should note that every one of the bracketed GDP cost figures in Table 3 are substantially higher than the estimates that I have seen for the GDP cost of the Kyoto target. In particular, they are anywhere from 1.5 to 4 times higher than those of Jaccard, Nyboer and Sadownik (2002), which represent, in my view, by far the most careful and responsible cost estimates I have seen to-date. See Table 4. At the other extreme, the bracketed cost calculations are as much as an order of magnitude, or more, higher than those generated by the MARKAL model, a model with a world-wide notoriety for lowballing Kyoto costs. They are also several times higher than the 1.2% to 1.6% (of GDP) *cost* estimates presented in the Annex to Canada's Climate Change Plan.

The reasons why the thought experiment calculations are so different from reported cost estimates should be clear: the thought experiment calculations assume that, beyond some point, attempts to achieve reductions in GHG emissions begin to run up against short-term technological limitations. As a result, further efforts to reduce GHGs must primarily affect the GDP variable, and thereby the GDP cost of reducing GHG emissions. Figure 2 illustrates. Beyond some point, attempts to further increase the rate of decline in the carbon intensity of output will incur rising marginal GDP costs. Figure 2 *qualitatively* compares the slopes of the GDP cost functions that are suggested by the MARKAL and CIMS models with that implied by my thought experiment.

Table 4: Estimates of GDP Cost of Canada's Kyoto Commitment

	% GDP reduction from BAU (reference) level
Canada Climate Change Plan[a] (Analysis and Modelling Group)	1.2 – 1.6
Markal Model[b]	0.5
Jaccard *et al.* (CIMS model)[b]	2.1
Green's "Thought Experiment"	3.8 – 8.4+

Notes: [a]Government of Canada (2002, Chart 2, p. 63).
[b]Jaccard, Nyboer and Sadownik (2002, Table 4.6, p. 87).

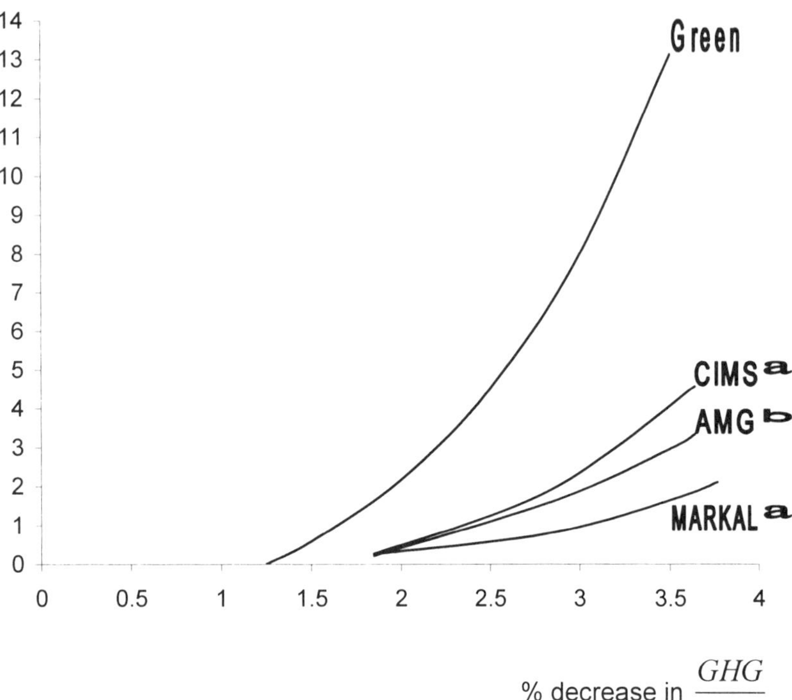

Notes: [a]For a comparison of CIMS and MARKAL models in terms of GDP costs, see Jaccard *et al.* (2002, ch. 3, especially pp. 87–88).
[b]National Climate Change Process, Analysis and Modelling Group. See Annex to Canada's Climate Change Plan.

There is, of course, a potential escape valve. If it is too costly for Canada to achieve even a modified (683 MT) Kyoto target by reductions at home, it could attempt to reduce costs somewhat by buying large amounts of emission permits on the international market. But at something like C$300 million for each 10

MT of permits, purchases of upwards of 50+ MT each year to meet commitments in a manner that does not unduly reduce the GDP growth rate would be a fiscally expensive proposition. In addition, such purchases may impact negatively on the balance of payments, causing further downward pressure on the Canadian dollar.

Conclusion

Any evaluation of the fiscal effects of Kyoto must take into account what is required to achieve the commitments in the first place. I have tried to show that even under the best of circumstances (a modified 683 MT target), it is highly unlikely that Canada can come close to achieving the required emission reductions. Furthermore, attempting to make large emission reductions is likely to be very expensive, incurring costs totally out of proportion to the prospective benefits (climate damages reduced) either globally or in Canada.

Still, there is a long-term global climate problem to be faced — and Canada must plan to do its share. In my view, facing up to the existence of a serious climate-change problem calls for abandoning costly and futile attempts to achieve short-run emission targets. After all, what affects climate is *not* annual emissions (a flow), but the *global* atmospheric concentration of GHGs (a stock). The relevant question is what will it take to stabilize the atmospheric concentration of GHGs at a level that avoids a "dangerous interference" with climate. Contrary to popular belief, including that of many climate policy-makers, the facile view (IPCC, WG III, 2001) that a combination of energy efficiency improvements and renewable energies are capable of achieving stabilization, has been shown to be fundamentally flawed (Hoffert *et al.*, 1998, 2002; Lightfoot and Green, 2001, 2002).

If the Canadian government wants to use its fisc to contribute to making a difference in stabilizing climate, it should focus its climate-change expenditures on the long-term development of technologies that, if successful, could be used not only in this country, but on a global scale, to eventually stabilize the atmospheric concentration of CO_2. Let me mention three possible projects, two in which, to the federal government's credit, it has already indicated a degree of interest or commitment.

Carbon capture and sequestration. As fossil fuels are likely to remain the dominant form of energy for much, if not all, of the twenty-first century, the capture of CO_2 emissions and their storage in depleted natural gas, oil wells, old coal beds, and saline acquifers is a technology that could begin to make a difference by 2020 to 2030. Canada's Climate Change Plan calls for investments in a clean coal demonstration project and CO_2 pipelines. This investment could be stepped up, and include expenditures on the research and development (R&D) into the capture of CO_2 and its conversion to a solid (and stable) state in a process that uses our plentiful supply of magnesium silicates. A further reason to pursue carbon capture and sequestration is that processes that would strip CO_2 from fossil fuels can produce hydrogen as a by-product.

Nuclear fusion. Despite closing down Canada's only fusion reactor (tokamak), at Varennes in Quebec, Canada is a backer of the International Thermonuclear Experimental Reactor (ITER). Canada is one of three countries or regions vying to host the ITER project (the other two are Japan and the EU). The host is expected to ante up 20 to 25% of the $5 billion basic cost of the project (*Science*, 28 February 2003, p. 1299). Canada has picked a potential site at Clarington, in Ontario (near Toronto). Although it is currently a private-sector initiative, common sense says that most of the basic R&D funding will have to come from the public sector.

Nuclear-generated electrolytic hydrogen. Any hope for a so-called "hydrogen economy" requires producing massive amounts of hydrogen without producing carbon dioxide emissions in the process. The focus, to-date, has been on electrolytic hydrogen using solar and wind sources of energy. But the diluteness of these renewable energy sources and the massive amounts of fresh water of distilled-water quality required to produce significant amounts of hydrogen (Lightfoot and Green, 2002), suggest looking elsewhere for a carbon-free source of electricity for the electrolytic process. An alternative source of carbon-free electricity is nuclear. One interesting proposal is to locate CANDU heavy water reactors in Canada's far north where there is plenty of fast running fresh water. The Canadian government could begin by investing in an experimental CANDU nuclear electrolytic hydrogen project.

Projects of the sort described, whether or not taken in partnership with some other countries, would require committed and long-term financing. I would suggest a small, earmarked carbon tax on all fossil fuels, with rebates in cases where the CO_2 is captured and sequestered. Undertaking such projects would

                                                                    Christopher Green

reflect a serious attempt to deal with climate change. While there is no assurance which of several plausible technologies for producing concentrated carbon-free energy will be successful, committed, long-term investment in them is the only path that is likely to produce stabilization GHGs at an acceptable level. Thus, if the federal government really wants to make useful investments on the climate-change front, it would do better to make investments that could really make a difference, rather than use those funds in a scattershot and eventually futile attempt to achieve essentially meaningless GHG emission targets.

References

Canada. Department of Finance (2003), *Budget 2003 — Budget Plan* (Ottawa: Department of Finance).

Canada. National Climate Change Process, Analysis and Modelling Group (1999), *Canada's Emissions Outlook: An Update* (Ottawa: Supply and Services Canada).

Government of Canada (2002), *Climate Change Plan for Canada* (December), at <www. climatechange.gc.ca>.

Hoffert, M.I. *et al.* (1998), "Energy Implications of Future Stabilization of Atmospheric CO_2 Content", *Nature* 395 (October), 881–884.

Hoffert, M.I. *et al.* (2002), "Advanced Technology Paths to Global Climate Stability: Energy for a Greenhouse Planet", *Science* 298 (November), 981–987.

Jaccard, M., J. Nyboer and B. Sadownik (2002), *The Cost of Climate Policy* (Vancouver: UBC Press).

Lightfoot, H.D. and C. Green (2001), "Energy Intensity Decline Implications for Stabilization of Atmospheric CO_2", Research Report No. 2001–7 (Montreal: Centre for Climate and Global Change, McGill University).

___________ (2002), "An Assessment of IPCC Working Group III Findings of the Potential Contribution of Renewable Energies to Atmospheric Carbon Dioxide Stabilization", Research Report No. 2002–5 (Montreal: Centre for Climate and Global Change, McGill University).

Science (2003), "ITER Negotiations Heat Up as All Sites Pass Muster", 28 February, 1299.

THE SOCIAL DIMENSION AND FISCAL ASPECTS OF HEALTH

LINKING ECONOMIC AND SOCIAL POLICY — TO BENEFIT *ALL* CANADIANS?

Frances Woolley, Carleton University

The 2003 budget is about connecting social and economic policy. The Department of Finance budget news release ran with the headline "Budget 2003 Supports Social and Economic Agenda While Maintaining Balanced Budgets". The budget documents contain a more explicit statement of the government's philosophy: "Budget 2003 recognizes the critical link between social and economic policy and how an integrated approach produces policies that benefit all Canadians" (Canada. Department of Finance, 2003, p. 8).

It is never entirely straightforward to separate social and economic dimensions of the budget. For example, is infrastructure spending on urban public transit about social goals (improving quality of life in our cities) or economic goals (attracting business to Canada)? Are language-related policies about social goals (furthering social cohesion) or economics (expanding the economic opportunities of specific linguistic groups)? Political imperatives require a coalition of interests behind various policies. More often than not these involve both parties with economic goals and ones with social objectives. Yet traditionally a distinction has been made between the economic and the social — evidenced, by, for example, the sectioning off of social policy in John Deutsch Institute Budget Conference volumes (this volume, and Hobson and Wilson, 2001).

Under the current Liberal government, however, social and economic policy have become increasingly intertwined. The National Child Benefit program is a classic example of the trend. On first inspection, it appears to be a policy with social goals, including child development and "quality of life."[1] Yet closer inspection shows that the National Child Benefit is explicitly an economic policy, designed to make work pay better than welfare, and "promote attachment to the workforce" (Federal, Provincial and Territorial Ministers Responsible for Social Services, 2003, p. 3). Health care, too, mixes social and economic policy:

> Canada's publicly funded health care system plays a key role in building the society we value. It is vital to our quality of life and a reflection of the values we share as a nation. *It is also at the leading edge where economic and social policies interact.* It provides Canada with the distinct economic advantage of a healthy, productive workforce and provides security in retirement. (Canada. Department of Finance, 2003, p. 12 emphasis added)

(Un)Employment Insurance, circa 1970s macroeconomics textbooks, was part of economic policy, an "automatic stabilizer". Yet increasingly, EI is being used for social policy goals.

In this paper, I will begin by looking at the budget numbers. Where is the money being spent? However, I will argue that dollar amounts are an incomplete guide to the significance of policy initiatives. Small programs can make a big difference, because they have a substantial impact on a tightly defined constituency, because of their cumulative effect over time, or because they are the levers of fundamental changes in incentives, in the way policy works. I will then go on to consider program developments that I consider particularly noteworthy: the changing nature of Employment Insurance (EI), policies relating to the integration of immigrants, visible and linguistic minorities into the labour force, and the division of the Canada Health and Social Transfer into separate Health and Social components.

---

[1] Quote taken from *Supporting Families and Children: Government of Canada Initiatives* available at <http://socialunion.gc.ca/nca/supporting_e.html>.

                                                    Frances Woolley

The budget policies are ostensibly designed to benefit all Canadians. However, as Jeffrey Simpson noted in his introductory remarks at this conference (Simpson, 2003), the spending initiatives in this budget are popular with the Liberal government's core constituencies, which include low-income women, immigrants, and francophones. Numerous policies outlined in this budget benefit exactly these constituencies. So, is this a budget for supporting an economic and social agenda? Or is it an agenda for political support? The only way to find out is by looking closely at the numbers.

Some Numbers

> You'll note that politicians no longer spend money, they invest it. Don't worry about paying more to the [IRS]. You aren't being taxed; you're taking a plunge on a fly-by-night stock issue.
> (P.J. O'Rourke, 2003)

Budget 2003 spending initiatives are divided into three categories: "Improving the quality of life of Canadians", "Making Canada's economy more innovative" and "providing essential public services" (Canada. Department of Finance, 2003, p. 223). The categories are mutually exclusive and jointly exhaustive — if something does not make Canada's economy more innovative, then it must improve the quality of life of Canadians or be an essential public service. The choice of words is deliberate: just as the average economist's eyes glaze over at the mention of "social dimensions", one suspects the average voter is more enthusiastic about spending to improve quality of life than social policy, however defined.

Quality of life spending is broken down into two broad categories: "Investing in Canada's health-care system" and "Investing in Canadian families and their communities". Table 1 summarizes these initiatives.

The first point to note is that health care dwarfs other components of the budget. Spending on health-care initiatives in the current fiscal year alone (2002/03) are more than twice the size of other social initiatives for

Table 1: Social Dimensions of the 2002/03 Budget

	2002/03	2003/04	2004/05
Health care			
Employment insurance compassionate family care leave benefit		86	221
Total health care	**4720**	**1369**	**2095**
Investing in Canadian families and their communities			
Families			
Early learning and childcare		25	81
Employability assistance for persons with disabilities		193	193
Child and family law strategy		27	26
Communities			
Affordable housing, residential rehabilitation and community partnerships		293	313
Infrastructure		100	150
Proceeds of crime		23	23
Aboriginal communities		**38**	**45**
Promoting Canadian culture and values		**188**	**233**
Total families and communities		**886**	**1065**
Revenue initiatives			
National child benefit supplement		200	300
Canadians with disabilities			
Child disability benefit		40	50
Tax assistance for Canadians with disabilities		55	110
Total revenue initiatives		**95**	**160**

2003–05 together. It is subtly revealing that the totals for health-care spending appear in bold font in the hard copy budget documents (Canada. Department of Finance, 2003, pp. 224–225), while other spending subtotals are in regular typeface. However, since Armine Yalnizyan's (2003) chapter in this volume provides a rich discussion of health care, I will stick primarily to other quality of life programs.

These quality of life initiatives are a disparate crew — everything from affordable housing to early learning and child care to (under Canadian culture and values) Katimavik and amateur sport and (under Aboriginal communities) first nations policing. Compared to the $4.7 billion allocated to health care in 2002/03 alone, the expenditure totals are small — $38 million for all programs "Strengthening Aboriginal Communities" in 2003/04 or $25 million for early learning and child-care services in that same year. Media discussions of the budget gave bigger spending numbers — $1 billion on child care, for instance — however, these large totals are derived from spending numbers aggregated over five years. Since future governments may not consider themselves bound by this year's budget plans, I will consider spending up to 2004/05 only.

Small programs can, however, make a difference. They matter, first of all, when they serve small target populations. Table 2 compares spending figures to target populations for selected programs. What is striking is that, relative to target populations, the various initiatives for Aboriginal com-munities are similar, in terms of per capita spending, to spending on health care, at just over $40 per capita. By way of contrast, the various early learning and child-care initiatives only work out to $14 for every child in Canada between 0 and 4.

The greater amounts received per beneficiary from narrowly targeted programs is the logic behind targeting programs more generally. Cheque writing has long been one of the things the federal government does best, as witnessed by programs such as Old Age Security and the Canada Pension Plan. This budget contains new cheque-writing programs. But they have tightly defined constituencies. The new compassionate family care leave, available through the EI program and worth up to $2,578, is available only to those with a gravely ill or dying family member and who meet EI eligibility criteria. A targeted, refundable, $1,600 Child Disability Benefit is available to those parents who have a disabled child, and whose family income is below $46,602 per year. An increase in the National Child Benefit Supplement (NCBS) of $150 per child as of July 2003 is available only to families with incomes below $33,487 (as of July 2003).

The size of the cheque — the amount received by each beneficiary — is inversely proportional to the number of people served by the program. For example, the NCBS served 2.7 million children and 1.5 million families between July 2001 and June 2002 (Federal, Provincial and Territorial Ministers Responsible for Social Services, 2003, p. iii). These 2.7 million

Table 2: Putting the Numbers into Perspective

	2003/04 ($million)	Target population (millions)	Benefit/ Target pop
Health care			
Employment insurance compassionate family care leave benefit	86	n/a	Max $2578
		15	**$5.73**
Total health care	**1369**	**31.50**	**$43.46**
Investing in Canadian families and their communities			
Families			
Early learning and childcare	25	1.71	$14
Employability assistance for persons with disabilities	193		
Child and family law strategy	27		
Communities			
Affordable housing, residential rehabilitation and community partnerships	293	1.8 to 3.1	$95 to $162
Infrastructure	100		
Proceeds of crime	23		
Aboriginal communities	**38**	**0.8 (1996)**	**$47.5**
Promoting Canadian culture and values	**188**	**31.5**	**$5.97**
Total families and communities	**886**		
Revenue initiatives			
National child benefit supplement	200	2.7 million children	Max $150 (July 1 2003 increase), average $75.
Canadians with disabilities			
Child disability benefit	40		Max $1,600
Tax assistance for Canadians with disabilities	55	3.6[a]	$15
Total revenue initiatives	**95**		

Note: [a]Figure taken from HRDC (2002).

children get at most $150 each. (I say "at most" because the amount budgeted for increasing the NCB supplement is $200 million in 2003/04 (Canada. Department of Finance, 2003, p. 228), which works out to be about $75 for each NCBS child).

It is hard to say for certain how many people will benefit from the Child Disability Benefit program since it is difficult to get firm data on the number of potentially eligible children. However, we can make some estimates by working backwards from the program's projected budgetary cost of $40 million in 2003/04. If each recipient family were to receive $1,600 then, based on the projected cost, we would expect to see 25,000 families benefiting from the program. If we take a more realistic figure of $1,000 per family (factoring in the effect of benefit tax-backs) the program benefits 40,000 families.

It is not clear why this program needs to be so tightly targeted. Targeting has a real equity cost. An average income, single-earner, two-parent family will have too high an income ($50,192 in 2001[2]) to be eligible for the Child Disability Benefit. Dual-earner families will not be eligible for the program unless their income is less than two-thirds the average.[3] Most lone parents of children with disabilities will benefit from the program. However, lone parents are not the only ones who need help. Having a child with special needs is a huge challenge for a family, regardless of family income level. There are indirect costs in terms of reduced income (it is hard to manage two jobs plus a special needs child), and direct costs such as modifying the home or Attends or purchasing adult-sized tricycles or computer software. Yes, low-income families need extra help to cope with a child's disabilities. But surely average income families could use a bit of help too?

The logic behind targeting seems to be that if we limit eligibility to a program, then we can afford a generous per capita benefit. It is better to provide a generous benefit to a small group of people than a small benefit to a widely defined constituency. There is a political logic to the argument.

---

[2]Market income, 2001, taken from <www.statcan.ca>, accessed August 5, 2003.

[3]An average dual-earner family's market income was $75,417 in 2001, <www.statcan.ca>, accessed August 5, 2003.

Suppose we begin with the assumption — commonly made in the public choice literature — that when a voter receives a transfer from political party X then he or she is more likely to vote for party X. Moreover, suppose that the larger the transfer, the greater the change in voting preferences. If the $40 million dedicated to the Child Disability Benefit was divided equally amongst all Canadian children, it would amount to about $5 per child or $8 per family. It is hard to imagine $8 changing anyone's vote. But a benefit of $800 or $1,000 or $1,600 per family, delivered to a marginal or organized or identifiable voting constituency, such as low-income women, could deliver votes.

Initiatives that are not targeted can end up falling into the category of "worthy causes but not enough money to make a difference". The initiatives in child care could, potentially, fall into this category. Child care is expensive: in 1998 the median fees charged for licensed care for children 18 months to three years was $603 per month in Ontario, $547 per month in BC, and averaged $477 per month across the country, according to Friendly, Beach and Turiano (2002). More recent (2001) figures estimate the mean monthly fee for 18-month to 3-year olds is $662 in BC, with the highest fees, $848 per month, in Richmond, BC (Forer and Hunter, 2001, p. 42). Even if we take the 2004/05 budget number ($81 million) and give a low-end estimate of $5,000 per year per place, this amounts to somewhere in the ballpark of 16,000 fully subsidized spaces. Quite a few spaces, yes, but compared to numbers such as "2.7 million children receiving NCBS supplement" or "1.7 million children between 0 and 4 in Canada" it is a tiny number.

Moreover, since the money is being transferred to the provinces and then spent provincially, there is a real possibility that increased federal funding will, to some extent, crowd out provincial funding. For example, Quebec already has a universal $5 per day child-care program. For Quebec, additional federal money simply reduces the provincial cost of an already existing program.

The same "worthy but small" label is true of the affordable housing initiatives. Yes, $313 million in 2004/05 is a nice chunk of money. But if we decompose this figure into component parts, and look only at the money going directly into affordable housing as opposed to residential rehabilitation and community partnerships, the figure shrinks to $50 million. Is this

                                                                    Frances Woolley

enough to make a difference? An optimistic scenario is that federal money can be used for "leveraging resources": small amounts of federal money can produce substantial amounts of housing, as in this CMHC success story:

> In 1999, the City of Nepean completed a $10 million, 66-unit life-lease project for seniors, called the Meridian. The project was self-financing with the help of a $45,000 proposal development fund loan from CMHC and a CMHC-insured $7.5 million mortgage loan to help finance the land purchase and construction. (CMHC, 2001)

A more pessimistic appraisal compares housing costs with the incomes of poor Canadians. A single parent with one child in Alberta will receive an income, from welfare, of under $12,000 per year, a couple with two children gets less than $20,000 from welfare. At the same time, the average rent for a low-end, two bedroom apartment in Calgary is $650 per month. Welfare incomes are not enough to pay housing costs.[4] When people do not have the wherewithal to afford housing, "leveraging resources" is not enough: subsidies are required. There are currently 1.84 million Canadians living on welfare,[5] 3.1 million with low incomes.[6] The affordable housing initiatives will help some of these people. Yet the entire bundle of initiatives works out to around $100 per low-income Canadian. I find it hard to get excited about a program that will have a limited impact on a large problem.

What's more interesting is the nature of policy, the fundamental philosophy driving program choices. A fundamental philosophy behind this budget is that social and economic policy can be brought together — two goals for the price of one. Somewhat explicit is the idea that good social policy

---

[4]Welfare incomes taken from National Council of Welfare (2003). Housing prices taken from CMHC (2003).

[5]National Council of Welfare (2003), *Fact Sheet: Welfare Recipients* <http://www.ncwcnbes.net/htmdocument/principales/numberwelfare.htm>, number of welfare recipients for March 2002.

[6]As of 2001, low-income data taken from Statistics Canada, <http://www.statcan.ca/english/Pgdb/famil19b.htm>.

strengthens economic performance. Less explicit is the idea that economic policies can be used to achieve social ends. But this is precisely the issue I want to talk about next: the social ends served by an economic program — Employment Insurance.

Employment Insurance

I will argue that, however much one may agree with the objectives of the EI changes (and I will be frank, I like these policies), we are seeing a fundamental shift in the nature of EI. This will lead to mounting pressure for reform of EI finance and, indeed, questions about the long-term sustainability of the current EI structure.

Figure 1 documents the rise in special benefits, relative to regular benefits, over the past five years. (Numbers are shown as a portion of regular benefits to facilitate comparison across data sources, to control for the effects of inflation on nominal benefit values, also to highlight the relative importance of different components of the EI program.) The first years are taken from Canada Employment Insurance Commission (2001) and preceding volumes; 2001 and 2002 numbers are based on the projections of the Chief Actuary, available from HRDC (2001) and subsequent volumes. What these figures show is relative stability in regular benefits claims, with the big changes being driven by program changes, particularly for maternity and parental leaves. The most dramatic change is the doubling of parental leave entitlements, which is projected to mean that, by 2002, for every dollar paid out on regular benefits, 36 cents will be paid out in special benefits.

Why does that matter now? The 2003 federal budget announced a new "Employment Insurance Compassionate Family Care Leave Benefit" (Canada. Department of Finance, 2003, p. 73). This benefit will allow "individuals who meet the eligibility requirements for EI special benefits, and have served the two-week waiting period" to receive "a six-week EI compassionate family care leave benefit to care for their gravely ill or dying child, parent or spouse" (2003, p. 73). The cost of the program is projected to be at $221 million once it is fully in effect. If the program had been in place in 2002, special benefits would have approached 39% of regular

                                                                 Frances Woolley

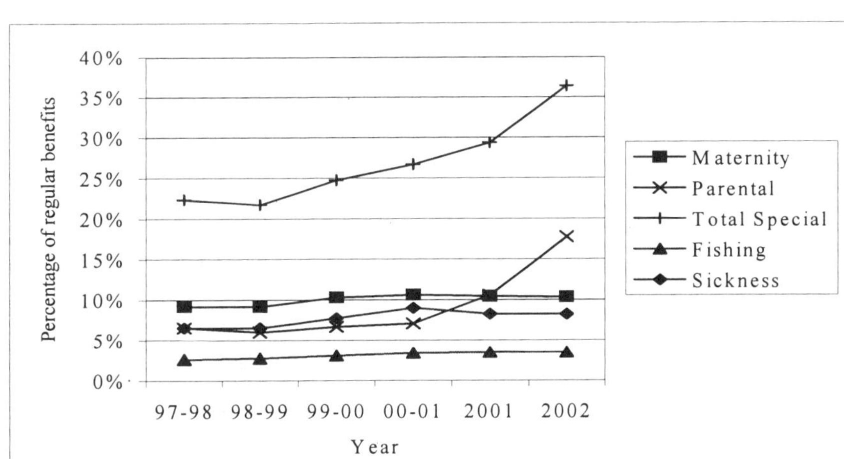

benefits, as shown in Figure 1. This is not a bad thing. Enhanced parental leave provisions in the previous budget have been very popular among new parents. With the aging population, more and more people find themselves caring for elderly relatives. I would be willing to bet that this will be one of the most popular measures in this year's budget. But at the same time, it raises some very interesting questions about the way policy gets made in Canada, and the best design for social policies.

The method by which this $211 million cost figure is arrived at is described in the Kirby report (Kirby, 2002). This report estimated that approximately 160,000 of those dying each year in Canada require palliative care (based on 1999 numbers). Providing EI at an average rate of $257 per week for six weeks for 160,000 caregivers would cost around $247 million, which is in the ballpark of the figure given in the budget. There are two reasons to think that this Kirby report estimate may be too low. First, it is based on number of deaths, so it excludes those who are gravely ill but survive for a period of time. It also appears that there is only one leave associated with each critically ill person: "eligible family members will be able to share the benefit" (2003, p. 73). However it is not obvious how easy a limit of one leave per critically ill person will be to enforce. At the same time, however, only about 50% of new births generate an EI maternity or parental leave claim. If the take-up rate for compassionate family care leave is similar to the take-up rates for maternity and parental leave, then the Kirby report figure may in fact be an overestimate.

One of the more interesting features of the compassionate family care leave provisions in the most recent budget, is that it funds a form of leave that many employers do not allow — leave to care for family members. Indeed, such a leave is not protected in provincial labour relations acts. When maternity and parental leaves were expanded, provincial legislation changed to force employers to allow employees to take advantage of more generous leave provisions. Will this happen again? For federal employees, the answer appears to be "yes": the budget promises changes to the Canada Labour Code to allow employees to take family care leaves. This is a very interesting case of changes in federal benefit programs driving regulation of the labour market.

And it again raises the question: Why do this through EI? The reason is fairly simple: the EI fund has a surplus of over $40 billion. In 2002 a break-event premium rate would have been $1.57 for every $100 of earnings, actual premiums were $2.20 (figures taken from HRDC, 2001). Sitting on top of a surplus and not using it does not work politically: "If there's such a surplus in the EI fund, why not cut premiums?" Cutting premiums, however, is risky. Each 2% increase in the unemployment rate increases the break-even EI premium level by about 30 cents (HRDC, 2001, p. 3). The EI fund could go from an annual surplus to an annual deficit position over-night. Even more crucially, cutting premiums and then raising them again when the unemployment rate rises is bad politics — electors will punish a tax increase more than they will reward a tax cut. And also bad economics, since it is a destabilizing fiscal policy.

So what better way to help families than to allow them to spend time together and support those who care for the sick and dying? Plus more care from family members relieves pressure on the formal, publicly funded health-care system. But this new EI initiative raises awkward questions: Who's in and who's out? Who has jobs that allow six weeks off to care for a sick relative, and who doesn't? And what about the self-employed? How much will this cost? Government estimates are simply ballpark figures — no one really knows what the take-up rate is likely to be for a program such

                                    Frances Woolley

as this one. In the case of a relatively long-lasting serious illness (e.g., Alzheimers), how many compassionate care family leaves are allowed to care for a single family member?

Fundamentally, however, it continues the evolution of EI from an employment-related program to a social program. Will contributors at some point say "employment insurance is insurance against job loss and I'm not paying into what is essentially a social program — that should be funded out of general tax revenues". Or will compassionate family care leave, by broadening the base of EI claimants into people with steady jobs (a middle manager at a Toronto bank or a nurse in a Vancouver hospital) actually serve to increase and maintain support for the program?

Integration of Immigrants and Linguistic Minorities

Liberal governments have a long-standing tradition of support for immigration and for language policies. Yet the past 20 years have seen fundamental changes in the nature of immigration and language policies in Canada. Immigration has changed: immigrants are increasingly coming from non-European countries or are members of visible minorities. There is evidence that immigrants did not do as well in the Canadian labour market in the 1990s as they did in, say, the 1960s and 1970s, suggesting that immigrants are integrating into the labour market at a declining rate. Communities such as Surrey or Richmond in British Columbia are suggestive of the emergence of racially segregated suburbs and communities, and a possible decline in social and cultural integration of immigrant and/or visible minority groups.

Language politics have also changed, because of the slow but steady decline of the relative importance of Quebec, and the French language more generally, in the Canadian confederation. In the most recent census, about 23% of Canadians had French as a mother tongue; 18% had a language other than French or English. Quebec's population has shrunk from 29%

of the Canadian total in 1951 to 23.7% today[7] — an 18% decline in population share. Census data show a respectable 18% of the Canadian population as bilingual in both French and English. However, the census question only asks if a person is able to carry out a conversation in each official language. Even a linguistically challenged individual such as myself, who can carry on very simple conversations on severely circumscribed subject matter (children, dogs, poutine) can answer "yes".

Policies regarding immigration and language are right on the nexus between social and economic policies. This budget contained a number of initiatives in this area. Some deal specifically with new immigrants:

- To encourage immigrants to settle in smaller communities throughout Canada, the government will invest $3.8 million over the next two years to work with its partners on more effective approaches to attract skilled workers to communities across the country (Canada. Department of Finance, 2003, p. 131).
- The federal government will invest $13 million over the next two years to work in partnership with provincial and territorial governments, regulatory bodies and employers to facilitate foreign credential assessment and recognition (ibid.).

The second of these two initiatives is particularly sensible. There is a fundamental inconsistency in an immigration policy that gives potential immigrants points for having needed skills such as training in engineering or medicine, but then fails to recognize that same training once immigrants arrive on Canadian soil. In fact, it would be wise to integrate the assessment of foreign credentials with the immigration process, so that potential immigrants with recognized credentials would be awarded more points and/or fast tracked in the immigration process.

Budget 2003 also represents a renewed commitment to official languages: "Linguistic duality is at the heart of Canada's collective identity. Knowledge of another official language is a matter of both cultural and economic enrichment" (ibid., p. 112). This is neither the time nor the place

---

[7] 1951 figures taken from <http://www.ucalgary.ca/applied_history/tutor/canada1946/chapter4.html>; most recent figures are calculated from 2001 census data, available at <http://www.statcan.ca>.

                                        Frances Woolley

to provide a detailed analysis of Canada's language policy. However, some facts and figures are revealing. Bilingualism levels are highest among young high school graduates — 24% know (according to the extremely weak census criterion) both official languages. This might suggest that Canada is at last becoming a truly bilingual country. A quick look at past censuses reveals that young high school graduates consistently have among the highest reported bilingualism levels. If we take those same high school graduates and follow them five years later — when they are no longer taking French or English at school, and when they, and not their parents, are answering the census questions — we see a fall in the reported bilingualism levels.

Language policies are experienced differently in different parts of the country. In Quebec, 40.8% of the population speaks both French and English. The corresponding figure for British Columbia is 7.0%.[8] Any policy designed to "enhance the use of Canada's two official languages in the public service" (ibid.) will have a disparate impact on people from different regions of the country. A policy requiring police officers to be taller than five feet ten inches will eliminate many women, Chinese-Canadians, and other applicants. In the same way, a policy requiring people in the public service to speak both French and English will have a particularly strong impact on people whose mother tongue is, say, Arabic or Mandarin or Urdu. Requiring such a person to speak both French and English before obtaining a public service position is a requirement for tri-lingualism, not just bilingualism.

The federal government is committed to increasing the representation of visible minorities in the public service. However, there is a real tension and conflict between the government's bilingualism policies and its multi-culturalism policies. Policies such as height requirements are now subject to strict scrutiny. Employers must demonstrate that the requirement is strictly necessary for the job. Often height requirements are replaced with other, more appropriate tests, such as strength requirements. In the same way, we need to provide government services in more than one language and in a way that is responsive to the needs and aspirations of all

---

[8]Calculated from 2001 census figures taken from <http://www.statcan.ca/english/Pgdb/demo19a.htm>.

Canadians. Yet this does not mean enshrining an official bilingualism policy developed for another era in Canadian political and economic life.

Official language legislation may look like a social policy. But it is one with serious economic implications. And here I believe we need to be particularly aware of where the Liberal government's policies come from. Recall who are the Liberal Party's core constituencies: low-income women, francophones, and immigrants. Earlier budgets delivered billions in tax cuts which did less, relatively speaking, for these groups. This budget gives immigrants and francophones something to hold onto.

Splitting up the Canada Health and Social Transfer

Sometimes the most significant budget items are ones that do not have a dollar sign attached. The 2003 budget announced the division of the Canada Health and Social Transfer into the Canada Health Transfer and the Canada Social Transfer. It is a move watched anxiously in the ivory towers, as academics ask "Is this good for universities or bad for universities?"

Splitting the Canada Health and Social Transfer into two limits provincial discretion over federal funds. Earmarking part of the transfer for health and part of the transfer for "social" programs (social assistance, postsecondary education) establishes minimum levels of spending in each category.

It also allows for differential increases in health and social spending, and allows differential allocation formula to be applied to different provinces. This is, *a priori*, a sensible thing to do. In general, one would expect lower income provinces to have higher social assistance caseloads and a greater need for social spending. At the same time, the lower cost of living in these provinces may reduce the effective cost of providing health-care services. Also provinces have differential needs for health-care spending because, for example, of demographic differences. Differentiating social and health allows for differential increases in the two parts of the budget.

Is it good for universities or bad for universities? It really depends upon the priorities of the federal government. If the federal government places a relatively high priority on health, it could harm universities.

                                                        Frances Woolley

A Note on Child Benefits

At the 2000 John Deutsch Institute Budget Conference, I was able to praise a footnote in one of the Annexes of the budget, which described government plans to reduce the rate at which child benefits are taxed back from 5% to 4.14%, lowering tax rates on hundreds of thousands of Canadian families (Woolley, 2001, p. 153). These plans appear to have been shelved. At least, reduction in tax-back rates has changed from a specific commitment to a vague promise. This is unfortunate. A two-child family in Toronto on a net income of $70,000 per year will struggle to buy a house in that city. Yet that family will receive no National Child Benefit Supplement, and will have had (taking July 2004 numbers to make the math easy) 73% of their Canada Child Tax Benefit taxed back. The tax recognition for caregiving those parents receive — $321 per child per year or $26.75 per child monthly — is less in real terms than middle-class parents received a generation ago, when a child was a tax deduction and moms got family allowance cheques each month.

All of this is old and familiar. What is unfortunate is that this old and familiar reasoning is being applied to new programs, specifically, the Child Disability Benefit.

Conclusions

Overall, it was not a bad budget. I would have liked to have seen a clearer focus. I worry that the small initiatives set up in this budget will simply become the targets for the next program review. This is particularly likely to happen if the programs require a large administrative apparatus relative to the benefits delivered, if the programs become discredited through being overly politicized, or if the constituencies served by the program are no longer seen as core. Programs such as Katimavik, affordable housing, or employability assistance for people with disabilities are examples of programs I would see as potentially vulnerable according to these criteria.

Ongoing program reviews are likely. The finance minister, John Manley, in his pre-budget consultations, made a commitment to program review. Without radical restructuring, which is unlikely to happen in the near term, health-care spending will continue to put pressure on other areas of the budget. Tax cuts announced in previous budgets have eaten away most of the budget surplus. A negative shock to revenues could push the budget into a deficit position, and generate pressure for spending cuts.

Employment Insurance is another program I see as being potentially vulnerable in the medium to long term, if dissatisfaction grows among employers or employees with EI being used as a social program, if new programs cost more than anticipated, or if an economic downturn pushes the fund from black to red.

Yet this budget contains initiatives in areas where the federal government has a responsibility to act, and where spending is needed. Aboriginal communities have some of the highest population growth rates and worst socio-economic outcomes of any community in Canada: there is scope for federal policy to make a difference. A small amount of coordinated federal spending to ease the entry of immigrants into Canada, especially through language training and credential recognition, could have huge future payoffs for individual immigrants and the Canadian economy. And the federal transfusion of funds into health care will ease, at least temporarily, the financial strain on the health-care system. So, overall, it was not a bad budget.

References

Canada. Department of Finance (2003), *Building the Canada We Want: The Budget Plan 2003* (Ottawa: Minister of Public Works and Government Services Canada).

Canada Employment Insurance Commission (2001), *Employment Insurance 2000 Monitoring and Assessment Report* (Ottawa: Human Resources Development Canada), available at <http://www.hrdc-drhc.gc.ca/ae-ei/loi-law/2000/2000mar. pdf>.

Canada Mortgage and Housing Corporation (CMHC) (2001), *A Guide to Developing a Municipal Affordable Housing Strategy,* Research Highlights Socio-economic Series No. 89 (Ottawa: CMHC).

__________, (2003) *2003 Canadian Housing Observer*. Available at <http://www. cmhc-schl.gc.ca/en/cahoob/cuhoma/cuhoma_09.cfm>, accessed August 6, 2003.

                                                         Frances Woolley

Federal, Provincial and Territorial Ministers Responsible for Social Services (2003), *The National Child Benefit Progress Report: 2002* (Ottawa: Minister of Public Works and Government Services Canada).

Forer, B. and T. Hunter (2001), *2001 Provincial Child Care Survey* (Victoria: British Columbia Ministry of Community, Aboriginal and Women's Services). Available at <http://www.mcaws.gov.bc.ca/childcare/ChildCar/research2001.htm>.

Friendly, M., J. Beach and M. Turiano (2002), *Early Childhood Education and Care in Canada 2001* (Toronto: Childcare Resource and Research Unit), available at <http://www.childcarecanada.org/ECECC2001/>.

Hobson, P.A.R. and T.A. Wilson (2001), *The 2000 Federal Budget: Retrospect and Prospect* (Kingston: John Deutsch Institute for the Study of Economic Policy, Queen's University).

Human Resources Development Canada (HRDC) (2001), *Outlook for EI Premium Rates in 2002*, available from <http://www.hrdc-drhc.gc.ca/ae-ei/loi-law/sept-outl-eng.pdf>.

__________ (2002), *The Strategic Plan of the Office for Disability Issues 2002–2007*, available at <http//www.hrsdc.gc.ca/asp/gateway.asp?hr=/en/hip/odi/documents/strategicPlan/chap2.shtml&hs=pyp#22>.

Kirby, M.J.L. (2002), *The Health of Canadians — the Federal Role*. Final Report on the state of the health-care system in Canada, Standing Senate Committee on Social Affairs, Science and Technology.

National Council of Welfare (2003), *Fact Sheet April 2003: 2002 Welfare Incomes and the Estimated Poverty Line by Province and Household Type*. Available at <http://www.ncwcnbes.net/htmdocument/reportwelfinc02/WelInc&PovLin02.htm>.

O'Rourke, P.J. (2003), "Signature Quotes: Politics", accessed at <http://www.urbin.net/EWW/sigs/pj_polysigs.html>.

Simpson, J. (2003), "The Politics of the 2003 Budget", in this volume.

Woolley, F. (2001), "Budget 2000: A Children's Budget?" in P.A.R. Hobson and T.A. Wilson (eds.), *The 2000 Federal Budget: Retrospect and Prospect* (Kingston: John Deutsch Institute for the Study of Economic Policy, Queen's University).

Yalnizyan, A. (2003), "The Health Care Budget: Did it Resolve the 'Crisis'?", in this volume.

THE HEALTH-CARE BUDGET:
Did it Resolve the "Crisis"?

Armine Yalnizyan, Canadian Centre for Policy Alternatives

It came as no surprise that health care took the spotlight in the February 2003 federal budget. Since 1997 there have been eight separate governmental bodies concerned with the future of public health care: five provincial commissions and advisory committees on the future of health care (Alberta, New Brunswick, Ontario, Quebec, and Saskatchewan), and three federal (the National Forum on Health; six volumes — and counting — of reports from the Senate Standing Committee on Social Affairs, Science and Technology; and the release, in November 2002, of the high profile and greatly anticipated report of the Romanow Commission, appointed by the outgoing prime minister, Jean Chrétien).

During this period of scrutiny, intergovernmental wrangling intensified, largely around the level and nature of financial contribution the federal government should make for public health care. Political squabbling was accompanied by increasing public concern over longer waits for access to care. These new pressures created a crescendo of policy debate about the "sustainability" of universal health care as we know it. Various attempts to contain the rising public costs in the mid-1990s were seen as having been ineffective at best, counterproductive at worst.

By September 2000, the first of two major federal-provincial-territorial (FPT) deals were struck, providing $21.2 billion in new federal funds for health spending over the next five years. This infusion of cash produced little noticeable improvement in reduced waiting times in the first two years. Rising public pressure for immediate improvements triggered another round of provincial demands for more federal money. Health care began to be framed as a public program in crisis, whose future was perhaps unaffordable.

In the new post-Romanow climate, the next FPT deal was expected to "save" medicare, and all eyes were on the federal government. The Health Accord of February 5, 2003 provided the blueprint for the federal budget's announcements of $34.8 billion in reinvestments in health care, making up the lion's share of new federal spending over the next five years. Did this "health budget" resolve the crisis?

This paper looks at how the February 2003 federal budget addressed three themes that have contributed to a sense of crisis in public health care in recent years, then discusses how these themes will continue to fuel public debates in the near-to-medium term:

- *How much is enough?*
The need for more money drives the "sustainability" theme, but touches on the fear that no amount is enough and that public health care as we know it is unaffordable.

- *Is health care a "national" program?*
Health care mirrors the tensions of the increasingly fractious and decentralized environment in which this "national" social program is delivered. Yet it also embodies a basic commonality of services needed for individuals and the economy to function well.

- *What are we getting for our money?*
Lack of transparency and accountability — with respect to both federal transfers for and provincial spending on health care — increase cynicism and concern about whether vast public expenditures are delivering value for money.

While progress has been made in each area, the same elements of tension exist now as before the budget. What has changed is the increased desire, at least on the part of citizens and policy experts, to monitor progress on improvements in the efficiency and the cost-effectiveness of the public system.

Armine Yalnizyan

How Much is Enough: Is Public Health Care on an "Unsustainable" Track?

There are two aspects to the sustainability question. First, how much should we spend on health care through the public purse? Second, how should those expenditures be cost-shared between the federal and provincial governments?

The sustainability question first emerged as a debate about the cost-shared dimension of funding. But within the space of a few years this discussion developed an additional, more existential theme — what is the nature of public health care in the twenty-first century? What should be in the basket of publicly insured goods and services, and should that basket look the same from coast to coast to coast?

Unsustainable: Unilateral Retrenchment of the Senior Partner in a Deal

The debate about whether public health care was affordable began, historically, with a clear message from the federal government that, at current rates of growth, it was not affordable. The shift to an "unsustainable" trajectory was initiated by unilateral moves by the federal government starting in the mid-1980s, as it stepped up its efforts to eliminate budgetary deficits that had become a fixture of federal governance since the late 1970s.

From 1986 to 1996, there were two changes in the funding formula governing how the federal government calculated its transfers to the province. The first slowed the rate of increase in transfers, the second froze the levels. It is estimated that the provinces lost about $23.6 billion in transfers from the federal government over this period (Canada. Standing Senate Committee on Social Affairs, Science and Technology, 2001, p. 14).

The period 1988 to 1992 saw public health-care costs soar. The combination of rapidly increasing costs and shrinking federal assistance triggered a flurry of attempts to contain costs at the provincial level, starting with the fiscal year 1991/92 and ending by 1997/98. Provincial cuts during this period totalled about $2.5 billion (CIHI, 2002).

The February 1995 federal budget increased pressures on the provinces by introducing the first absolute cuts to federal funding of medicare since it was launched in the 1960s. That budget introduced the Canada Health and Social Transfer (CHST), which henceforth provided federal cash and tax transfers to the provinces in one block fund covering health care, postsecondary education, and a range of social assistance support programs, to be allocated as the provinces saw fit. Promoted as offering greater "flexibility" for the provinces, the new fund transferred less money for these programs than had previously been provided federally. This shifted the political heat for decisions to cut spending from the federal to the provincial governments. Between 1994/95 and 2000/01, using the benchmark of how transfers were allocated when the current government came to power in 1993–94, it is estimated that federal cuts for health care alone would total $8.7 billion.[1] Almost all of this was due to reductions in the CHST.

The Era of Cuts
- 1985/86 – 1995/96: The federal government unilaterally changed funding formula, twice. Lost transfers to provinces estimated at $23.6 billion.
- 1991/92 – 1997/98: Provinces cut own health budgets, cumulative loss of $2.5 billion.
- From 1994/95 to 2000/01: Federal government cuts to cash transfers for health alone estimated at $8.7 billion.

Unsustainable: Dramatic Cost-Containment

The degree of cost-containment was unprecedented in the history of public health care, as can be seen from Figure 1, and highly unusual in the international context as well. The denominator, or gross domestic product (GDP), was not the driving factor behind the trend lines in this period, as GDP growth was quite stagnant from the recession of 1990/91 until the late 1990s. No other

---

[1]Calculated from Canada. Department of Finance (2000, p. 7), using 1995/96 allocations for health care as the base year. This series provides the federal cash and tax transfers for health care from 1975 to 2000. To state this cash amount as a share of provincial expenditures on health care, reference has been made to Canadian Institute for Health Information (2001, Table 9).

                                                        Armine Yalnizyan

Figure 1: Health Spending as Percent of GDP, Canada 1975 to 2001

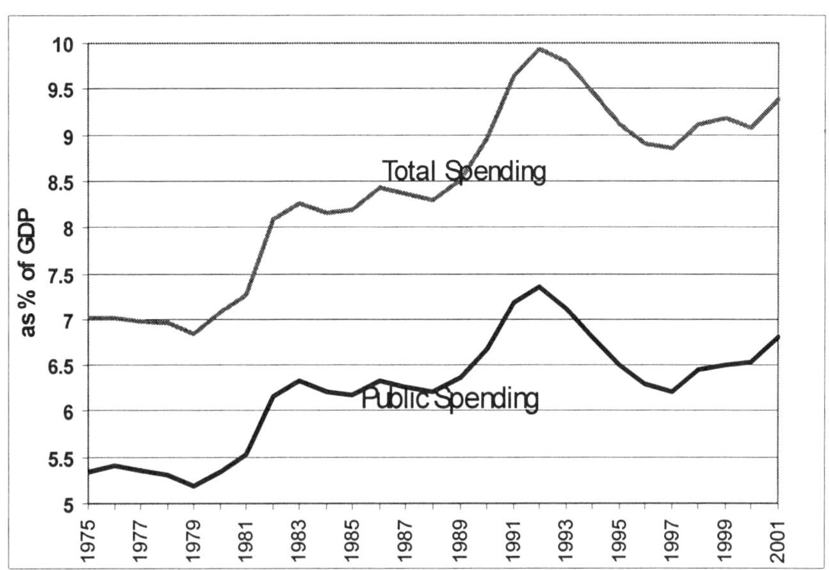

Source: CIHI (2001).

Organisation for Economic Co-operation and Development (OECD) nation matched this stark downward trend, except for Finland, whose decreasing ratio of health-care spending to GDP was driven by a rapidly increasing GDP (OECD, 2002, Table 10).

Health care is arguably the single most politically difficult service cluster to cut. As can be seen from the previous page, provinces cut, but not to the degree that federal supports for health care were cut. But the scale of cuts that occurred in the mid-1990s were sufficient in impact that the consequent rationing of the system produced widespread concern about waiting times for access to primary care, diagnostics and treatment.

Unsustainable: More Spending on a "National" Program, Less Help from the Feds

The constraints that became endemic throughout the public system predictably launched new calls for private-sector "solutions" that could shorten patients' waiting times. These ideas can be lumped into three broad categories: individual out-of-pocket purchases or user fees that permit people to avoid or jump the queue; new financing and billing schemes, such as medical savings accounts, or a system of co-payments or credits through the tax system; and the provision of new supply (of facilities, not labour), levered through private investment and/or ownership.

Figure 2: Federal Real Per Capita Health Support is at Historic Lows

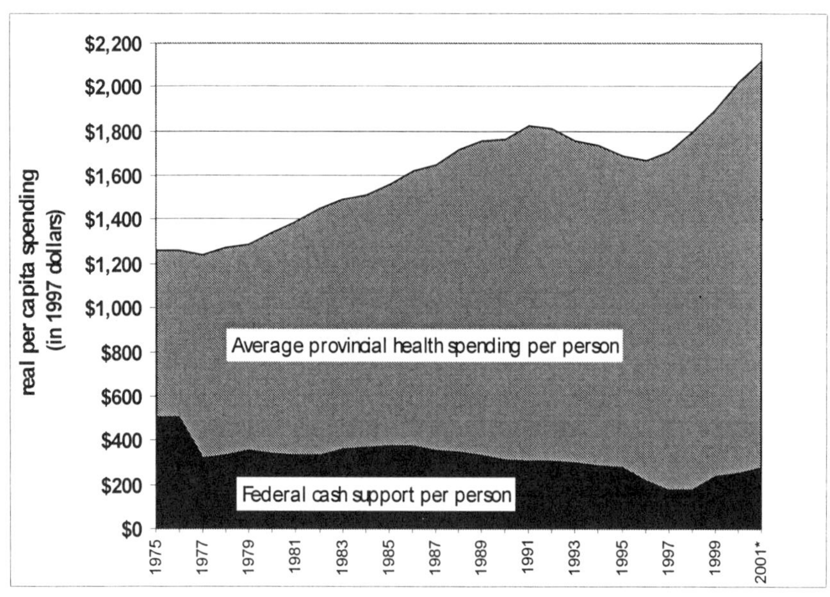

Source: Provincial data CIHI (2001, Table B4.7); federal data calculated from Finance Department data, updated to reflect the September 2000 agreement.

                                                      Armine Yalnizyan

Although these options were and remain highly contested, they are very potent in an atmosphere where the provinces continue to do most of the heavy lifting to meet the costs of increased health-care demands. Indeed, collectively the provinces have never spent more on health care, per person, in inflation-adjusted dollars, and the trend lines show no sign of flattening.

The demand pressures of a population expecting to live longer and remain more active throughout its life, combined with an explosion in technological possibilities that can make those expectations a reality, means the health-care system cannot stand still. But clearly, in a context where growth of demand will always outpace expansion of supply, there is a limit to what can be done. This places more intense visibility on the fact that federal support for the social program that Canadians most value has languished, even taking into account renewed contributions.

Unsustainable: Concerns about Growth in a No-Growth Environment

After the cuts of the early to mid-1990s, continued constraint was not a political option. Elected officials who ignored the growing strains in the public health-care system were likely not to get re-elected. Starting in 1998, public spending on health care increased, with growth first funded just from provincial coffers, then fuelled by funds from both senior levels of government.

Long-term trends in health-care spending show that the past few years were not a period of unusually rapid expenditure growth, even though it is an unusually high profile period of reinvestment and ideas for health-care reform (see Figure 3). Indeed, expenditures for health care grew far more rapidly from the mid-1970s to 1980s, but at that time there was notably little debate about the sustainability of the promise of universal public health care.

However, this recent period of accelerated spending has become another cause for concern. Though widely acknowledged to be at least in part a "catch-up" phase, reversing the earlier cuts, the renewed rate of growth in spending is viewed as unsustainable because of a particular context: almost every jurisdiction (federal and provincial) has committed itself to no- or

Figure 3: Why is the Growth in Health-Care Spending Considered Out of Control Now?

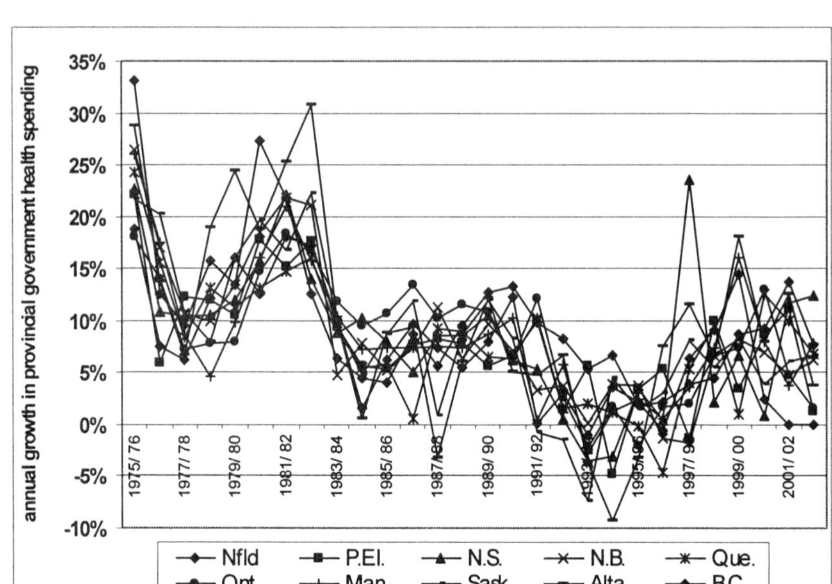

Source: CIHI (2002, Table A1).

slow-growth policies for government spending, with a priority on balanced budgets and tax cuts.

Unsustainable: Health Care Taking a Bigger Bite Out of Provincial Coffers

What makes the current period of expansion doubly challenging from the point of view of those who deliver public health care is that it is unclear if the provinces and territories will be caught on the hook for a program that is expected to be there for all Canadians when they need it, but that is not publicly resourced in a manner that reflects a commitment by the more senior level of government.

Armine Yalnizyan

The previous figures show the degree to which provinces and territories are increasingly carrying the burden to provide what Canadians want from public health care. However, pervasive commitments to balanced budgets and tax cuts, combined with continued public pressure to make sure health care is universally available, has meant that cost-containment is taking place in other areas of government expenditure. The result is that health care is taking a bigger bite out of provincial expenditures with every passing year.

Unsustainable: Commitment to Revenue Constraints

While it is true that the provinces are doing more for health care than was the original bargain, it is also true that their demands on the federal government for more money have occurred at the same time as they have opted to forego revenue from their own sources.

Since 1996, in both times of budgetary deficit and surplus, the provinces have used different rationales to introduce or accelerate tax cuts. The federal government also embarked on a serious tax-cutting exercise starting in 2000.[2] In most jurisdictions the tax-cut platform has become coincident with rising GDP, with the happy result that government revenues from income taxes have in most cases increased, albeit at a slower rate. But as of 2001 this dynamic was beginning to change, with federal revenues from taxation falling absolutely, and relative to GDP, and provincial own-source revenues dropping as a share of GDP (Canada. Department of Finance, 2003b, Tables 1, 2, 31).

---

[2]The federal government announced a five-year $100 billion tax-reduction plan in October 2000. The October 2000 "mini-budget" estimated that the fiscal impact of these cuts would be $20 billion for 2002/03, $25 billion for 2003/04 and $31 billion for 2004/05. These amounts have been increased by subsequent budgets which have added other initiatives to further reduce personal and corporate income taxation. Together, the federal and provincial governments have foregone at least $40 billion in revenues in 2002/03, $48 billion in 2003/04 and $61 billion in 2004/05, making tax cuts a far greater fiscal priority than any single spending expenditure in this period.

Table 1: Health Care is a Rising Share of Provincial Spending Everywhere[1]

	Nfld.	PEI	NS	NB	Que.	Ont.	Man.	Sask.	Alta.	BC	YT	NWT	Nun.
						(in percent)							
1990/91	30	26	33	30	30	36	35	34	30	35	11	16	
1991/92	29	28	34	30	30	36	33	27	31	33	12	17	
1992/93	28	27	31	30	29	36	35	34	31	34	12	17	
1993/94	29	23	33	30	30	36	34	29	32	34	14	16	
1994/95	29	28	31	31	30	37	35	33	30	34	16	15	
1995/96	30	29	31	32	29	35	36	34	30	33	14	16	
1996/97	30	30	33	31	29	38	35	36	32	33	14	16	
1997/98	32	29	39	30	30	38	35	37	34	34	15	17	
1998/99	34	30	37	31	31	37	36	36	35	26	17	20	
1999/00	38	29	38	30	30	39	38	35	36	36	16	16	18
2000/01	37	30	38	32	32	43	40	36	31	39	16	18	18
2001/02	39	32	39	35	32	44	41	39	32	41	16	18	20
Increase	**34**	**18**	**13**	**19**	**6**	**21**	**26**	**46**	**5**	**26**	**32**	**3**	

Note: [1]Excluding debt charges.
Source: CIHI (2002, Table A5).

Population growth over the last decade requires increased resources to expand basic infrastructure, and some related operating costs. An extensive but aging infrastructure has also put capital-intensive pressure on public resources. Just maintaining the level of public goods and services we currently enjoy is increasingly a challenge, given widespread commitments to keeping governments small and reducing existing debts.

Accelerated economic growth is widely viewed as the solution to these dilemmas, and the current conventional wisdom is that tax cuts are the best mechanism for achieving such a state. It is not clear if tax cuts have been the main policy responsible for broad-based economic growth since about 1999. However, it seems unlikely that a focus on continued tax cuts will meet the objectives of public governance over the medium to long term, especially when rates of growth start to decline as they do in any business cycle. At some point new revenue requirements will need to be addressed, or major elements of public provision, such as health care, will need to move away from its universal mandate.

Unsustainable: No Consensus on What is the "Fair Share"

When universal access to doctors, hospitals and some extended health services was originally envisioned, it was based on a deal for cost-sharing between federal and provincial governments. The "fair share" for both levels of government was roughly equivalent investments so that service levels and quality could be roughly equivalent across Canada.

That deal broke in the 1980s, a casualty of the war on the deficit. But even after deficits turned to surpluses, the federal share of health spending remained at historically low levels.

What started as a 50/50 deal for the costs of doctors and hospitals was transformed in 1977 by the Established Programs Financing (EPF), a funding mechanism that broke out federal support from straight cash cost-sharing to a mix of cash transfers and tax points. (Federal cost-sharing never reached half of total provincial expenditures even prior to the introduction of EPF because the provinces always provided some level of service that was not included under medicare, such as drug programs, or long-term care.)

Table 2: Tax Cuts, Not Health Care, Were the Priority for Most Provinces Since 1996

	1996–97	1997–98	1998–99	1999–00	2000–01	2001–02	2002–03	2003–04	2004–05	2005–06
					(in $millions)					
Nfld.	60	–30	–34	–58	–112	–146	–134	–148	–160	–173
PEI	0	7	6	3	–6	–8	–1	–2	–3	–4
NS	0	–150	–159	–171	–163	–169	–76	–203	–268	–293
NB	0	–155	–192	–225	–291	–338	–308	–360	–390	–419
Que.	651	1422	1387	972	–154	–2,938	–2,308	–3,337	–3,952	–4,544
Ont.	–1,171	–3,121	–4,950	–7,556	–8,793	–10,586	–11,905	–13,269	–15,944	–17,470
Man.	–7	–8	–54	–142	–231	–303	–325	–362	–400	–436
Sask.	–55	–238	–278	–415	–497	–606	–639	–742	–797	–852
Alta.	–73	–173	–458	–515	–1,438	–2,796	–1,932	–2,190	–2,415	–2,569
BC	–96	–104	–157	–402	–785	–2,281	–2,341	–2,568	–2,761	–2,945
Total Tax Cuts	**–691**	**–2,550**	**–4,890**	**–8,509**	**–12,469**	**–20,173**	**–19,969**	**–23,180**	**–27,090**	**–29,705**

Source: Provincial estimates and Finance Canada estimates, unpublished backgrounder to *The Fiscal Balance in Canada: The Facts*, January 2002, Department of Finance Canada (updated October 2002).

Figure 4: Federal Cost-Sharing of Provincial Spending on Health Care Has Fallen

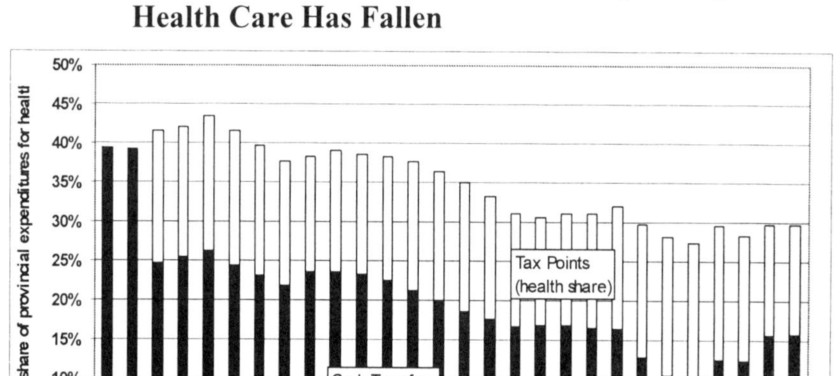

Note: 2001–02 and 2002–03 are forecasts for provincial expenditures and use the Finance Department's revised methodology for calculating tax points.

Source: Calculated from Canada. Department of Finance (2000), data from the September 2000 agreement; Finance Canada's Backgrounder, Federal Transfers to Provinces and Territories, October 2002; and CIHI (2002, Table A1).

The direct cash share was roughly half of this new funding vehicle, so that between 1977 and 1985 something close to a quarter of all provincial expenditures for public health care came from federal cash supports. Reductions in funding formulae meant that the level of federal support dropped consistently after 1985, falling to a low point, in 1998, when federal cash transfers for health care were estimated to have fallen to about 10% of what the provinces were spending for health care. (Tax transfers did not actually decrease during this period. Since the mid-1980s the focal point for provinces was, and remains, what share of the cash outlays for health care are being reimbursed by the federal government.)

Even with the landmark FPT agreements for renewed federal transfers, the federal cash share of health expenditures rose only to 14% immediately

The Health-Care Budget: Did it Resolve the "Crisis"? 243

subsequent to the September 2000 agreement.[3] It stood between 18% and 21% at the start of the period covered by the 2003 Health Accord, but is poised to fall back to 18% or lower after 2003/04. (The variability comes from elements of the accord that are not permanent, and the accuracy of projections for provincial spending. The share only rises to 21% if all provinces draw down their total share of the $2.5 billion CHST supplement in 2003/04 and provincial spending does not exceed $76.1 billion.) In the years ahead, this proportion is expected to once again fall, however, because the fastest growing parts of provincial spending on health care (drugs, long-term and home care, and public health measures) are not cost-shared elements, and because some of the funds in the accord are time-limited sources of money.

The Federal Share of Provincial Spending on Health Care
- between 1977 and 1985 about 25% cash (another 15–17% in tax transfers)
- by 1989 cash share down to 19%
- by 1993 cash share down to 17%
- by 1998 cash share down to 10%
- September 2000 agreement brought it up to 14%
- 2003 Health Accord raises it further, to roughly 18% in 2003, but it will fall again over the duration of the accord

Is this a fair share? Certainly the provinces and territories don't think so. Notwithstanding the billions announced in late 2000, and the billions more announced mere months ago, there is renewed pressure for the federal government to do more.

---

[3]Such calculation by the federal Finance Department is often considered contestable because the very intent and design of a block fund is that it is not transferred with specific allocations to different uses. The Finance Department's calculations are based on historic uses of the EPF by the provinces and territories, which showed health-care expenditures averaged between 59 and 62% of all provincial expenditures on health care and postsecondary education.

 Armine Yalnizyan

Is Health Care a "National" Program?

A major area of tension in the funding of public health care is that the provinces and territories want more fiscal resources from the federal government, but they do not want Ottawa to have too large a say in how health-care services are provided in different jurisdictions. This raises the question: Is health care a national program or not? Should Canadians expect roughly equivalent levels and scope of service regardless of where they live? And why should the feds provide more cash if they have no say over how that money is spent?

Chronic funding shortages have led to trade-offs in what is, and is not, publicly funded. The choices made have not been the same in every part of the country.

The creation of regional boards throughout most of the country (excluding Ontario) has devolved decision-making to yet another subsidiary level. This has accelerated the degree of balkanization of service and made it even more difficult to coordinate service flows between regions to mitigate the impact of further rationing.

The result is variation in access to and waits for services between provinces, and between regions of provinces. A federal statutory right of access to physicians and hospitals exists, but is not qualified by how long such access might take. Waiting times are dependent on the number of doctors, nurses, and technicians who are available in a particular area, as well as the quantity of equipment and beds available.

Increasingly Canadians want greater access to diagnostic and curative technology, including drugs and services outside the hospital setting. Provinces and territories have responded. But growth in services that are not cost-shared with the federal government have become even more variable than growing disparities in access to doctors and medical procedures, both between and within jurisdictions.

Much of this variation is defined by what (and who) the public health system in any province or territory commits to covering under its public insurance scheme. Immigrants and refugees are eligible for services in some provinces, but not in others. Some provinces have a three-month residency requirement for eligibility for new residents, both Canadian and out of country, some do not. Some provinces offer pharmacare to all residents, some provide protection from catastrophic drug costs, some offer limited support only to the elderly and those on social assistance. There are significant differences as to what drugs are covered by provincial formularies. Despite a trend toward shortened length-of-stay in hospitals virtually everywhere across the country, access to home care and long-term care is highly unpredictable, with no uniformity of eligibility, amounts and standards of care, or its cost. The differences in service multiply for rural and remote populations, most particularly among Aboriginal populations.

And yet the Canada Health Act makes access to health care a right of citizenship, one of the defining features of being Canadian, and a distinct competitive advantage for our economy. So as the differences increase, so does the pressure on the federal government to increase its involvement in establishing the conditions for more consistent access.

Since these pressures have emerged at the same time as calls for greater federal financial contributions to health care, and since the federal government has in part responded to these calls for more money, it could have been assumed that the "new" money would be used to buy change and improvement.

With so much expectation placed on them, what did the two FPT deals buy?

The first agreement, on the eve of a federal election in September 2000, maintained the "hands off", decentralist approach of the federal government. Billed as a health agreement, the bulk of the money was a reinfusion of cash transfers through the CHST which, as mentioned, funds a range of programs, from health care and postsecondary education to a range of social assistance supports.

In addition to the general increase of $18.9 billion to the CHST, there were three distinct funds. Two were truly targeted: one for the purchase of medical and diagnostic equipment ($1 billion to be shared in a per-capita division of resources by all jurisdictions over the course of two years); one for informatics in the health sector ($500 million in one year for the entire country, but not

                                                            Armine Yalnizyan

Table 3: The September 2000 Agreement[1]

	2000–01	2001–02	2002–03	2003–04	2004–05	2005–06	Total
			(in $billions)				
General increase		2.5	3.2	3.8	4.4	5	18.9
Med equipment fund	0.5	0.5					1
Primary care fund		0.2	0.2	0.2	0.2		0.8
Health info. tech	0.5						0.5
Increase for "health"	**1**	**3.2**	**3.4**	**4**	**4.6**	**5**	**21.2**

Note: [1]The September 2000 agreement also provided $2.2 billion over five years specifically for an Early Childhood Development Fund — something that could not be guaranteed if the money flowed through the CHST — bringing the final total of new transfers to the provinces to $23.4 billion. This $2.2 billion cannot be counted in resources transferred to the provinces to meet their public health-care pressures.

apportioned to the provinces). The third, providing $800 million over four years for primary care reform, was so vague in its terms that it essentially did not count as a targeted fund, though it did occasion a few announcements of joint "new" initiatives in health care over the coming months. Overall, the September 2000 agreement really was aimed at redressing the cuts of the mid-1990s, speaking to the "fair share" argument which was getting harder to duck given two back-to-back federal budgetary surpluses and a third one on its way.

After more than a decade of unilateral federal retrenchment, the first major announcement for new federal funding would have created more political problems than it solved if it was tied to conditions for what the provinces had to do to get the money. (Tied funding for housing and early child development/child care funds has proven this point amply.) Furthermore, the new monies were transferred through a block fund, and it is virtually impossible to trace how much new money would end up in the individual programs supported by that block fund. The new CHST money could go to health care, but just as easily it could be used for other priorities of provincial and territorial governments.

Though marketed as a deal for health care, the September 2000 agreement was basically a non-conditional increase in support from the federal government. It could be viewed as a way of making amends for the hard years of the 1990s. This was politically important.

On the verge of a federal election which prominently featured the politics of regional difference and discord in the federation, the September 2000 agreement was a concrete proposal for restoring federal-provincial relations, made just before the election by the party in power. It was a deal that competing parties would find hard to undo, and just as hard to better given the prevailing political climate was promoting tax reduction and smaller governments. The bulk of the money was unconditional, as the provinces viewed renewed federal re-engagement in the health-care file with a jaundiced eye, seeing the potential for renewed centralism with every new initiative.

The September 2000 agreement was pitched as a health deal — even though it was not strictly about health — because the electorate was transfixed by genuine problems in health-care delivery across the country. The resonance of the deal was that the party in power could do something to reverse the obvious deterioration of services everywhere across the country without actually being interventionist about it.

However, the succession of provincial and federal reports on health care over time made it apparent that the new money did little to improve things. By the end of 2002, both the Senate and Romanow Commission reports spoke of the need for "transformative" change. It was widely agreed that new money was needed, but that new money had to be tied to changing how health care was delivered. In report after report, the desire to "buy change" with clear objectives and timelines for reform was reiterated. The Romanow report also suggested ways that new monies could be used to strengthen the federation.

The subtext was that growing disparities and regional differences in service needed to be mitigated. But federal contributions for health care were still historically low, and it was not clear which recommendations the federal government would act on. Without a clear picture of what the federal share would rise to and settle at, it was premature to be talking about forming "national" standards and objectives via the new infusion of funds.

                                                    Armine Yalnizyan

Yet an emerging conformity regarding the direction of improvement is inherent in virtually every health policy document. Every jurisdiction wants to reduce waiting times. Every jurisdiction wants reforms to primary care, so that emergency rooms do not become the health-care system of default. Every jurisdiction wants to use more care in the community, not just in acute-care and long-term care settings, particularly with more effective use of home care. Every jurisdiction wants to get a better handle on expenditures on drug programs, to relieve the growing strains on provincial coffers and increased incidence of financial hardship for individuals who rely on costly drugs to stay alive. Every jurisdiction has backed-up capital needs (for facilities and equipment) that hamper efficient care of patients. Every jurisdiction needs to address the massive short-comings of the information system in health care so as to facilitate more effective case management and clearer identification of supply blockages (and possible alternatives) in the system. And every jurisdiction is dealing with the rising costs connected to the most pressing element of shortage in health care: the care itself, and the shortage of health professionals, not just in Canada but around the world.

These are problems common to every jurisdiction, yet movement toward common resolution of these problems is viewed as inappropriate centralist intervention. Nonetheless, each of these areas requires additional resources to "buy change", and given an unprecedented string of budgetary surpluses at the federal level, the immediate and obvious place to look for more resources for everyone's needs was the federal government.

Given the complex history leading up to the 2003 federal budget, and the Health Accord that underlies it, the question posed by this paper is: Did the federal budget address the conflicts and needs described? And were these measures sufficient to "buy change", and move public health care off a track deemed "unsustainable"?

What Are We Getting for our Money?

There are three questions that address whether the new federal money offered in the 2003 budget resolved the "crisis" in health care. First, will the timeliness and quality of public health care be improved? Second, does the infusion of federal funds resolve the issue of fair share between the federal and provincial governments? And third, does this latest initiative clarify and stabilize what is, and what is not, covered by public insurance?

The answer, in each case, is a rather Liberal "somewhat". Although progress has been made in the right direction in each area of concern, all the points of tension remain.

The February 2003 accord sought two things for public health care: *stability* and *improvement.* The federal budget allocated $34.8 billion in new funds over the next five years. Of this amount, over $5 billion ($5.29 billion) is spent directly by the federal government for Aboriginal health, nationwide research initiatives, investments in information technology (which can be cross-jurisdictional in scope), and other health initiatives in support of reform such as immunization and patient safety programs, health promotion programs, technology assessment, Employment Insurance supports to caregivers, GST rebates, and creation of a Health Council.

Of the remaining $29.5 billion in new transfers to the provinces, $12 billion flows through the CHST, the mechanism that finances not just health care but postsecondary education and social assistance related programs.

Some of the $12 billion is not rolled into the base of CHST transfers to the provinces. This is the CHST "supplement", worth $2.5 billion, and widely viewed as a "signing bonus" for getting the provinces and territories simply to agree to the deal. As such, it is even less conditional than the loose terms of the CHST, in that it may or may not be used for health purposes at all. For example, in Ontario the full amount of the supplement was drawn down to balance the 2002/03 budget. It is finessing the argument to say any of this money was used to improve health care.

This leaves $9.5 billion in increased federal transfers to the province through the CHST. [Some of this amount ($3.9 billion) is simply the rolling out of the last three years of the September 2000 agreement. A further $5.6 billion is the implication of extending the September 2000 agreement into fiscal years 2006/07 and 2007/08.] Year one of the deal increases base funding by $700 million. Thereafter, the base is increased by an additional $600 million every year. By April 1, 2004 the remaining $8.8 billion in increased CHST transfers to the provinces will be divided into two separate funds: the Canada Health

                                                          Armine Yalnizyan

Table 4: Increased Federal Cash for Health Care in Budget 2003 (covers 2003/04 to 2007/08)

	2003–2004	2004–2005	2005–2006	2006–2007	2007–2008	Total
			(in $millions)			
TRANSFERS: Canada Health and Social Transfer (CHST) cash						
Cumulative increase (2000)[1]	700	1,300	1,900	2,500	3,100	9,500
*CHST supplement[2]	1,000	1,000	500			2,500
HEALTH REFORM						
Health Reform Fund	1,000	1,500	3,500	4,500	5,500	16,000
*Diagnostic/medical equipment[3]	500*	500*	500*			1,500*
*Health information technology[4]	200*	200*	200*			600*
*Research hospitals						
(Canada Foundation for Innovation)[5]	100*	100*	200*	100*		500*
Direct Health Accord initiatives	221	336	341	341	346	1,585
Other health initiatives in support of reform	337	253	258	258	258	1,364
First Nations and Inuit health	180	230	280	280	280	1,250
Annual increase (above 2002/03 base)	4,238	5,419	7,679	7,979	9,484	34,800
*Of which surplus funding provides	1,800*	1,800*	1,400*	100*		5,100*
Cumulative funding increases	4,238	9,657	17,336	25,315	34,800	

Notes: *These amounts are financed from the 2002/03 budgetary surplus.

[1]Includes an increase of $1.8 billion over 2006/07 ($600 million) and 2007/08 ($1.2 billion).

[2]$2.5 billion to be paid to a third-party trust and accounted for in 2002/03 by the federal government. Profile based on an assumed drawdown by provinces and territories.

[3]$1.5 billion to be paid to a third-party trust and accounted for by the federal government in 2002/03. Profile based on an assumed drawdown by provinces and territories.

[4]$600 million to be paid to Canada Health Infoway and accounted for by the federal government in 2002/03.

[5]$500 million to be paid to the Canada Foundation for Innovation and accounted for by the federal government in 2002/03.

Source: Canada. Department of Finance (2003a, p. 68).

Transfer (CHT) and the Canada Social Transfer (CST). The Canada Health Transfer will receive 62% of these funds, meaning that the provinces will receive an additional $5.5 billion over the next four years strictly for the purposes of health care. This money will disappear into the maw of a massive system that needs to grow to survive, as the next section explains.

More than half the $29.5 billion made available through the 2003 accord is directed to the provinces and territories, in principle, to improve health-care delivery. Of the $17.5 billion that they will receive over the next five years for these purposes, $1.5 billion is available, on a per capita basis, to buy new medical and diagnostic equipment over the next three years. (As noted earlier, the September 2000 agreement also had a medical equipment fund, worth $1 billion over two years.) This is the only truly tied funding. The bulk of innovation is to be financed by the five-year $16 billion Health Reform Fund. This fund makes money available for initiatives in primary care, home care, and programs that provide coverage for catastrophic costs of drugs. It is so loosely structured, however, that almost anything to do with health care can be partly financed out of this money. Improvements to existing programs are not required to access the funds.

What Are we Buying this Time? Stabilizing Public Health-Care Delivery

Just keeping public health-care systems functioning at a steady level of service requires huge resources. Global human resource shortages in the health-care sector lead to wage increases in order to retain the pool of labour that we have, and premiums and incentives to attract new people. Since labour represents over 80% of input costs in health care, this is a significant cost push in the system.[4] One conservative estimate of the contractual obligations of existing collective agreements with doctors and nurses over the period 2000 to 2002 puts the figure at approximately $2.5 billion at the national level. This represents the extra cost of hanging on to

---

[4] Health care is highly labour-intensive, with some 85% of total expenditures flowing to labour costs. Calculations based on 1996 open-model multipliers using Statistics Canada, National Model, Input-Output tables, obtained from Jacobson Consulting Inc.

 Armine Yalnizyan

this particular pool of health professionals.[5] It does not finance the costs of one more doctor or nurse.

Attempts to reverse under-investment in equipment and facilities, one of the first variable costs to be deferred in periods of constraint, are similarly costly. Such deferral means a bulky period of reinvestment to catch up with the population growth that has taken place in the interim. Capital-intensive pressures exist in transportation, water and sewage, and other infrastructure systems, including the pressing need to expand and maintain the existing stock of equipment, hospitals, community clinics, and long-term facilities. Much of this stock was built half a century ago, in the post-war reconstruction phase that began in 1948. At the time, at least a third of these capital needs were financed by public borrowing through the federal government (Perry, 1997, p. 184). Though there have been no estimates as to the infrastructure needs of the health-care sector, it clearly runs into the billions, though this amount, unlike operating costs, can be amortized.

Rising costs in the form of higher utilization and increased use of newer, more expensive prescription drugs means drug programs are yet another area where simply maintaining the system requires billions more every few years. Using different scenarios (rates of growth from the last decade, last five years and last three years), the additional costs associated with growth in existing drug programs will range between $2.1 and $3.5 billion over the next three years.[6]

---

[5]Author's unpublished review of collective agreements active in 2000 across Canada. Length of agreement, expiry dates, and timing of increases vary from agreement to agreement. The total cost implication of this survey of settlements is about $2.4 billion between 2000 and 2002, with no less than $2 billion flowing to the 58,000 practising physicians over the next two to three years and about $400 million in higher wages flowing over the same period to a subgroup of the 230,000 employed registered nurses, not all of whom work in the public sector. These calculations do not reflect the cost implications of collective agreements for other allied health professionals and workers. It mostly does not reflect nursing costs outside the hospital sector. It refers to fees and wages, but does not generally include the cost of enhancements to benefits or other incentive pay schemes, making the figure a conservative estimate.

[6]Author's unpublished calculations, based on average of provincial and territorial trends; data from Canadian Institute for Health Information (2001).

The new money that the federal budget makes available through the CHST/CHT will be absorbed quickly, with not much to show for it. This is simply the cost of shoring up the basic systems we have. While the new federal money will unquestionably help, it will not address the fundamental sources of cost push: health human resource shortages, growing reliance on pharmacare, and a long over-due period of attention to capital investment, both for maintaining aging infrastructure and expanding capacity.

What Are we Buying this Time? Improvements, Efficiencies, Equity

Both the new funds to the provinces and direct federal spending will indeed generate some improvements in the form of increased efficiencies and could potentially generate greater equity in access to health services. Many individual provinces have independently initiated various elements of this plan.

The list of intended purposes for the money is long:

- Information (standardization of medical records, electronic formatting and transmission).
- Training and better utilization of the full spectrum of health workers (through primary care reforms and specific recruitment and continuing education initiatives).
- Moving toward improved and standardized coverage for pharma-therapy.
- Broadening use of home care (upstream versus downstream use of home care such as the use of home care to reduce reliance on the acute-care system, not just to facilitate quicker release from hospital).
- Better coordination and integration of all aspects of health care.
- Reduced wait times (more, better use of diagnostics and community-based services).

It should be noted, however, that the $16 billion Health Reform Fund (HRF) is back-end loaded, with most of the money flowing at the end of the five-year period. The provinces and territories only received, collectively, $1 billion for all these objectives in the 2003/04 year. While this is,

                                                   Armine Yalnizyan

arguably, fiscally prudent, it again delays investments that could have saved costs *and* improved the efficiency of public health care sooner than later.

Over the first three years of the accord, the HRF and the Medical and Diagnostic Equipment Fund together will provide a total of $7.5 billion for the express purposes of buying change. (The previous section showed how the $3.9 billion in additional base transfers through the CHST over the next three years, and the $2.5 billion CHST supplement, could easily be absorbed by the cost-push inherent in the massive expenditures of the existing health-care system.) If one adds in new funding for health informatics, the figure over the next three years rises to $8.1 billion.

As a point of reference, the Romanow report recommended an initial three-year investment of $15 billion for the purposes of buying "transformative" change, while the Senate Committee's Volume 6 of the Kirby Report recommended more than $19.5 billion for the same purposes over the same period.[7]

What Are we Buying this Time? Greater Transparency

Much of the corrosive "he said/she said" wrangling that has characterized these past few years of federal/provincial disputes has been over the different views of how much financial support the federal government actually provides for health care. The reason is in the very design of the funding vehicle, the CHST. As a block fund for a variety of programs, it offers no indisputable way to calculate what is being transferred for the purposes of health care.

---

[7]Both the Romanow and the Kirby reports recommended that existing federal government contributions to the provinces and territories for health care be supplemented by $6.5 billion, then increased according to different proposals for escalator mechanisms. The Romanow report ramped up to the $6.5 billion by the third year of the reinvestment phase; the Kirby report (Volume 6) suggested starting immediately with an infusion of $6.5 billion more for health-care and growing. (The Kirby proposal is often characterized as requiring $5 billion a year more in new funds, but the increased transfers for health included an additional $1.5 billion redirected from GST revenues.) For a comparison and analysis of the Romanow, Kirby, and provincial positions in the run-up to the February 2003 Health Accord, see Yalnizyan (2003).

The CHST was a failure as a fiscal mechanism for a social program under increasingly intense scrutiny. It provided no transparency, no account-ability, and no enforceability.

The federal 2003 budget, in combination with the terms of the February 2003 Health Accord, offered several ways to improve transparency and accountability.

What did the budget deliver?

*   A clear definition of base spending for health, by dumping the CHST and creating a new funding vehicle expressly for health care, the Canada Health Transfer, using 62% of the old block fund (65% if the Health Reform Fund is included as part of the new funds being transferred to the provinces and territories).
*   Stability over a multi-year horizon, with clear increases over time.
*   A series of "soft" objectives for improvement, particularly in areas that go beyond the traditional cost-shared aspects of the Canada Health Act.
*   An implicit, if not explicit, agreement that cash transfers are what count, and an increase in the federal share of provincial/territorial cash outlays for the full spectrum of health care.
*   Plans for a Health Council, to monitor how these new funds would lever improvements and movement toward the stated goals of the accord.

Notwithstanding these advancements, notable gaps remain unresolved.

*   There is no escalator in the new funding formula for the CHT (only population growth). This means multi-year deals are now the norm (with five-year horizons being the new standard for commitment) and negotiations for improvement are almost continuous within that horizon.
*   There is no explicit resolution to the "fair share" debate. The new funds initially bring the federal cash share of projected provincial expendi-tures to between 18% and 20%, but after 2004/05 the share starts to decline below 18%.
*   Funding is still largely unconditional with no clear objectives, standards, or conditions tied to the $16 billion Health Reform Fund.

                                                   Armine Yalnizyan

- Funding is insufficient to implement Kirby or even Romanow's plans for transformative change to put health care on a long-term sustainable track.
- There was no plan to deal with health human resource issues, which is the linch-pin for resolving the issue of waiting lists in such a labour-intensive sector.

What Does this Mean for Future Debates Around Health Care?

The public debate on the future of health care was characterized by three themes going into the 2003 Health Accord and federal budget: sustainability, national character, and value for money. These points of contention are far from resolved, and will play themselves out in continued debate in the arenas of budget-making and policy formulation. In addition, continued pressures around patient waiting times and reluctance to raise public debt for capital projects is leading to new controversy in the arena of legislative definitions of statutory rights and government obligations.

Future Budgetary Negotiations for Health Care Will Continue to be Noisy

The context for health-care budgeting and cost-shared deals is an easy recipe for continued noise-making: No deal will ever be enough. There is always more that can be done (for example, improvements in pharmacare, extension of home care and support services, access to emerging technologies and preventive therapies). The demand for health care will always outweigh supply, and all the more so in a society with an aging population.

This simple fact has been made doubly potent by the institutionalization of FPT fights. The 2003 budget, like its predecessor mini-budget of October 2000, relies on five-year deals, negotiated through the fractious FPT process. Neither deal articulated a new formula for increasing transfers, nor a commitment to what the federal share of provincial and territorial costs for health care would be. This escalates the politicization of the deals.

Finally, latest forecasts show that, together, the provinces and territories spent over $74 billion on health care in 2002/03. The sheer amount — the scale of which occasions even slow rates of growth to require billions more every year — coupled with growing differences in how health care is delivered across the country, provides ample opportunity for controversy about when and how public expenditures on health care provide the best value for money. But increased pressures to document just how the money is being used are meeting with resistance.

One reason the September 2000 agreement was not deemed a success was due to the lack of perceptible improvement in health care, despite enhanced funding. Partly because of this, the 2003 Health Accord was crafted to be conditional on the creation of a new Health Council of Canada which could monitor progress of the implementation of the terms of the accord. Though the money has flowed, the monitoring capacity has not, due to provincial reluctance to participate in the creation of a national (not federal) body that requires transparent and comparable indicators of service provision and health outcome.

Unresolved Policy Arenas Will Grow Increasingly Costly to Address

The federal approach to restoring the sustainability of public health care has thus far failed to address three major areas of public policy concern. The outbreaks of SARS and "mad cow" disease in 2003 raised a fourth area, public health, that also demands a national strategy and resources for effective management.

But public health issues pale in comparison to the cost considerations related to the future of spending for drugs, long-term care/non-acute care, and human resources for health care. Effective management of these public costs is critical to resolving the "sustainability" debate.

Drugs. The growing array of new drugs and increased utilization of pharmatherapy to prevent, treat and control medical conditions have pushed drug costs at, or close to, double-digit rates of inflation for over 20 years. This is straining the capacity of both public and private benefit plans to continue to provide effective coverage, and creating catastrophic financial

                                                              Armine Yalnizyan

circumstances for a growing number of people who have no coverage. Without a comprehensive strategy, provinces (and businesses) will increasingly reduce coverage in the face of growing costs, leaving individuals increasingly vulnerable. This is the least cost-effective way of dealing with health care from a macroeconomic perspective.

Long-term care and home care. As the practice of health care continues to shift from acute care and hospital-based care to the increased provision of preventative, managed and/or chronic care in the community, the resources have not necessarily followed. An aging population will make more demands on the most expensive part of the system, acute care, if more resources are not put into supports in the community, a balance between institutional and home-based, long-term care and more rapid access to a range of primary care. (Long-term care was conspicuously absent from this round of federal scrutiny.) The costs of an aging society are more likely to increase if there is no change in the modality of care provided.

Health human resource shortages. The biggest pressure point in the health-care system, whether in the community or in hospitals and clinics, is the shortage of health-care human resources. As mentioned, at least 80% of input costs for health care go to labour. The health-care sector accounts for about one-tenth of the economy. Given the demographic profile of employed physicians and nurses, the sector is facing a worrying situation: up to half of these health professionals may retire in the next five years if current rates of attrition apply. Enrolments in medical and nursing schools are insufficient to guarantee enough graduates to meet this emerging gap. Though these dynamics have been known for years, there is still no national strategy to educate and recruit new health professionals, or retain and retrain the existing labour force. Both approaches have enormous cost implications. Without a national strategy, individual provinces will be competing with each other and international jurisdictions, raising the costs further still.

Vast though the public resources for health care may be, current levels of public funding appear to be inadequate to meet the costs of looming capital and labour shortages and the growing reliance on pharmatherapy. Private-sector solutions (for capital, labour or drugs) cost citizens more, as individuals and as a society, because they rely on price signals through the market. The higher bidder always wins, but the prices have been inflated for everyone. As supply costs rise, scarce public funding grows increasingly insufficient to meet needs, leading to more rationing and seemingly intractable waiting lists in the public system. This dynamic, now unfolding, raises new issues in health-care debates.

New Terrains of Debate

Two themes that have been inherent in policy debates may emerge as explicit themes in the next few years. Both issues flow from the ambiguity of the Canada Health Act.

- Comprehensiveness
  What's in and what's out of the basket of publicly insured services? Currently this debate is about care guarantees to basic acute-care services, and to a more limited extent the interprovincial variability of prescription drugs coverage and access to home care. What technologies, drugs and community-based supports can be expected to be publicly covered in future? Will the range of service become more, or less, equivalent from coast to coast to coast? Will the federal government commit to contributing to the full range of public expenditure on health care, or participate in initiatives on an ad hoc basis?

- Public Administration
  The legislation is ambiguous regarding how public money gets used. The principle of public administration requires that administration of health care be carried out on a non-profit basis by a public authority. This, however, has led to debate about ownership and the scope of the for-profit service sector. For instance, should public money be used to lease investor-owned hospitals or clinics, essentially financing such construction for the private-sector owners through the terms of lease? Or should public finances only flow to publicly-owned infrastructure? Under what conditions can profits be made from public spending on health care? If it is legal in some instances, for example, laboratory services, is it legal for surgery or cancer treatment?

There will be continued visibility of these debates for three reasons:

                                             Armine Yalnizyan

- Though the Romanow Commission has finished its work, the Standing Senate Committee on Social Affairs, Science and Technology (the Kirby Committee) continues to produce research and reports on issues concerning the future of public health care.
- Health Council of Canada and its evolution may become a forum for discussion of issues under contention, depending on the degree to which it becomes an accepted mechanism of federal-provincial relations.
- Grassroots resistance to "privatization" or, more accurately, public-private partnership initiatives and investor-owned service delivery is becoming more organized in many provinces, extending to applications for legal injunctions against signed agreements. Similarly, legal action has also been instituted to challenge governments' ability to prevent queue-jumping for those with the ability to pay for necessary medical services.

Conclusion

The budgetary issues that remain outstanding in the wake of the February 2003 federal budget are the ones that framed the "crisis" in public health-care in the first place:

- Sustainability
    - How much is enough to stabilize core health services? How much is necessary to buy improvements? How would taxpayers know if they are paying enough, or not, for the system they say they want?
    - Is the future of public health care sustainable given current approaches to funding and demands for care?

- National character of program
    - Should the provision of public health care be roughly equivalent from coast to coast to coast?
    - What conditionality should be associated with the transfer of federal funds to the provinces for health care (standards of care, objectives for improvement)?
    - What should be the federal share for Canada's most valued social program?

- Transparency
  - What are the provinces and territories doing with the new infusions of federal cash for health care?
  - What are we getting for $75 billion a year and rising? Is the growth in spending buying improvements? If not, why not?

Though the 2003 budget made real progress in mechanisms and funds to address these issues, the issues remain, and therefore so does the potential for "crisis talk" about the future of public health care, the social program most treasured by Canadian citizens.

The debate will remain vital in the coming months and years because as resolutions to these points of tension emerge, they will define not just the parameters of a public program; they will define the role of the state and the nature of civic society in Canada in the twenty-first century.

References

Canada. Department of Finance (2000), *Backgrounder on Federal Support for Health in Canada* (Ottawa: Department of Finance).

___________ (2003a), *The Budget Plan 2003* (Ottawa: Department of Finance).

___________ (2003b), *Fiscal Reference Tables* (Ottawa: Department of Finance), October.

Canada. Standing Senate Committee on Social Affairs, Science and Technology (2001), *The Health of Canadians — The Federal Role, Volume One: The Story so Far*, Interim Report (Ottawa: Public Works and Government Services Canada).

Canadian Institute for Health Information (CIHI) (2001), "Provincial/Territorial Government Sector Health Expenditure, by Province/Territory and Canada 1975 to 2001 – Current Dollars", *National Health Expenditure Trends* (Ottawa: Depository Services Program).

___________ (2002), *Preliminary Provincial Territorial Government Health Expenditures Estimates, Series F,* November.

Organisation for Economic Co-operation and Development (OECD) (2002), *Health Data* (Paris: OECD).

Perry, D. (1997), *Financing the Canadian Federation, 1867 to 1995: Setting the Stage for Change* (Toronto: Canadian Tax Foundation).

Yalnizyan, A. (2003), "Health Care Talks: The Constitutional Debate Revisited", *Paying for Keeps*, No. 3 (Ottawa: Canadian Centre for Policy Alternatives).

THE EVOLUTION OF THE CHST IN THE 2003 BUDGET

Michael Mendelson, Caledon Institute of Social Policy

Two budgets ago, I found myself contemplating what Ottawa's budget would look like if the prime minister had more complete command of the process. We got the answer in this budget. My overall review is that the prime minister's budget looks good from a social perspective. Of course, there is still much in the 2003 budget with which I would disagree. Like all good Canadians, I can always find something about which to gripe, but my assessment is more positive than negative.

There were several initiatives in the budget on the social side. Most have already been mentioned in other presentations. The major initiative on the social side was the increase in transfers to provinces associated with the Health Accord, through the Canada Health and Social Transfer (CHST) and allied health funds. In addition, there is a schedule of increases in the child benefit, improved child-care transfers, various measures with respect to disability, a housing initiative, changes in Employment Insurance (EI), and several other social initiatives that may be modest in total cost, but will have a substantial impact on a smaller number of Canadians; for example, initiatives with respect to Aboriginal housing.

While my assessment of the budget as a whole from a social perspective is positive, my comments here are on one of the initiatives about which I am mainly, although not wholly, critical; namely, the most costly and highly publicized social initiative — the increase in transfers to provinces under the CHST, soon to be divided into separate health and social transfers. Will the increase in the CHST accomplish anything useful?

To assess the impact of the increase in CHST, we have to identify the purpose of the CHST and the likely effect of the increase in accomplishing that purpose. The CHST is meant either to promote fiscal objectives or programmatic objectives, or a little of each. If the objective of the CHST is fiscal, then its effectiveness must be determined by the extent to which the CHST assists provinces to meet fiscal goals. If the objective of the CHST is programmatic, then its effectiveness has to be measured by the extent to which it results in provincial programs conforming to Ottawa's program design objectives.

Fiscal objectives.

If the purpose of the CHST is fiscal, it is a strange design. The CHST pays equal per capita transfers. Under what *fiscal* premise would Ottawa make transfer payments to Alberta or Ontario? Alberta's fiscal capacity is much greater than that of the Government of Canada's. Ontario's fiscal capacity must also be greater than the Government of Canada's since the federal government's fiscal capacity is just the composite of the fiscal capacity of all the provinces, with the exclusion of a few minor sources of revenue that provinces cannot access and a few major sources of revenue that the federal government cannot access, namely natural resources and gambling. In aggregate, the fiscal capacity of the provinces is greater, not lesser, than that of the federal government. So, what could be the *fiscal* objective of an equal per capita transfer?

From the perspective of a wealthy province such as Ontario, equal per capita transfers play a perverse fiscal role. Every dollar that Ontario gets from the federal government through an equal per capita transfer costs Ontario taxpayers some not insignificant amount more than a dollar — my rough estimate is between $1.05 and $1.10. This is because money that Ottawa transfers on an equal per capita basis to Ontario is also paid to other provinces. The federal government must raise this money from federal taxpayers in the provinces, and, of course, in total the residents of wealthier provinces make a larger per capita tax contribution to the federal program. Ontario taxpayers are obviously net losers, as are Alberta taxpayers, except even more so. I do not know whether

                                                    Michael Mendelson

BC taxpayers are also net losers in sum. This would require a more detailed analysis.

None of this is unknown and astonishing news to provincial finance officials, or even to provincial politicians. So what, then, would cause Ernie Eves and Ralph Klein to demand higher CHST payments to the provinces — that is, increased equal per capita transfers to provinces? There are only two possible explanations. One explanation is that the premiers of wealthy provinces have been overcome with generosity and patriotism. Given this explanation, Eves and Klein are just anxious to see that there are significant transfers from Ontario and Alberta taxpayers to their fellow Canadians in other provinces. That is one explanation. Somehow I do not find it quite plausible.

The other possible explanation is that Eves and Klein would like to avoid accountability to their taxpayers for raising taxes, but still get the political benefit of spending the money. Perchance the premiers would rather be seen to be cutting their own taxes while spending transfer funds obtained by federal taxes, even if the federal money comes at a premium? This is a much more plausible explanation. As usual, the public treats government financing as issuing from somewhere in the heavens, and so Ontario taxpayers never ask from whence the federal transfers come. Nor does the media delve into such complicated questions. So no one asks why Ontario and Alberta do not just raise their own taxes, if they need more money for health care, rather than begging from the federal government, as raising their own taxes would be cheaper for Ontario and Alberta taxpayers?

Premiers mention none of this. Premiers argue that the purpose of the CHST is to correct so-called fiscal imbalances between the federal and provincial orders of government. But the provinces have constitutionally mandated, unfettered access to all of Ottawa's main tax sources, plus a few important tax sources of their own that Ottawa cannot access, so an imbalance in fiscal capacity is impossible in Canada between the orders of government collectively. The provinces altogether have greater fiscal capacity than Ottawa. However, a fiscal imbalance is possible *between* provinces, as some provinces have more fiscal capacity than others. The CHST does go someway to addressing this second order of fiscal imbalance, by transferring fiscal capacity from wealthier provinces to poorer provinces, but the CHST is a highly inefficient mechanism for doing so. If Ottawa's fiscal objective were to redress a perceived imbalance in fiscal capacity among the provinces, then a program that would be closer to equalization rather than an equal per capita transfer would be more sensible. In sum, if the objective of the CHST is fiscal, the CHST is not a particularly well-designed transfer program.

Does the CHST have a programmatic objective?

To analyze whether the CHST is meeting program objectives we have to see whether the transfer changes the behaviour of the provinces with respect to targeted programs, mainly health programs, so that those programs are more likely to reflect federal program design parameters. In other words, if the objective of the transfer is to do something with respect to health programs, then the way to measure whether that objective is being attained is to see whether or not there is a change in health programs as a consequence of the transfer. How does the CHST change the behaviour of the provinces, which are the delivery agents and the regulatory authorities with respect to targeted programs, such as health programs, so that those programs are more likely to achieve federal objectives? There are two ways in which the CHST might affect the behaviour of recipient provinces. One way is by the *amount or the level* of the CHST, and the other is through *conditions or incentives* tied to the receipt of transfer payments.

With regard to the level of the CHST, to what extent is the amount of money in the CHST a factor in changing the health programs of provincial recipients of that money? Or, to put this question in another way, what do provinces do differently in their health programming than they otherwise would have done, as a consequence of an increase or decrease in the level of the CHST? For those have-not provinces for which the CHST increases fiscal capacity, an increase in CHST may result in increased funding for health care, compared to the funding that otherwise would have been available. However, this would just be a consequence of the have-not province having greater fiscal capacity, so a targeted fiscal transfer could achieve the same effect more efficiently. For the wealthier provinces, the CHST detracts from fiscal capacity and the argument could be made that the overall result of an increase in the CHST is likely to *decrease* health funding in the wealthier provinces, just as a consequence of decreasing fiscal room. So, in respect of the amount of the CHST, there may be an indirect effect for programs through changing fiscal capacity, but if this is what the CHST is supposed to do, it is, as already noted, rather poorly designed.

                                                            Michael Mendelson

In contrast, federal transfers such as the CHST, and its forerunners, may have a direct impact on provincial behaviour through conditions or incentives. The conditions on the CHST are the five principles of medicare set out in the Canada Health Act. These have been important in the design of health-care systems in the provinces, as can be seen by minimization of extra billing and user charges throughout Canada. The enforcement of the Canada Health Act conditions is through withholding transfer payments to implement a financial penalty. The effect of these penalties is mainly symbolic and political, not fiscal. It means nothing fiscally to Alberta to have $15 million or $20 million withheld. The impact of financial penalties is as a visible, political marker. But this has been sufficient up until at least the last year or two to keep the provinces more or less in conformity to the conditions in the Canada Health Act.

The same cannot be said for the postsecondary component of the CHST. This component of the transfer is entirely unconditional, as were its forerunners. In fact, the postsecondary component of the CHST is simply a fiscal transfer to provinces, for better or for worse. The question then is: Why have a so-called postsecondary transfer component as part of an equal per capita transfer? If it is unconditional it serves no objective, except a fiscal objective and that is better achieved through a fiscal transfer. The so-called postsecondary transfer is irrelevant to postsecondary education. In reality, there is no such transfer and there has not been such a transfer except in name for many decades.

My conclusion is that it is the conditionality and not the level of the CHST that has an effect on provincial programs, except through redressing fiscal im-balances between provinces; and this latter task would be better accomplished through a differently designed transfer. This view is consistent with the evidence from my own first-hand experience. Since the early 1970s I have had many decades of access to or sat in on Cabinet meetings or Treasury Board meetings in two provinces: Manitoba, a "have-not" province, and Ontario, a "have" province. In all that time, never once during the setting of a health budget, let alone a post-secondary education budget, has the amount of the federal transfer for health or for education been mentioned or even noted in any way, shape, or form. My own experience is that the amount of the federal transfer for health was simply not a factor in setting the provincial level of expenditure in health, and certainly not for postsecondary education. Internal provincial demands, both political and perceived public needs, were always the determining factor and all that was discussed. Federal transfers are just another source of revenue, discussed at a quite different time in the budget-setting process.

There is, in addition, a third component of the CHST: social assistance and social services. These were the services previously cost-shared under the Canada Assistance Plan (CAP). Unlike the block transfers under the CHST and its predecessors, CAP provided 50 cents in federal funding for every provincial (or municipal) dollar spent on approved services. In contrast to block funding, 50-cent dollars were an important consideration in bringing forward new programs. The availability of 50-cent dollars was discussed at Cabinet, at Treasury Board, in minister's offices, and so on, especially in Manitoba. Based on my own broad but admittedly anecdotal experience, cost-shared dollars did have an important behavioural impact on provinces, shaping what they would fund and the design of their programs. But, of course, CAP has been cancelled and rolled into the CHST. As with postsecondary education there are effectively no conditions on social assistance and social services in order to receive full CHST funding. The only condition is that provinces are required not to discriminate on the basis of past residency (e.g., recent migration from another province). Tangentially, we might note the odd fact that this condition is not applied to postsecondary services where provinces routinely discriminate against Canadians coming from out-of-province. Aside from this one condition, equal per capita funding for social assistance and social services under the CHST serves no discernible programmatic purpose.

I have argued in the above that the CHST must either serve a fiscal or a programmatic objective, that the CHST makes no sense just as a fiscal transfer, but that the CHST does work as a programmatic transfer for health services, but only for health services among the three components of the CHST, since health is the only area where there are meaningful conditions associated with the funding.

But most of the discussion of the CHST and allied transfers is neither about fiscal objectives nor about program objectives, rather it is about directing federal money to specific targeted areas, mainly in the health-care field, where provinces are expected to spend the money so as to increase funding for that designated area. This concept of designated funding for targeted areas has snuck up on us over the last several years, and it has not been subject to much analytic scrutiny.

                                                Michael Mendelson

One of the primary characteristics of money is that it is perfectly fungible. That means that any Canadian dollar is fully and completely substitutable for any other; five dollars are exactly and fully substitutable for five one-dollar coins. Since money is perfectly fungible, once a sum enters an account with other money, there is no sensible way in which we could "track" what happened to any particular money. In fact, the question, "What did you do with *my* dollar?" does not make sense, although this would not prevent hordes of auditors and other financial types from spending large quantities of public funds seeking an answer to this very question. When I was teaching, I tried to explain the implications of the fungible nature of money to my students with the following example: Imagine that every week you spend $100 on groceries of which $10 is spent on milk. This week I give you $5 and I say, "I want you to spend *my* $5 on milk". Now you do your regular shopping trip and you buy your regular $100 worth of groceries, including $10 on milk as usual. When you return I ask, "Well, did you spend my $5 on milk?" You say, "Yes, I sure did. I wrote a little "M" on it and circled it and if you go to the till of the grocery check-out you will see that it is in there." So, I am satisfied that you spent *my* $5 on milk. I am happy, and presumably Canadian citizens are happy, too, to see that provincial governments are spending *those* designated federal dollars on health care.

In fact, the whole notion of accountability through tracing how dollars were spent is nothing but a great illusionist act. The federal government is anxious to perpetuate this illusion so it can be seen as doing something about health funding (or substitute child care or any other designated area) without getting into a tussle with the provinces by attempting actually to do something with federal dollars. The provinces are pleased to maintain this fiction because they then get federal money without real strings attached. There is an old joke about the Soviet Union. "In the Soviet Union we have a social contract: we pretend to work and they pretend to pay us." Well, Canada has its own version: "In Canada, Ottawa pretends to give the provinces money for health care and the provinces pretend to spend it on health care." The same joke could be made about child care or any of the other areas where Ottawa provides funding that is unconditional, except that it must supposedly be spent on a specially designated service.

Rather than the question, "What did you do with *my* dollar?" we should ask, "How did my giving you a dollar change your spending?" To return to my grocery-shopping example: imagine that upon receipt of my $5 you spent $102, including an extra $2 for a chocolate bar that you would not have otherwise bought. You might insist that you had spent my $5 marked with the little "M" on milk, just as I asked, but the real effect of the $5 grant was that you bought a chocolate bar and saved $3. If I ask what affect my grant had on your behaviour, milk had nothing to with it.

What does this mean for our analysis of the changes in the CHST announced in the recent budget? The budget increased dramatically, or some would say restored, transfers to provinces "for health". The proposal is that a Health Council will provide accountability by ensuring that the money is spent on health care. Aside from the challenges facing the federal government in actually getting the Health Council up and running, as we have seen there is precious little substance to the idea of tracing the use of the money. If the Health Council can provide an ongoing evidence-based assessment of the state of health care in Canada, it will certainly be worth while, but it will still not permit "accounting for how the money is spent" to be a substitute for conditionality of the transfer. What remains in place are the five existing conditions. It is hoped that the added money will strengthen the resolve of all governments to abide by these conditions, and perhaps the Health Council can also play a useful intermediary role in providing unbiased documentation of potential infringements of the conditions.

With respect to postsecondary education, social services and social assistance, the budget promises to set up a separate transfer program. But there are at present no real conditions proposed for the new Canada Social Transfer, so the status quo will be preserved: the CST will be much like the CHST with respect to postsecondary education, social services, and social assistance — irrelevant, or at best a sham. Perhaps advocates will be able to press for some sort of conditionality to be associated with the CST, but the precedents do not raise one's hopes. Moreover, the advocates are just as likely to get side-tracked into an ultimately useless attempt to ensure that the provinces "spend the money" in specifically designated areas. The illusion remains alive and quite seductive, since it offers a seeming compromise between provinces' stiff resistance to conditionality and simply leaving the money with no strings attached at all. The compromise, however, is no compromise at all; it is just a way to appear as if there are some strings attached when there are in reality none at all.

So all in all, what has the increase in the CHST in the budget accomplished? The increase may leverage a Health Council into existence, although how

                                                          Michael Mendelson

useful the Council really is still remains to be seen. The increase redistributes some fiscal capacity among the provinces and, given the imbalance in fiscal capacity between provinces that is so evident today, this is likely a good thing, even if it could more sensibly be achieved by a differently designed transfer. The increase also strengthens the federal moral authority to maintain the existing Canada Health Act conditions. These are useful ends, although one may be left speculating whether these accomplishments are not somewhat modest for the vast sums involved.

FISCAL SUSTAINABILITY AND THE 2003 FEDERAL "HEALTH" BUDGET

Paul Boothe, University of Alberta

Introduction

In her paper "The Health Care Budget: Did it Resolve the 'Crisis'?" Armine Yalnizyan gives an excellent description and analysis of the 2003 federal budget initiatives related to health care. In this brief essay, I will attempt to complement her analysis by focusing on fiscal sustainability — one of the major concerns that prompted the recent federal government reports by Kirby and Romanow and the speculating on whether the initiatives in this budget will successfully address this critical issue.

The Nature of the Problem

A glance at their mandates reveals that two fundamental concerns underlie the recent federal reports on health-care reform by Kirby and Romanow as well as a host of provincial reports by Mazankowski, Fyke and others. The first concern is related to access. Citizens are asking whether quality care will be available when they need it. The second concern is related to fiscal sustainability. Governments are asking how they will continue to finance health systems when costs are growing substantially faster than total revenues. Both concerns are related because a health system that is not fiscally sustainable must eventually collapse as citizens become increasingly intolerant of the required tax increases or expenditure reductions in other areas.

The fiscal sustainability problem is easy to describe. According to figures provided in the Romanow report and by Finance Canada, over the last five years public-sector health spending in Canada grew at an average annual rate of 7.1%, while combined federal-provincial revenues grew at an average annual rate of 4.3%. As a result, health spending is taking a growing share of provincial government program spending, and crowding out other public services.

Some have argued that the current trajectory of health spending simply reflects "catching up" after the anti-deficit reductions of the 1990s. The question begged is: Catching up to what? As Yalnizyan shows, real per capita health spending has now far surpassed its earlier peak at the beginning of the 1990s and shows no signs of slow down. Others claim that the growth of health spending relative to other government services simply reflects rational choices by voters. Yet, when was the last time voters were confronted with the real choices: higher taxes, less education, transportation, or environmental spending in order to expand health spending?

Medium-term projections suggest that revenue growth for all Canadian governments will be in the 4–5% range — in line with the nominal growth of the economy. Without fundamental changes, the cost of public health care in Canada could easily continue to grow at 7% or higher. What do we need to do to preserve our equity-based, single-payer system for providing health care?

The Nature of the Solution

At least since the federal CHST cuts of the early 1990s, Canadians have been told that the answer to the health system's access problems was more money. For that last five years, billions of dollars have been added to health budgets without any lasting impact. Waiting lists for diagnostic procedures and non-emergency treatments continue to grow.

                                    Paul Boothe

Provincial and federal politicians have obscured the real issue while bickering over who should bear the responsibility for financing the rampant expansion of the health system. What gets lost in the arguments about the share that each order of government should be paying is the fact that costs are rising faster than the revenues of all governments. Further, the same taxpayers are the source of these revenues.

If throwing more money at the health system is demonstrably not the solution, what does a viable solution look like? In short, the root of the health system's fiscal problems is that currently, care is "free on demand" to both providers and consumers. Everything that can be done must be done, and medical research is providing new, costly treatments every day. Beyond a desire to be good citizens, providers and consumers have little incentive or the information required to use the health system responsibly and make the kind of trade-offs that we face elsewhere in the public sector and, indeed, in everyday life.

What the New Federal Money Will Do

Federal health money in the 2003 budget comes in two varieties: unconditional increases in transfers to provinces and conditional money to "buy" change. The federal money will, temporarily at least, restore some of the cuts to transfers that came as part of the federal deficit-reduction efforts of the 1990s. However, given the growth of public health spending, the federal share will ultimately begin to decline anew. The increase in federal transfers comes at the cost of future federal flexibility to respond to emerging issues since, over the life of the agreement, transfers grow substantially faster than projected revenues, and thus commit much of future federal surpluses. Despite this unsustainable increase in transfers, it will not be enough to close the gap between provincial revenue and expenditure growth. Provinces can be expected to return to Ottawa soon with new demands for additional health dollars.

New money to expand services in areas such as diagnostics and home care may provide some temporary improvements in access. However, given that the amounts are less than provinces were likely to increase such spending, the results may not be noticeable. The growth in spending in these areas has been particularly rapid so that beyond a one-time increase in services (or wages and salaries of providers), waiting lists can be expected to begin climbing again soon. Finally, new money to improve infrastructure, especially in the area of information, and primary care may well lead to improvements in the quality of care, but should not be expected, by itself, to lead to reductions in the growth of expenditures.

Accountability

One of the themes common to both the Kirby and Romanow reports was that health system accountability needed to be improved. The conditions attached to additional federal funding underscore this concern. No doubt such concerns stemmed from the fact that past, substantial increases in funding for health care failed to secure fiscal sustainability or more than temporarily improve access. Canadians and their federal politicians wanted to know where the money went and why it did not have the intended effect. Unfortunately, a lack of accountability is not at the core of the health system's sustainability problems. In fact, no other area of the public sector provides anywhere near the level of performance and other accountability information currently provided by the health sector. As a result of the previous First Ministers' Health Accord, provinces are even providing this information in a way that facilitates comparisons across jurisdictions. Rather than a lack of accountability, it is because the measures embraced do not work that Canadians are not seeing the results they expect from increased health-care funding.

Conclusion

As Yalnizyan makes clear in her paper, the 2003 federal budget did not resolve the fiscal sustainability problems of the health system. It is not because Ottawa did not spend enough money, but because spending more money was not the solution. The substantial increase in federal transfers cannot "buy" lasting change. Only a new set of incentives for providers and consumers can.

The 2003 federal "health" budget did postpone the day of reckoning for a year or two as well as substantially reduce the next prime minister's ability to address emerging issues. It seems that Canadians and their political leaders are not yet ready to face up to the fact that free-on-demand health care can never be affordable in a world of rapid technological change and rising public expectations and that more radical reforms will be needed to preserve our equity-based, single-payer health-care system. Until they do, our health system will continue to be in "crisis".

CONTRIBUTORS

Paul Boothe — Institute for Public Economics, University of Alberta and C.D. Howe institute

Thomas J. Courchene — School of Policy Studies, Queen's University and Institute for Research on Public Policy, Montreal

Bev Dahlby — Institute for Public Economics and Department of Economics, University of Alberta

Peter Dungan — Institute for Policy Analysis, University of Toronto

Rick Egelton — BMO Financial Group, Toronto

Pierre Fortin — Département des sciences économiques, Université du Québec à Montréal

Christopher Green — Department of Economics, McGill University

Richard Harris — Department of Economics, Simon Fraser University

Jonathan R. Kesselman — Public Policy Program, Simon Fraser University

Alan Macnaughton — School of Accountancy, University of Waterloo

Michael C. McCracken — Informetrica Limited, Ottawa

Ross McKitrick — Department of Economics, University of Guelph

Michael Mendelson — Caledon Institute of Social Policy, Toronto

Steve Murphy — Institute for Policy Analysis, University of Toronto

William Scarth — Department of Economics, McMaster University

Jeffrey Simpson   *The Globe and Mail*, Ottawa

John Wiersema   Office of the Auditor General of Canada, Ottawa

Thomas A. Wilson   Institute for Policy Analysis, University of Toronto

Frances Woolley   Department of Economics, Carleton University

Armine Yalnizyan   Canadian Centre for Policy Alternatives, Toronto

Queen's Policy Studies
Recent Publications

The Queen's Policy Studies Series is dedicated to the exploration of major policy issues that confront governments in Canada and other western nations. McGill-Queen's University Press is the exclusive world representative and distributor of books in the series.

John Deutsch Institute for the Study of Economic Policy

Canadian Immigration Policy for the 21st Century, Charles M. Beach, Alan G. Green and Jeffrey G. Reitz (eds.), 2003   Paper ISBN 0-88911-954-6
Cloth ISBN 0-88911-952-X

Framing Financial Structure in an Information Environment, Thomas J. Courchene and Edwin H. Neave (eds.), Policy Forum Series no. 38, 2003
Paper ISBN 0-88911-950-3 Cloth ISBN 0-88911-948-1

Towards Evidence-Based Policy for Canadian Education/Vers des politiques canadiennes d'éducation fondées sur la recherche, Patrice de Broucker and/et Arthur Sweetman (eds./dirs.), 2002   Paper ISBN 0-88911-946-5 Cloth ISBN 0-88911-944-9

Money, Markets and Mobility: Celebrating the Ideas of Robert A. Mundell, Nobel Laureate in Economic Sciences, Thomas J. Courchene (ed.), 2002
Paper ISBN 0-88911-820-5 Cloth ISBN 0-88911-818-3

The State of Economics in Canada: Festschrift in Honour of David Slater, Patrick Grady and Andrew Sharpe (eds.), 2001 Paper ISBN 0-88911-942-2 Cloth ISBN 0-88911-940-6

The 2000 Federal Budget: Retrospect and Prospect, Paul A.R. Hobson and Thomas A. Wilson (eds.), Policy Forum Series no. 37, 2001   Paper ISBN 0-88911-816-7
Cloth ISBN 0-88911-814-0

School of Policy Studies

Canada Without Armed Forces? Douglas L. Bland (ed.), 2004
Paper ISBN 1-55339-036-9 Cloth 1-55339-037-7

Campaigns for International Security: Canada's Defence Policy at the Turn of the Century, Douglas L. Bland and Sean M. Maloney, 2004
Paper ISBN 0-88911-962-7 Cloth 0-88911-964-3

Understanding Innovation in Canadian Industry, Fred Gault (ed.), 2003
Paper ISBN 1-55339-030-X Cloth ISBN 1-55339-031-8

Delicate Dances: Public Policy and the Nonprofit Sector, Kathy L. Brock (ed.), 2003
Paper ISBN 0-88911-953-8 Cloth ISBN 0-88911-955-4

Beyond the National Divide: Regional Dimensions of Industrial Relations, Mark Thompson, Joseph B. Rose and Anthony E. Smith (eds.), 2003
Paper ISBN 0-88911-963-5 Cloth ISBN 0-88911-965-1

The Nonprofit Sector in Interesting Times: Case Studies in a Changing Sector, Kathy L. Brock and Keith G. Banting (eds.), 2003
Paper ISBN 0-88911-941-4 Cloth ISBN 0-88911-943-0

Clusters Old and New: The Transition to a Knowledge Economy in Canada's Regions, David A. Wolfe (ed.), 2003 Paper ISBN 0-88911-959-7 Cloth ISBN 0-88911-961-9

The e-Connected World: Risks and Opportunities, Stephen Coleman (ed.), 2003 Paper ISBN 0-88911-945-7 Cloth ISBN 0-88911-947-3

Knowledge, Clusters and Regional Innovation: Economic Development in Canada, J. Adam Holbrook and David A. Wolfe (eds.), 2002 Paper ISBN 0-88911-919-8 Cloth ISBN 0-88911-917-1

Lessons of Everyday Law/Ledroit du quotidien, Roderick Alexander Macdonald, 2002 Paper ISBN 0-88911-915-5 Cloth ISBN 0-88911-913-9

Improving Connections Between Governments and Nonprofit and Voluntary Organizations: Public Policy and the Third Sector, Kathy L. Brock (ed.), 2002 Paper ISBN 0-88911-899-X Cloth ISBN 0-88911-907-4

Institute of Intergovernmental Relations

Canada: The State of the Federation 2002, vol. 16, *Reconsidering the Institutions of Canadian Federalism,* J. Peter Meekison, Hamish Telford and Harvey Lazar (eds.), 2004 Paper ISBN 1-55339-009-1   Cloth ISBN 1-55339-008-3

Federalism and Labour Market Policy: Comparing Different Governance and Employment Strategies, Alain Noël (ed.), 2004 Paper ISBN 1-55339-006-7 Cloth ISBN 1-55339-007-5

The Impact of Global and Regional Integration on Federal Systems: A Comparative Analysis, Harvey Lazar, Hamish Telford and Ronald L. Watts (eds.), 2003 Paper ISBN 1-55339-002-4 Cloth ISBN 1-55339-003-2

Canada: The State of the Federation 2001, vol. 15, *Canadian Political Culture(s) in Transition,* Hamish Telford and Harvey Lazar (eds.), 2002 Paper ISBN 0-88911-863-9 Cloth ISBN 0-88911-851-5

Federalism, Democracy and Disability Policy in Canada, Alan Puttee (ed.), 2002 Paper ISBN 0-88911-855-8 Cloth ISBN 1-55339-001-6, ISBN 0-88911-845-0 (set)

Comparaison des régimes fédéraux, 2^{e}éd., Ronald L. Watts, 2002 ISBN 1-55339-005-9

Available from: McGill-Queen's University Press
c/o Georgetown Terminal Warehouses
34 Armstrong Avenue
Georgetown, Ontario L7G 4R9
Tel: (877) 864-8477
Fax: (877) 864-4272
E-mail: orders@gtwcanada.com